JOE PRUETT

SZYMON KUDRANSKI

B.E.K.
BLACK EYED KIDS

VOLUME

1

THE CHILDREN

GUY MAJOR

MARSHALL DILLON

FRANCESCO FRANCAVILLA

AFTERSHOCK

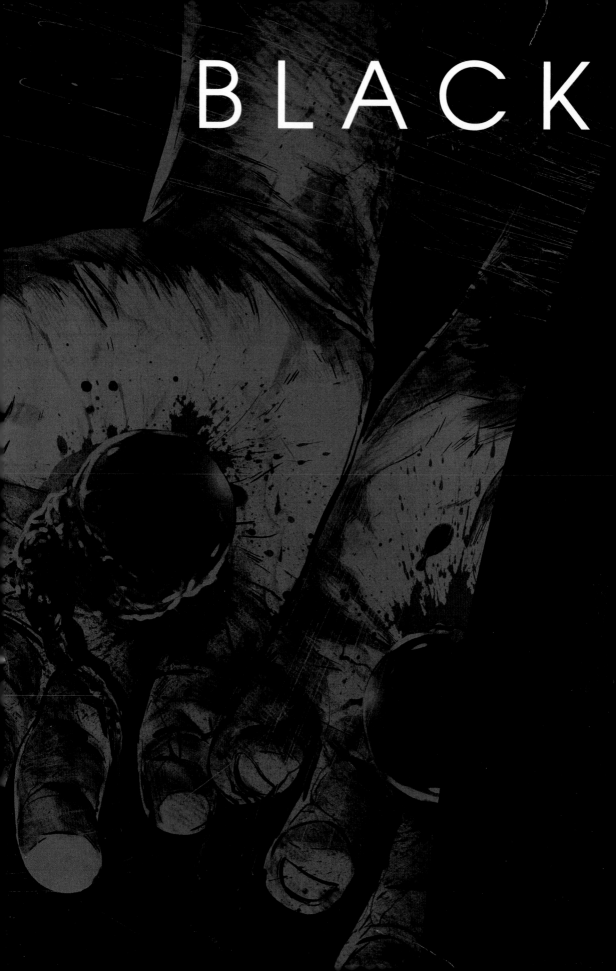

BLACK

EYED KIDS
VOLUME 1
THE CHILDREN

JOE PRUETT co-creator & writer

SZYMON KUDRANSKI co-creator & artist

GUY MAJOR colorist

MARSHALL DILLON letterer

FRANCESCO FRANCAVILLA front & original series covers

MICHAEL GAYDOS, PHIL HESTER &
SZYMON KUDRANSKI variant covers

JOHN J. HILL book & logo designer

MIKE MARTS editor

AFTERSHOCK ™

MIKE MARTS - Editor-in-Chief • **JOE PRUETT** - Publisher • **LEE KRAMER** - President
JAWAD QURESHI - SVP, Investor Relations • **JON KRAMER** - Chief Executive Officer
MIKE ZAGARI - SVP Digital /Creative • **JAY BEHLING** - Chief Financial Officer • **MICHAEL RICHTER** - Chief Creative Officer
STEPHAN NILSON - Publishing Operations Manager • **LISA Y. WU** - Social Media Coordinator

AfterShock Trade Dress and Interior Design by **JOHN J. HILL**
AfterShock Logo Design by **COMCRAFT**
Proofreading by **J. HARBORE** & **DOCTOR Z.**
Publicity: contact **AARON MARION** (aaron@fteenminutes.com) &
RYAN CROY (ryan@fteenminutes.com) at **15 MINUTES**

AFTERSHOCKCOMICS.COM   Follow us on social media 🐦 📷 f

INTRODUCTION

I've been fascinated about the legend of the Black-Eyed Kids
for years...so when Joe Pruett and I stumbled across our shared
penchant for the mystery of the B.E.K., our night soon went from
a quick drink at the convention bar to a several hour discussion. I
had long wanted to be the first person to write about the B.E.K. in
comics, but I'm very pleased that Joe and Szymon beat me to it.

BLACK-EYED KIDS by AfterShock is the perfect marriage of the
innocence of youth, the terrifyingly creepy and that evil little shit
who lives down the block.

These things don't go "bump" in the night—*they knock on your
goddamn door!*

I can't wait for more B.E.K., and I'm saying it right here and now:
if there isn't a "Chief" character at some point there will be some
conversations had.

—Aaron Douglas,
September 13, 2016

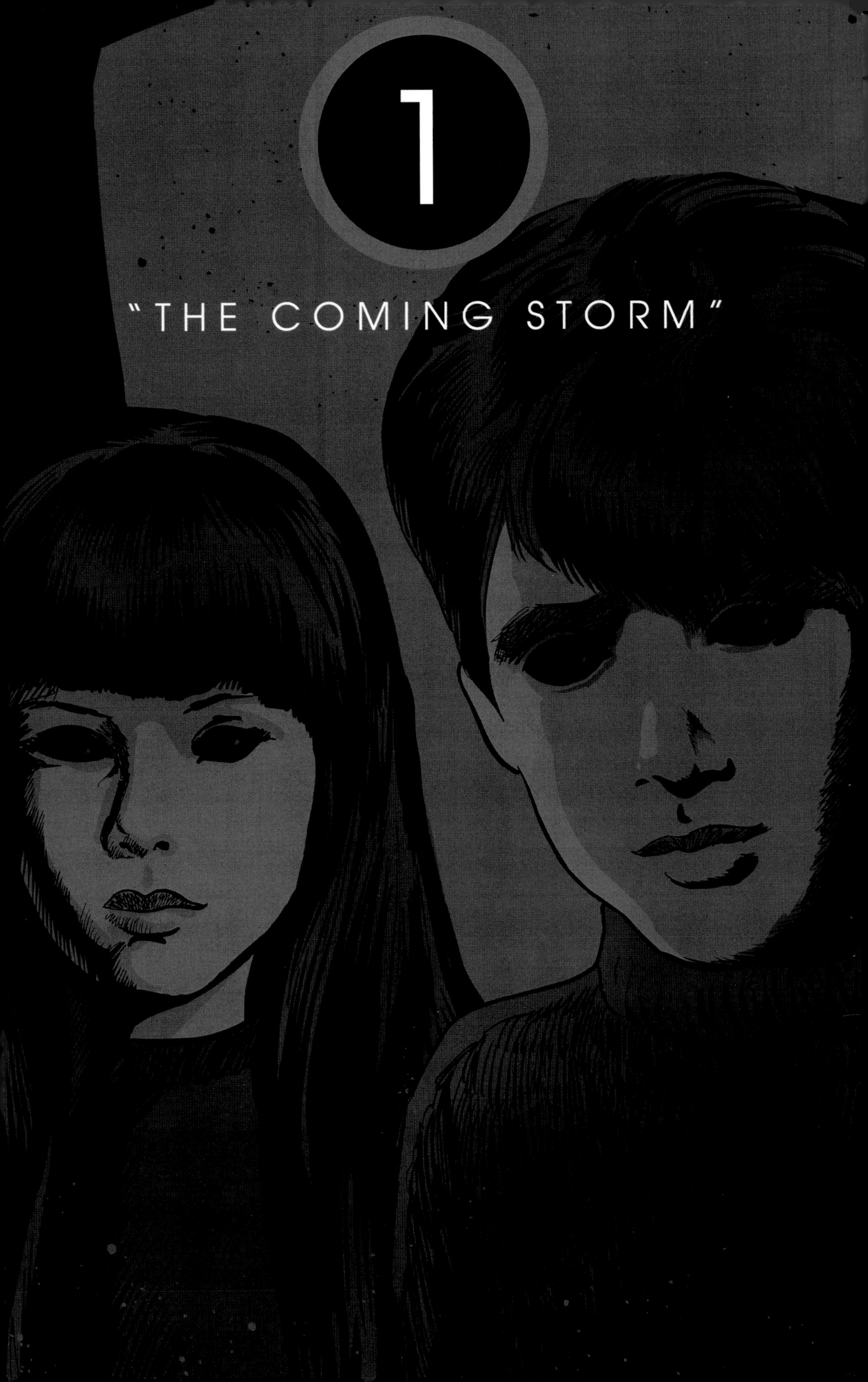
1
"THE COMING STORM"

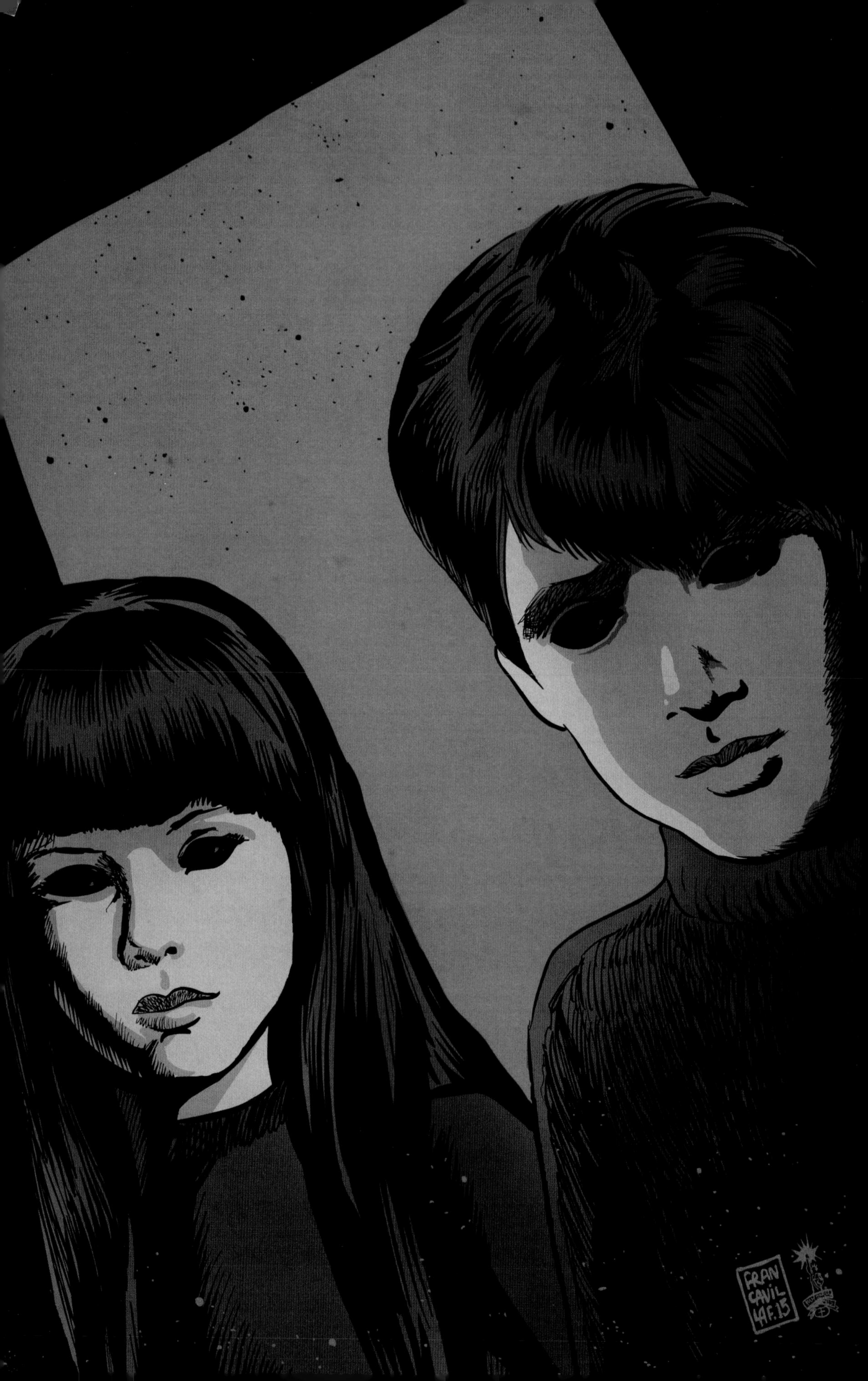
FRAN
CAVIL
14F.15

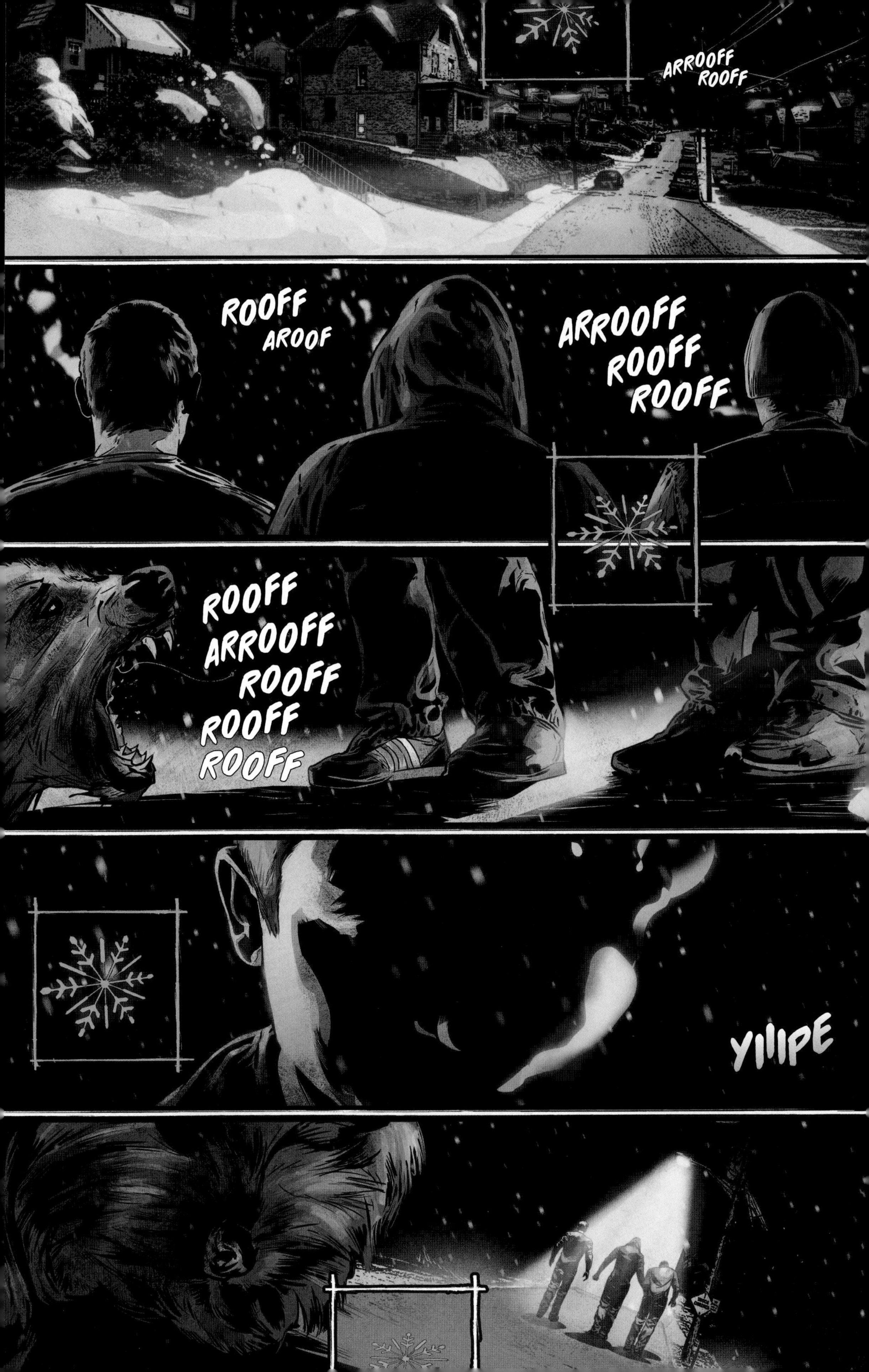
ARROOFF
ROOFF
ROOFF
AROOF
ARROOFF
ROOFF
ROOFF
ROOFF
ARROOFF
ROOFF
ROOFF
ROOFF
YIIIPE

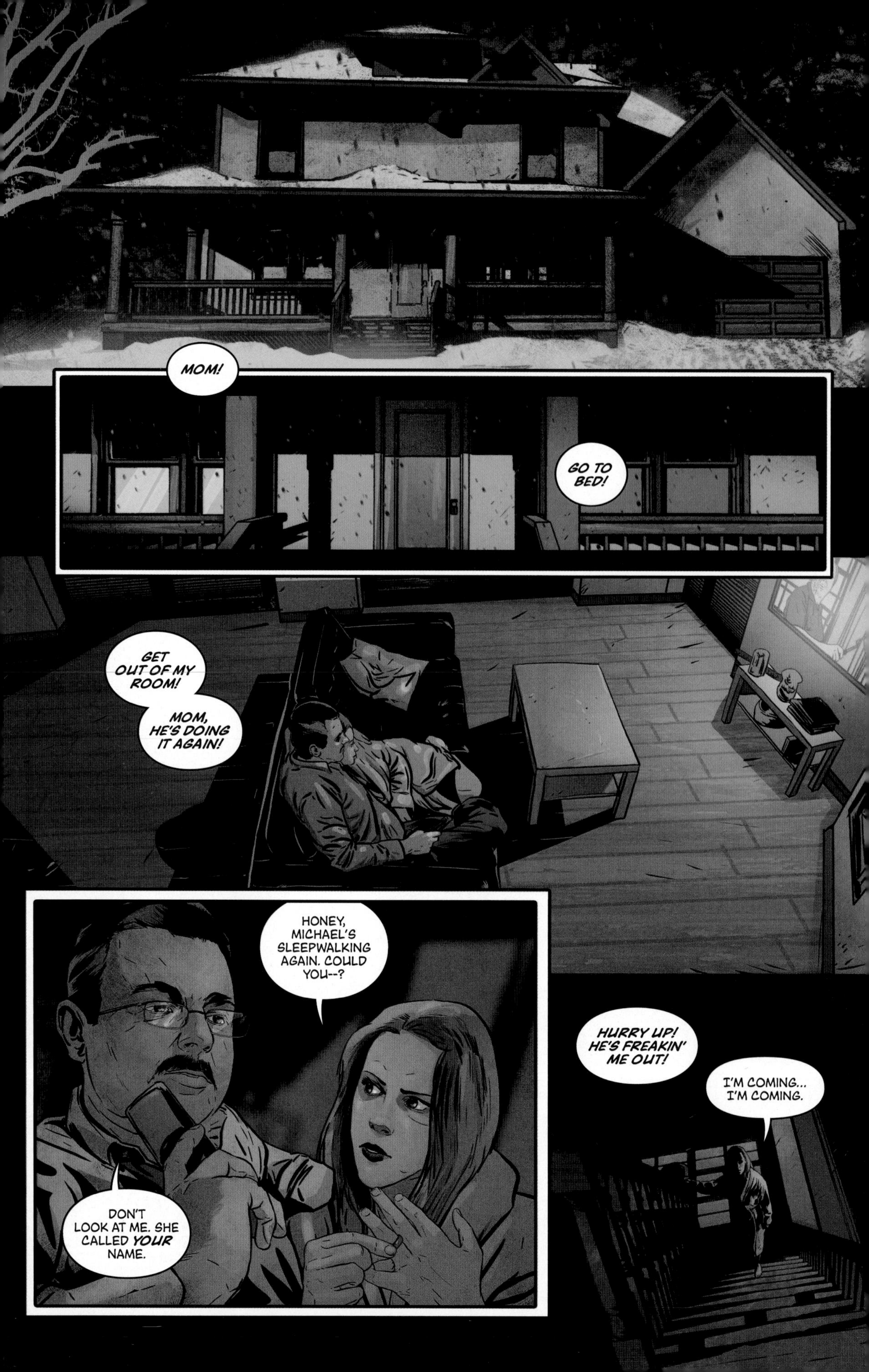
MOM!
GO TO BED!
GET OUT OF MY ROOM!
MOM, HE'S DOING IT AGAIN!
HONEY, MICHAEL'S SLEEPWALKING AGAIN. COULD YOU--?
DON'T LOOK AT ME. SHE CALLED *YOUR* NAME.
HURRY UP! HE'S FREAKIN' ME OUT!
I'M COMING... I'M COMING.

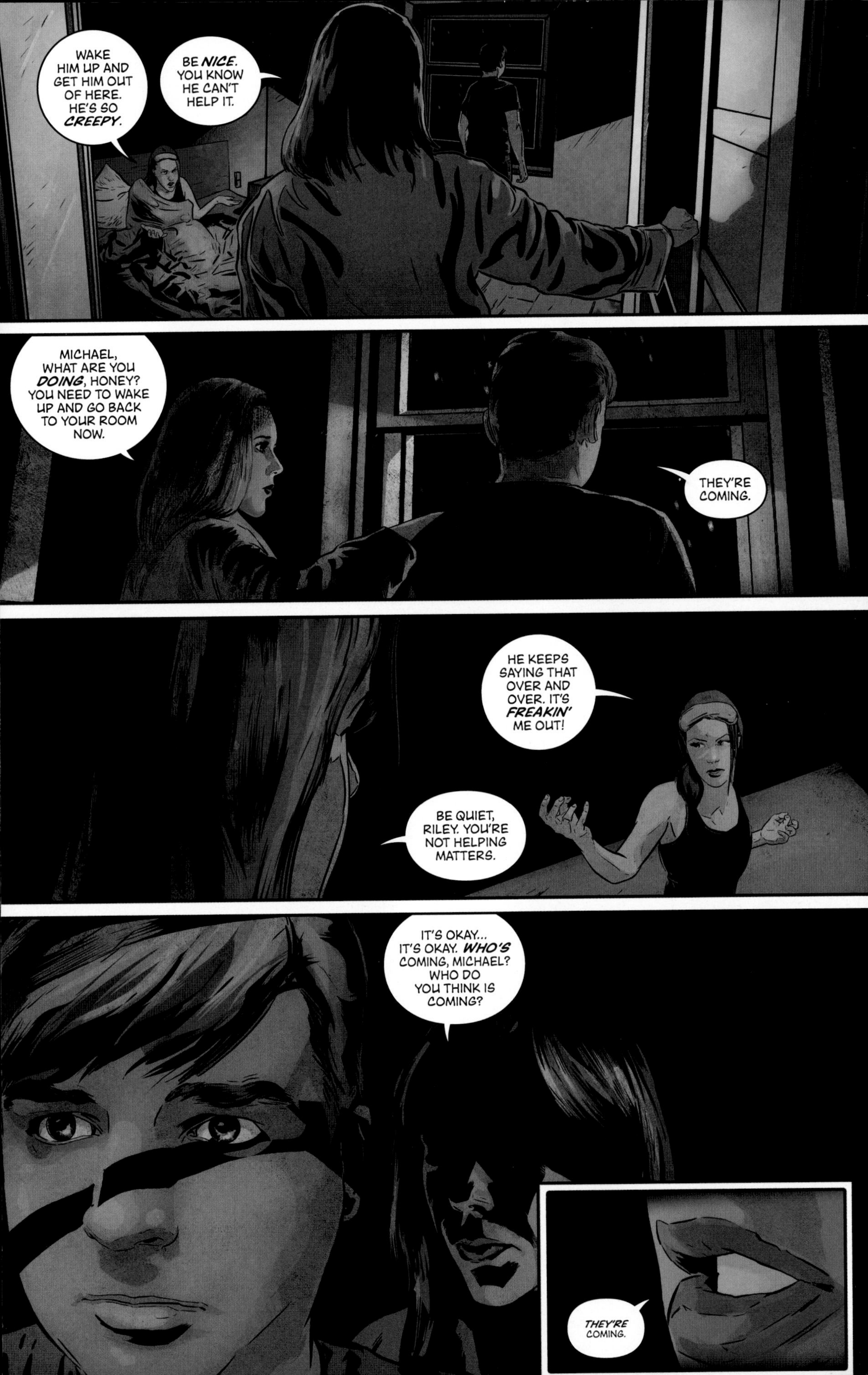
WAKE HIM UP AND GET HIM OUT OF HERE. HE'S SO CREEPY.
BE NICE. YOU KNOW HE CAN'T HELP IT.
MICHAEL, WHAT ARE YOU DOING, HONEY? YOU NEED TO WAKE UP AND GO BACK TO YOUR ROOM NOW.
THEY'RE COMING.
HE KEEPS SAYING THAT OVER AND OVER. IT'S FREAKIN' ME OUT!
BE QUIET, RILEY. YOU'RE NOT HELPING MATTERS.
IT'S OKAY... IT'S OKAY. WHO'S COMING, MICHAEL? WHO DO YOU THINK IS COMING?
THEY'RE COMING.

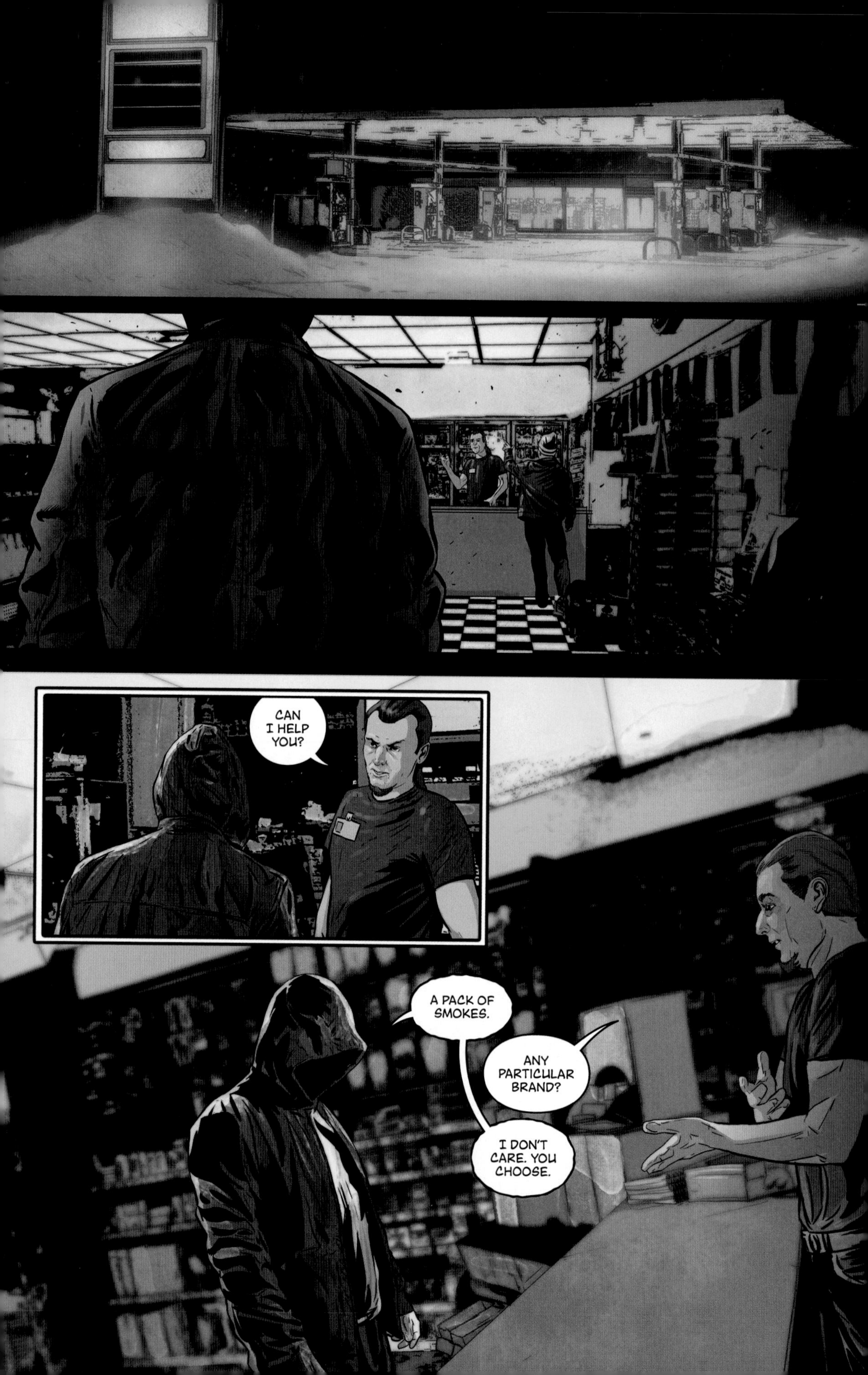
CAN I HELP YOU?
A PACK OF SMOKES.
ANY PARTICULAR BRAND?
I DON'T CARE. YOU CHOOSE.

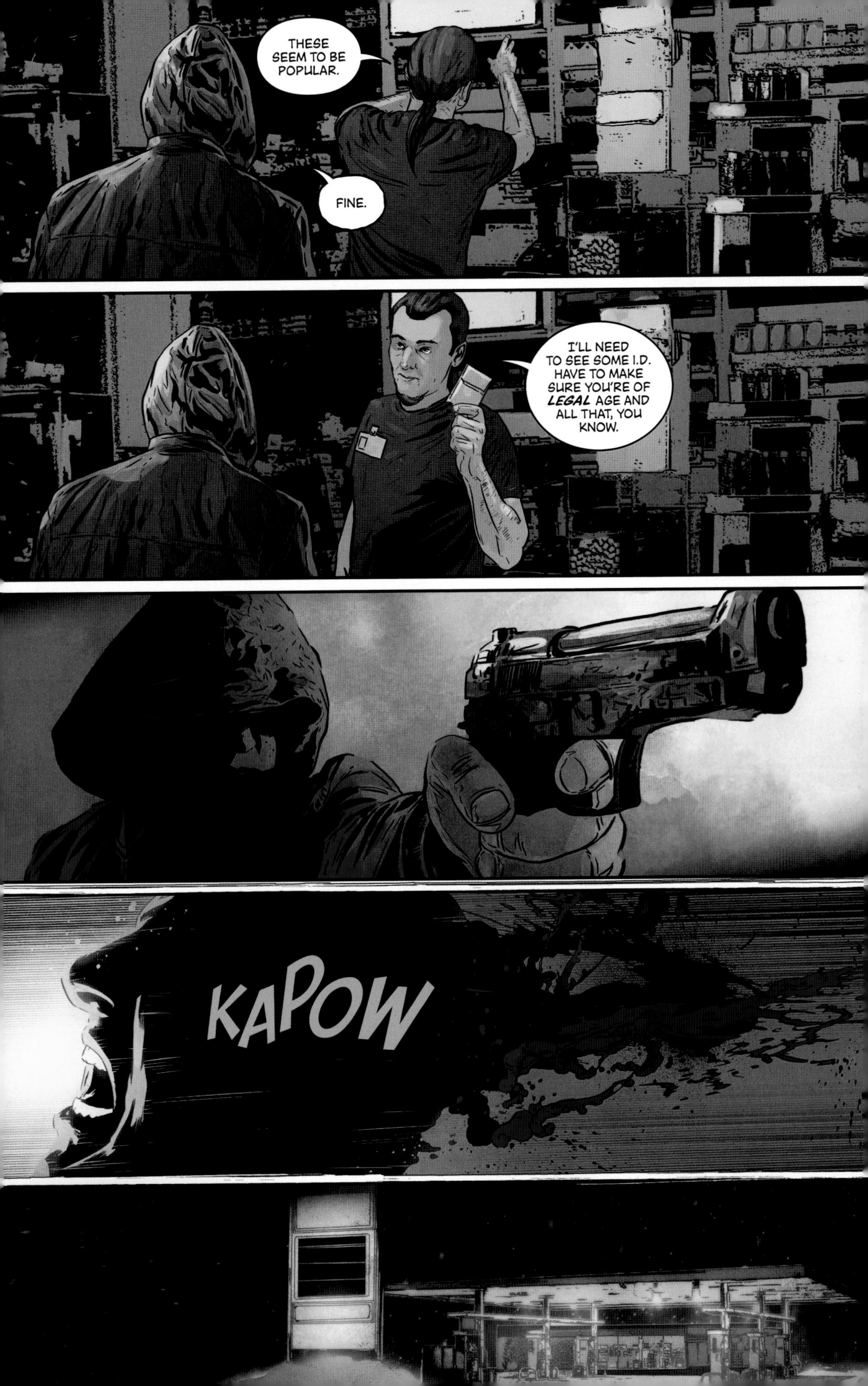
THESE SEEM TO BE POPULAR.
FINE.
I'LL NEED TO SEE SOME I.D. HAVE TO MAKE SURE YOU'RE OF LEGAL AGE AND ALL THAT, YOU KNOW.
KAPOW

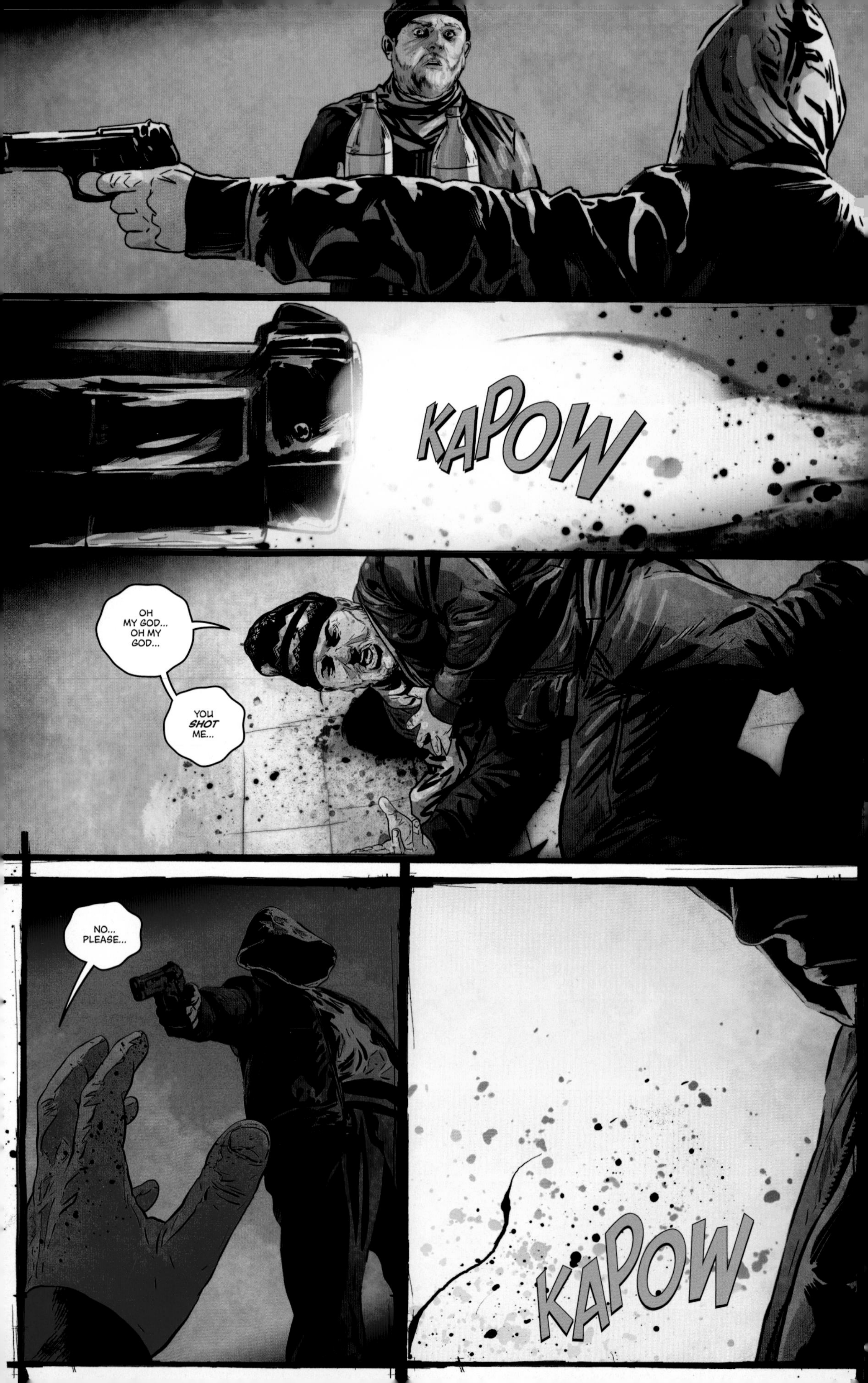
KAPOW
OH MY GOD... OH MY GOD...
YOU SHOT ME...
NO... PLEASE...
KAPOW

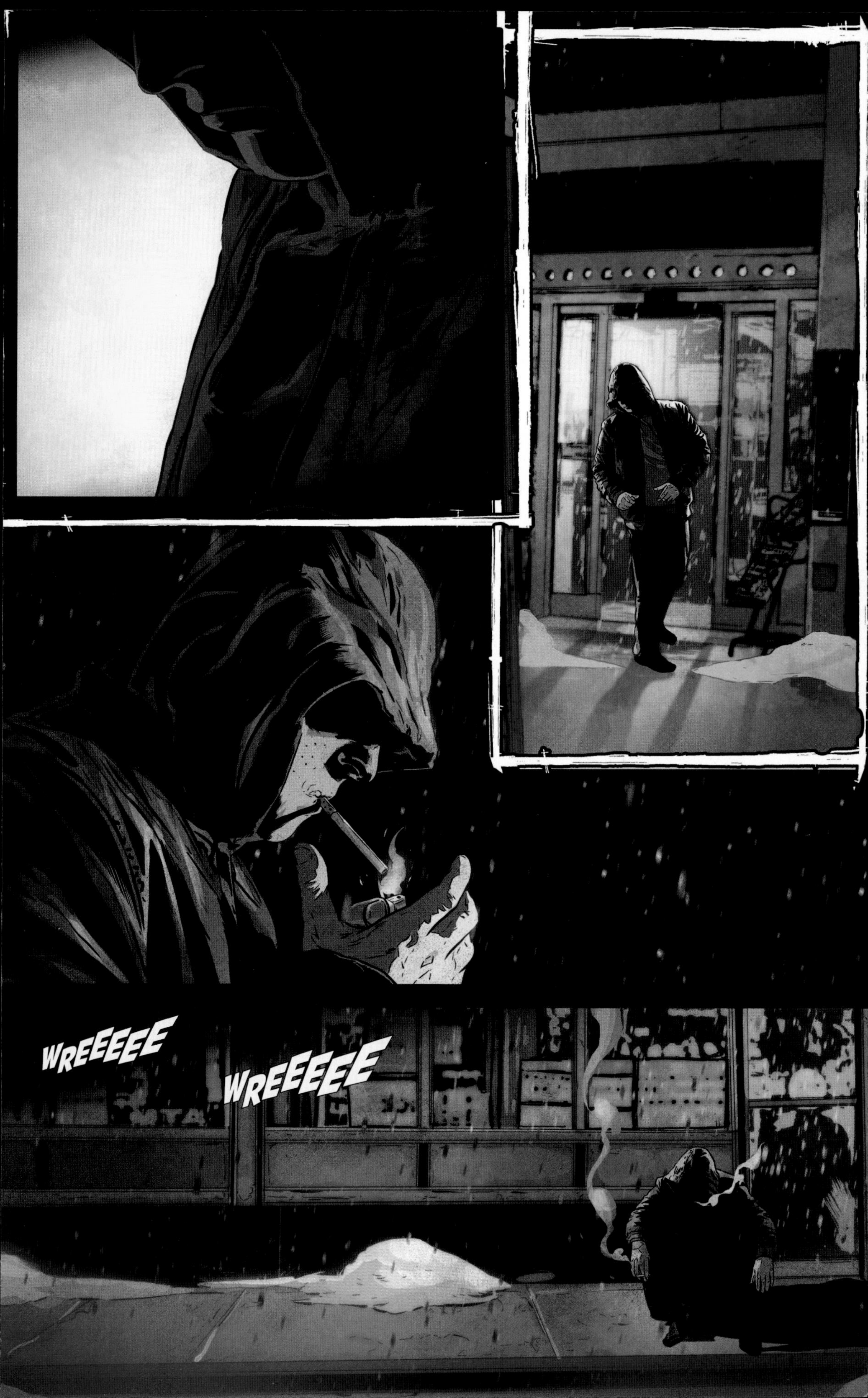
WREEEEEE
WREEEEEE

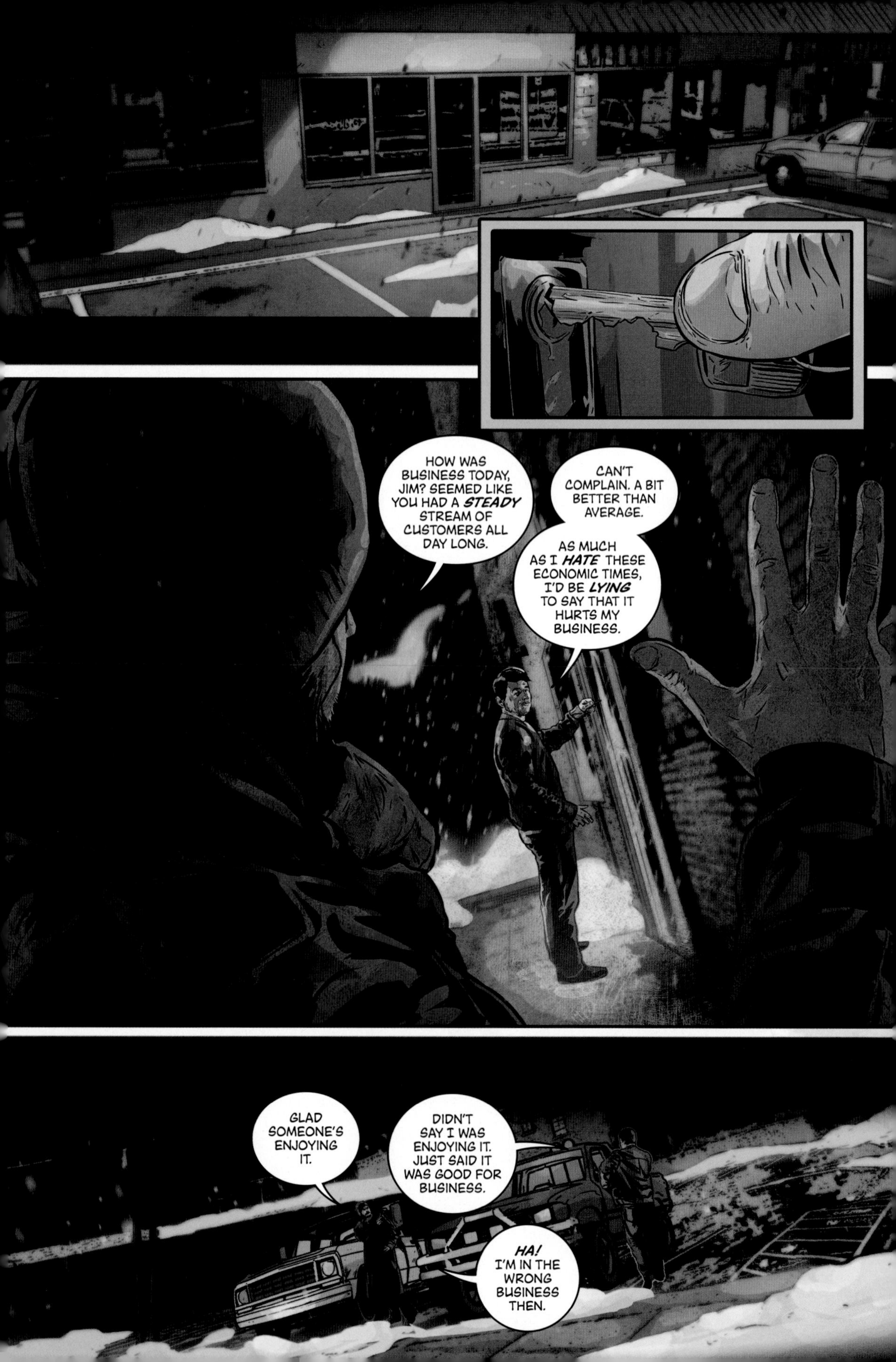
HOW WAS BUSINESS TODAY, JIM? SEEMED LIKE YOU HAD A STEADY STREAM OF CUSTOMERS ALL DAY LONG.
CAN'T COMPLAIN. A BIT BETTER THAN AVERAGE.
AS MUCH AS I HATE THESE ECONOMIC TIMES, I'D BE LYING TO SAY THAT IT HURTS MY BUSINESS.
GLAD SOMEONE'S ENJOYING IT.
DIDN'T SAY I WAS ENJOYING IT. JUST SAID IT WAS GOOD FOR BUSINESS.
HA! I'M IN THE WRONG BUSINESS THEN.

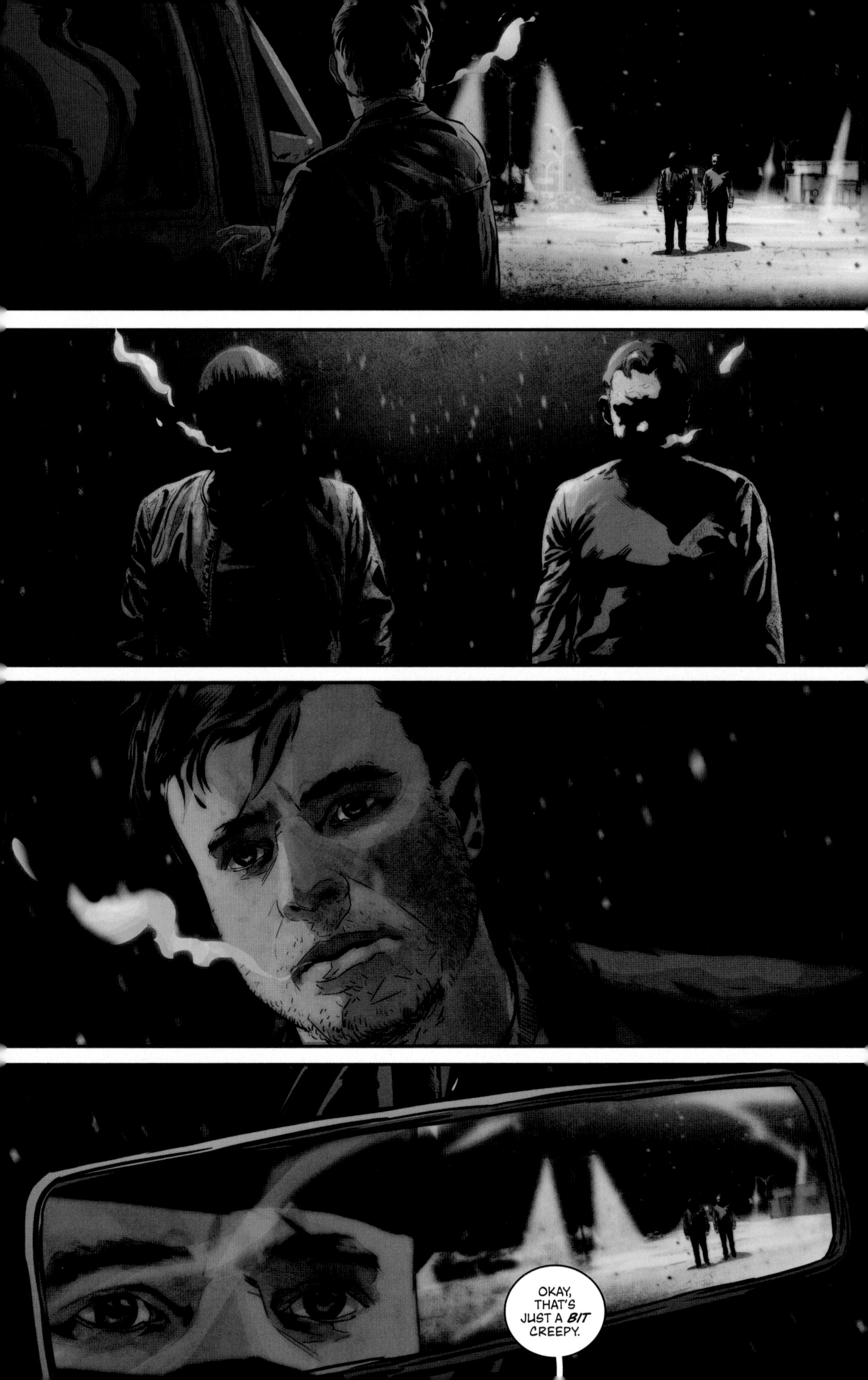
OKAY, THAT'S JUST A *BIT* CREEPY.

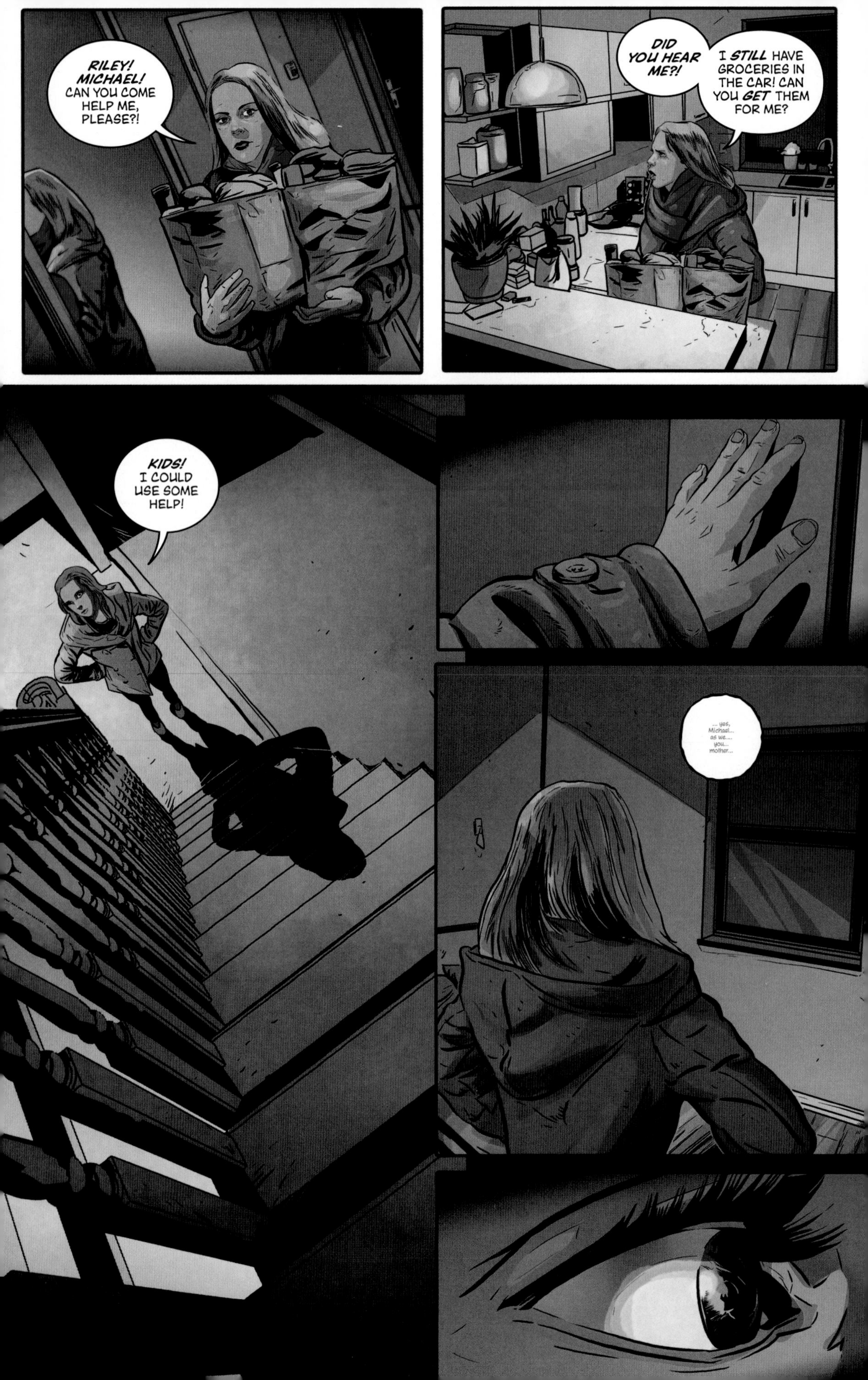
RILEY! MICHAEL! CAN YOU COME HELP ME, PLEASE?!
DID YOU HEAR ME?!
I STILL HAVE GROCERIES IN THE CAR! CAN YOU GET THEM FOR ME?
KIDS! I COULD USE SOME HELP!
... yes, Michael... as we.... you... mother...

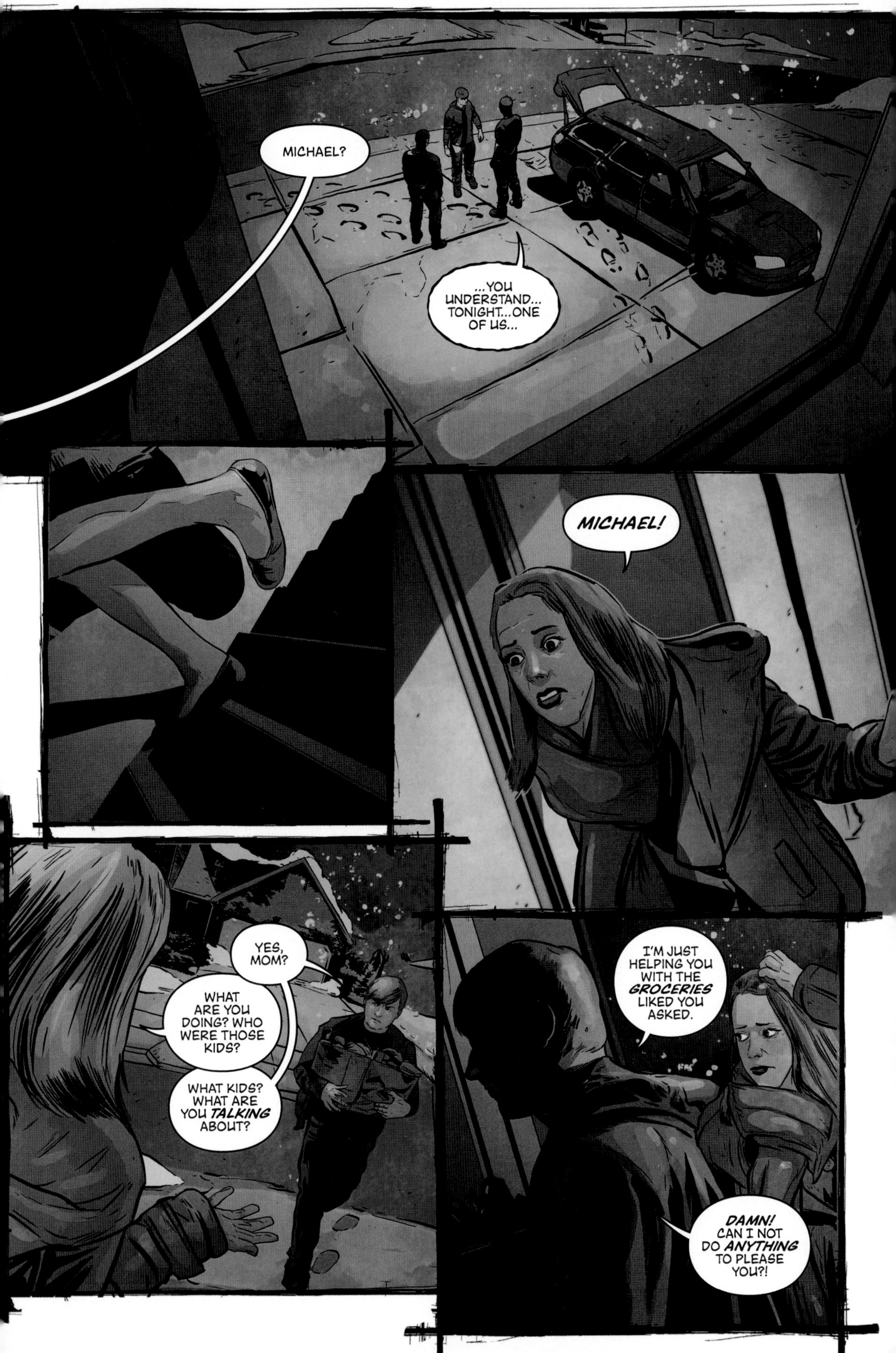

MICHAEL?
...YOU UNDERSTAND... TONIGHT...ONE OF US...
MICHAEL!
YES, MOM?
WHAT ARE YOU DOING? WHO WERE THOSE KIDS?
WHAT KIDS? WHAT ARE YOU *TALKING* ABOUT?
I'M JUST HELPING YOU WITH THE *GROCERIES* LIKED YOU ASKED.
DAMN! CAN I NOT DO *ANYTHING* TO PLEASE YOU?!

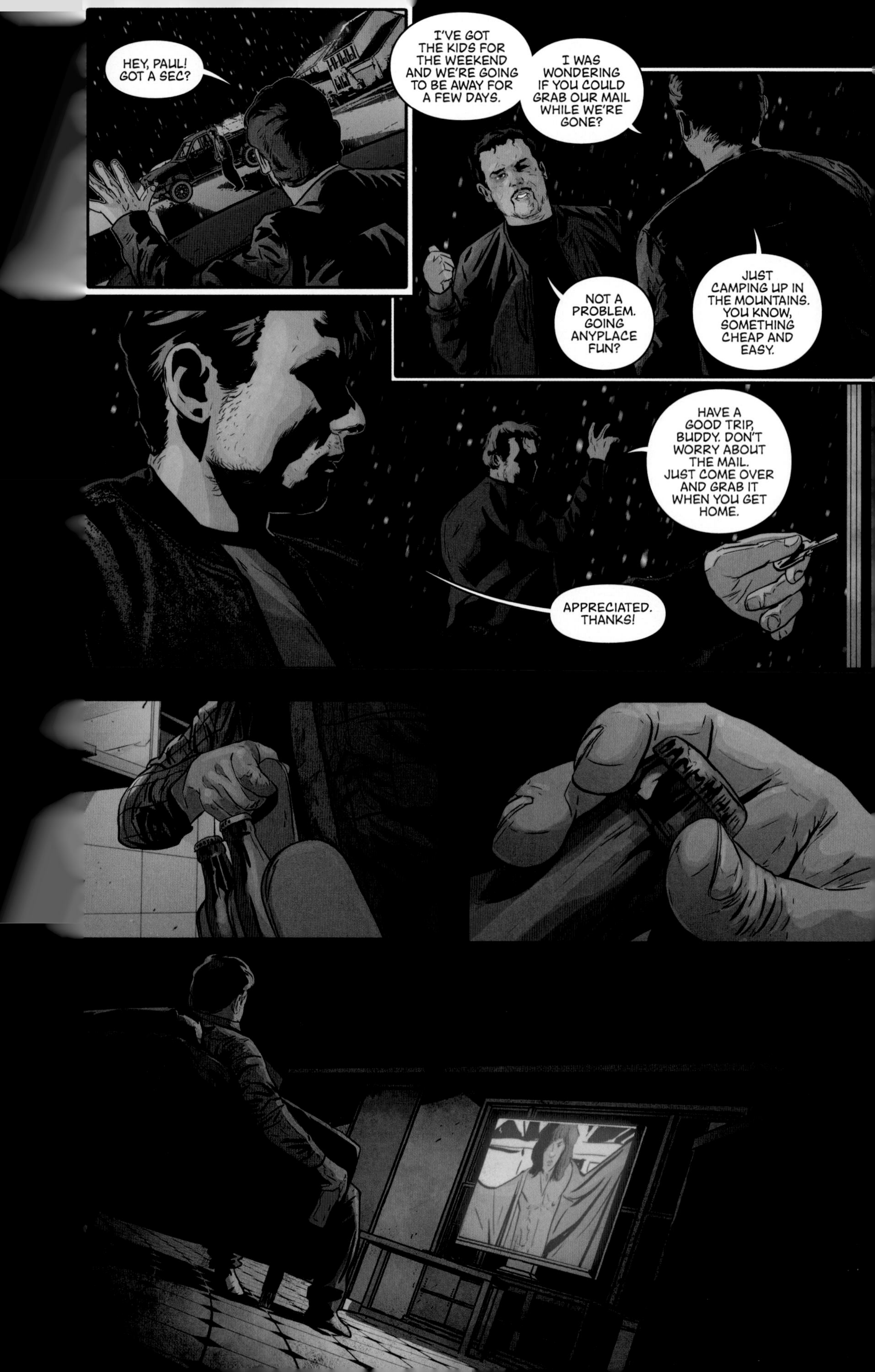
HEY, PAUL! GOT A SEC?
I'VE GOT THE KIDS FOR THE WEEKEND AND WE'RE GOING TO BE AWAY FOR A FEW DAYS.
I WAS WONDERING IF YOU COULD GRAB OUR MAIL WHILE WE'RE GONE?
NOT A PROBLEM. GOING ANYPLACE FUN?
JUST CAMPING UP IN THE MOUNTAINS. YOU KNOW, SOMETHING CHEAP AND EASY.
HAVE A GOOD TRIP, BUDDY. DON'T WORRY ABOUT THE MAIL. JUST COME OVER AND GRAB IT WHEN YOU GET HOME.
APPRECIATED. THANKS!

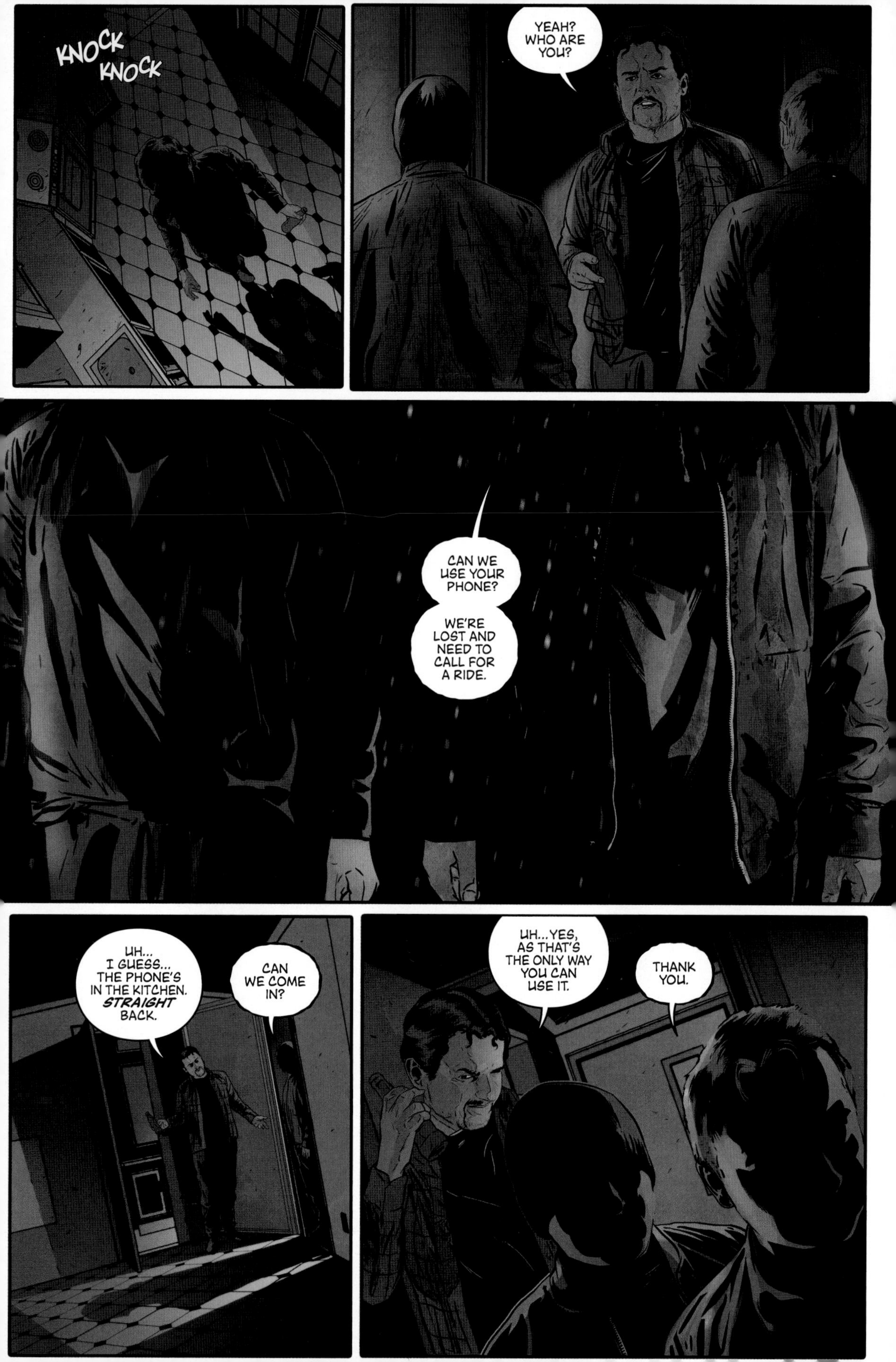
KNOCK KNOCK
YEAH? WHO ARE YOU?
CAN WE USE YOUR PHONE?
WE'RE LOST AND NEED TO CALL FOR A RIDE.
CAN WE COME IN?
UH... I GUESS... THE PHONE'S IN THE KITCHEN. STRAIGHT BACK.
UH...YES, AS THAT'S THE ONLY WAY YOU CAN USE IT.
THANK YOU.

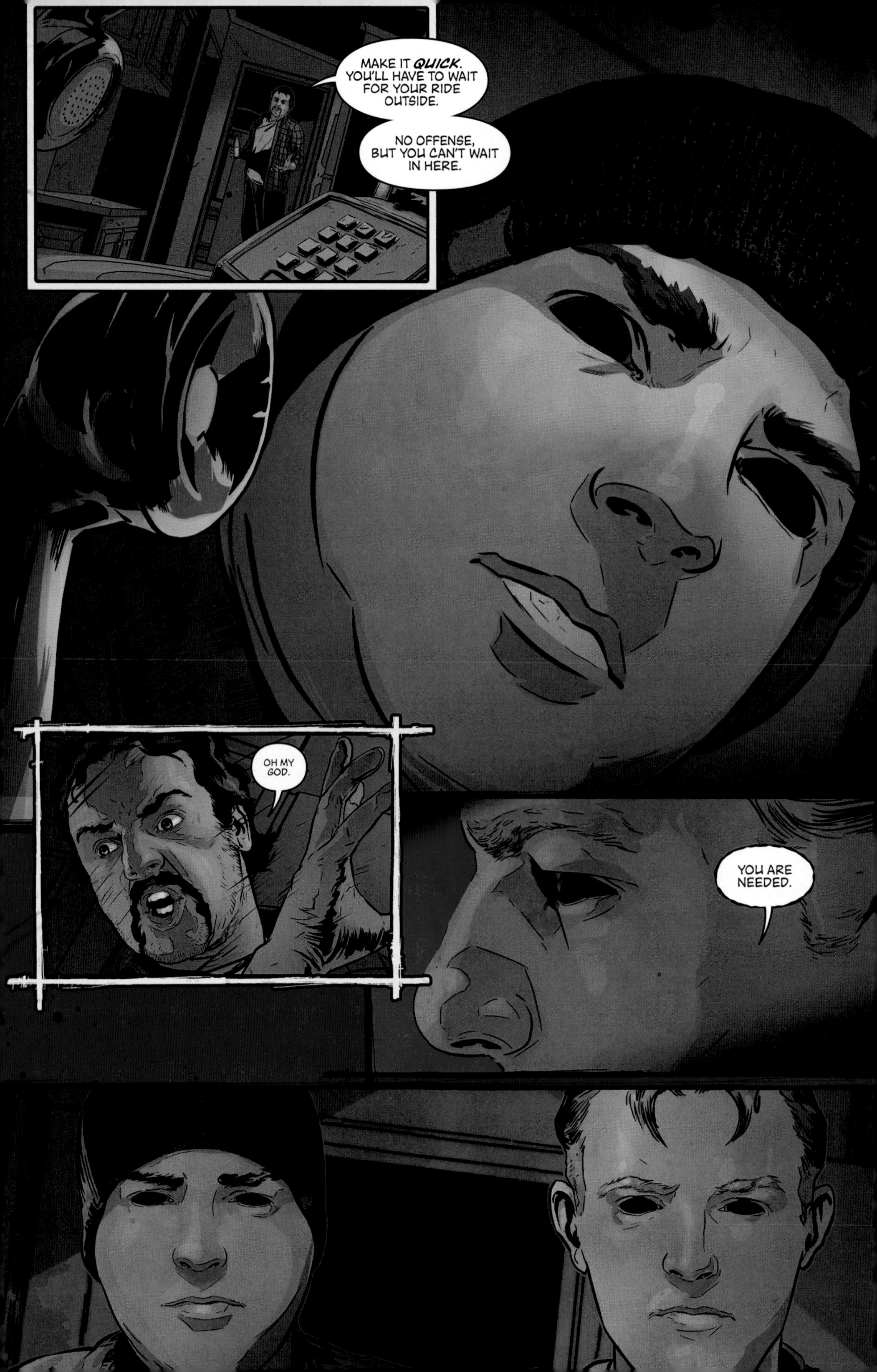
MAKE IT QUICK. YOU'LL HAVE TO WAIT FOR YOUR RIDE OUTSIDE.
NO OFFENSE, BUT YOU CAN'T WAIT IN HERE.
OH MY GOD.
YOU ARE NEEDED.

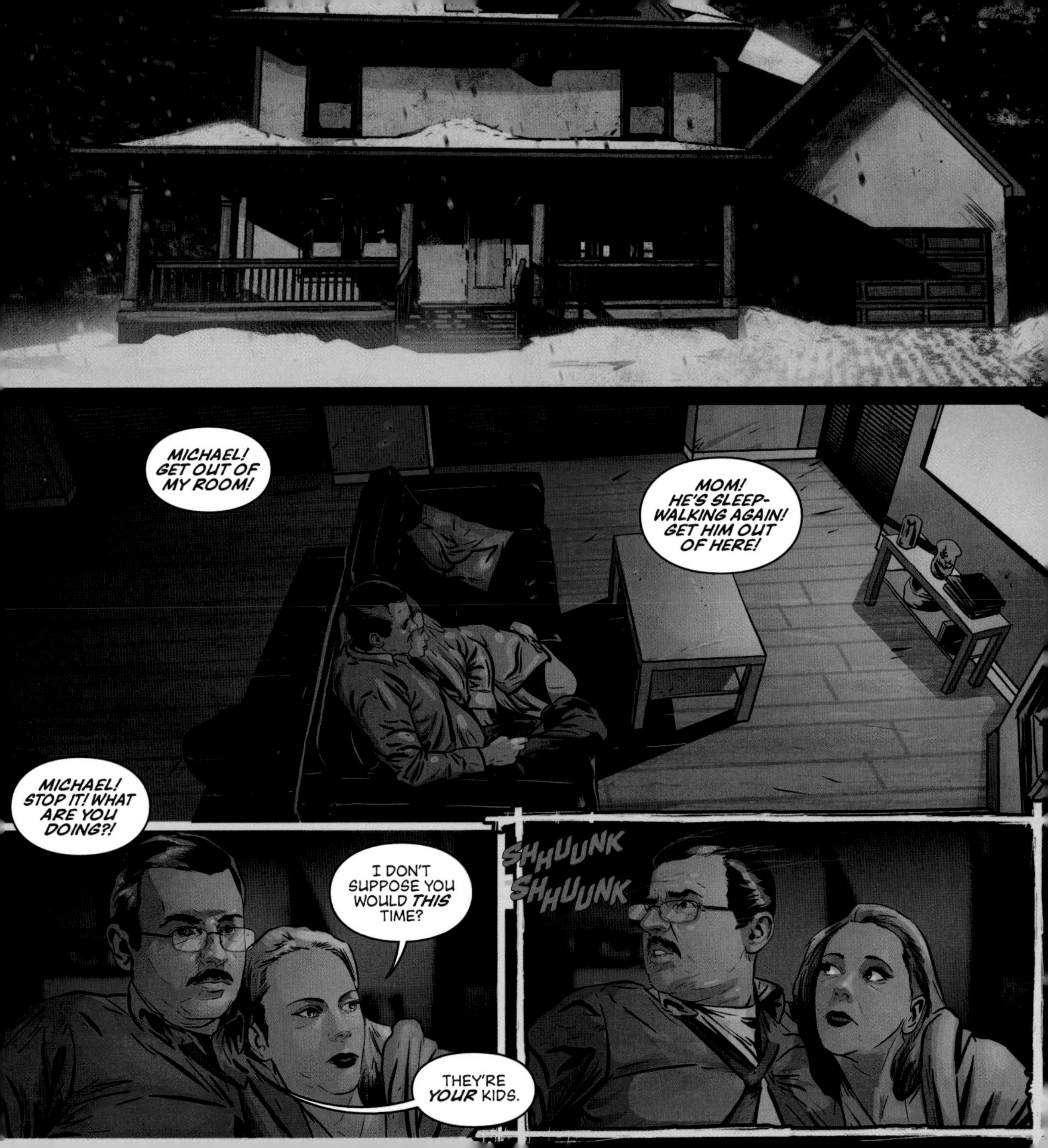
MICHAEL! GET OUT OF MY ROOM!
MOM! HE'S SLEEP-WALKING AGAIN! GET HIM OUT OF HERE!
MICHAEL! STOP IT! WHAT ARE YOU DOING?!
I DON'T SUPPOSE YOU WOULD THIS TIME?
THEY'RE YOUR KIDS.
SHHUUNK
SHHUUNK

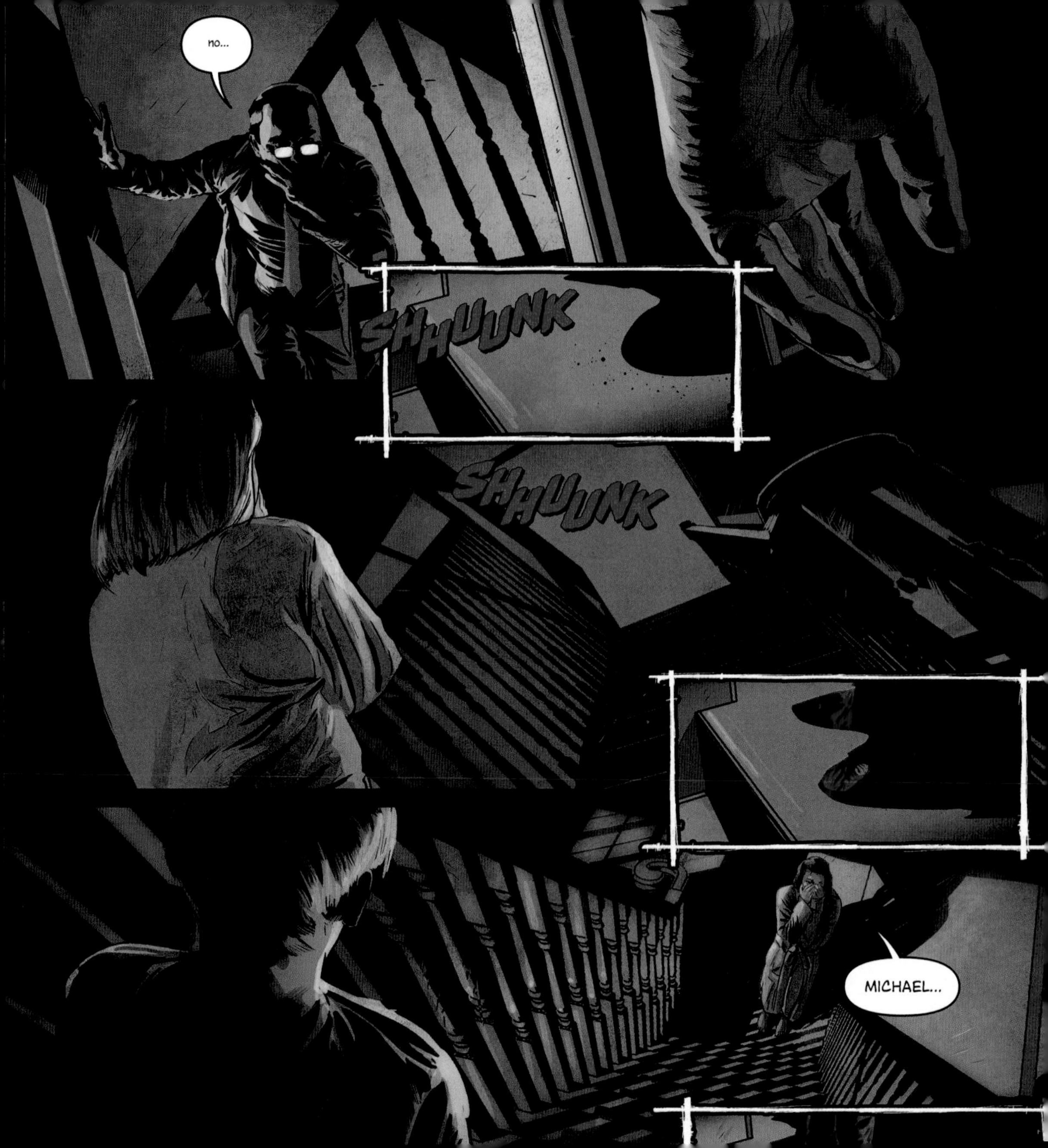
no...
SHHUUNK
SHHUUNK
MICHAEL...

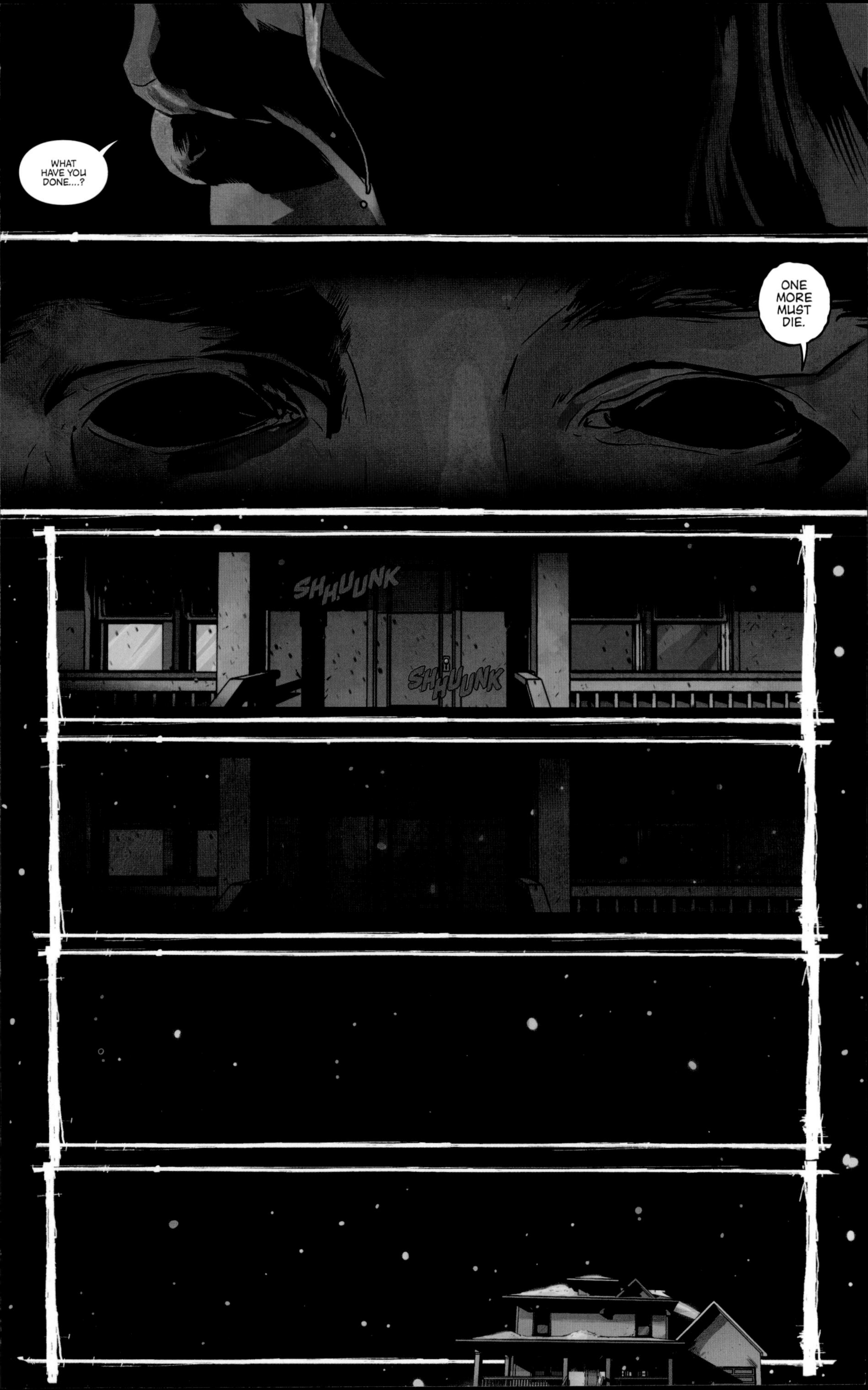
WHAT HAVE YOU DONE....?
ONE MORE MUST DIE.
SHHUUNK
SHHUUNK

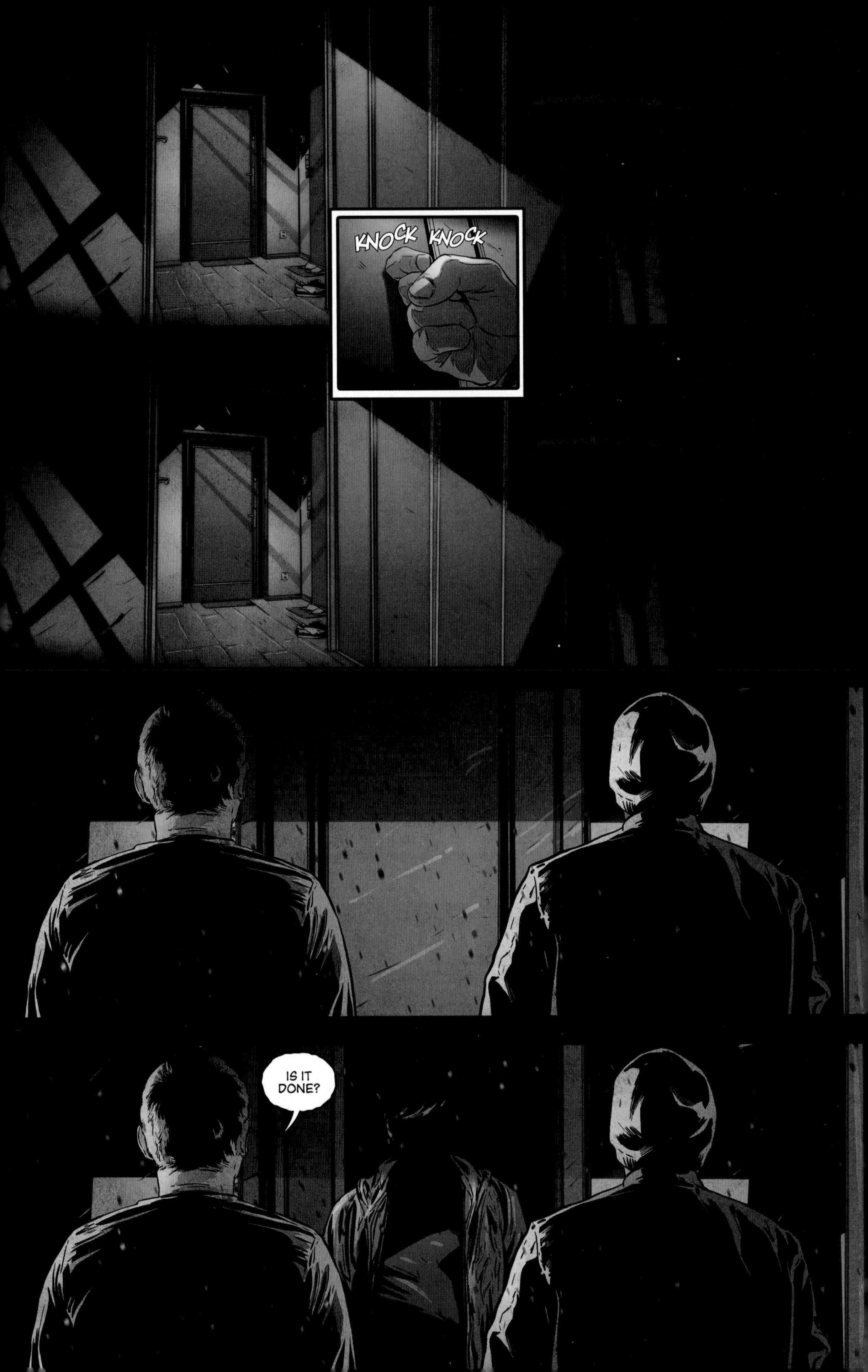
KNOCK KNOCK
IS IT DONE?

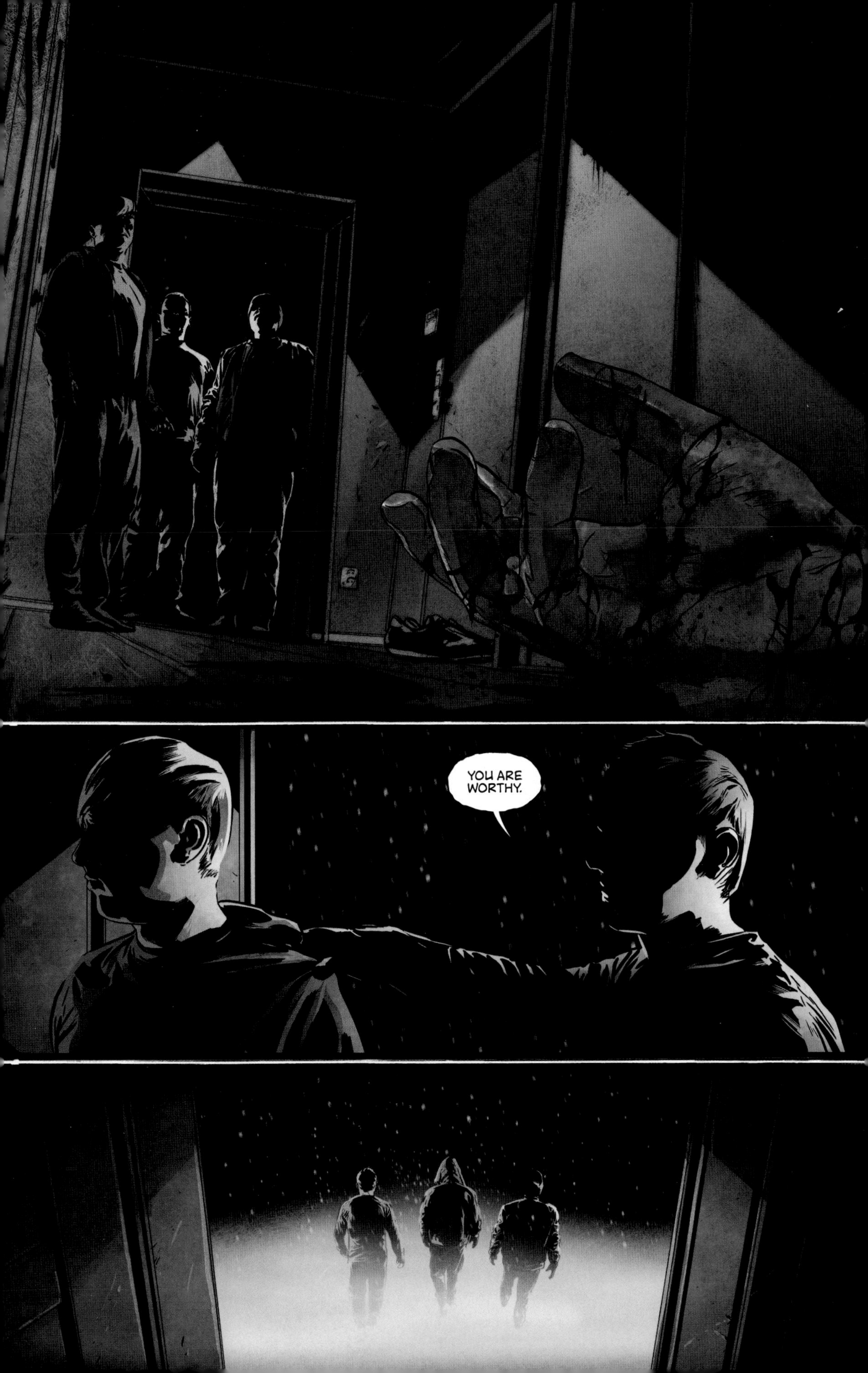
YOU ARE WORTHY.

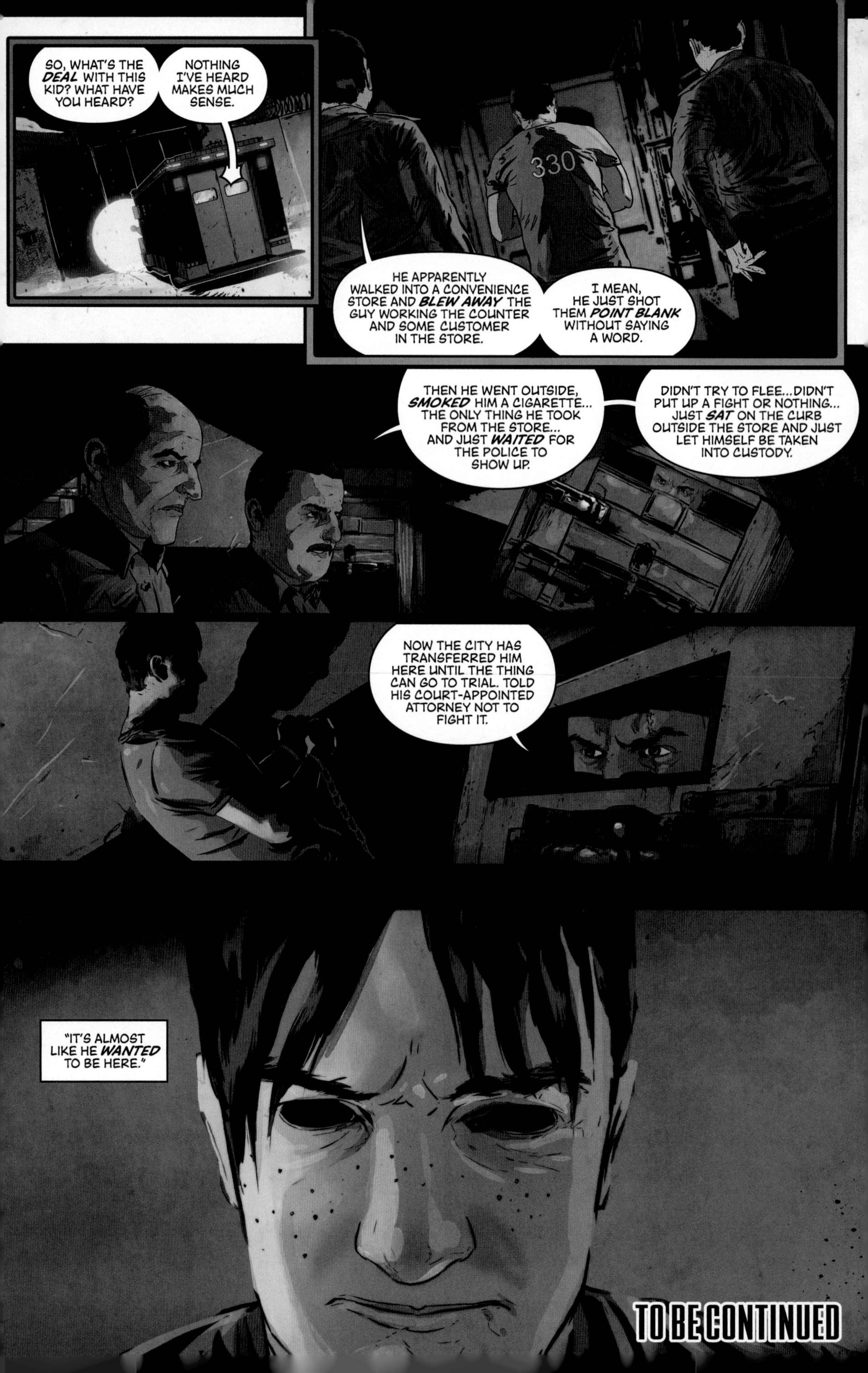
SO, WHAT'S THE DEAL WITH THIS KID? WHAT HAVE YOU HEARD?
NOTHING I'VE HEARD MAKES MUCH SENSE.
330
HE APPARENTLY WALKED INTO A CONVENIENCE STORE AND BLEW AWAY THE GUY WORKING THE COUNTER AND SOME CUSTOMER IN THE STORE.
I MEAN, HE JUST SHOT THEM POINT BLANK WITHOUT SAYING A WORD.
THEN HE WENT OUTSIDE, SMOKED HIM A CIGARETTE... THE ONLY THING HE TOOK FROM THE STORE... AND JUST WAITED FOR THE POLICE TO SHOW UP.
DIDN'T TRY TO FLEE...DIDN'T PUT UP A FIGHT OR NOTHING... JUST SAT ON THE CURB OUTSIDE THE STORE AND JUST LET HIMSELF BE TAKEN INTO CUSTODY.
NOW THE CITY HAS TRANSFERRED HIM HERE UNTIL THE THING CAN GO TO TRIAL. TOLD HIS COURT-APPOINTED ATTORNEY NOT TO FIGHT IT.
"IT'S ALMOST LIKE HE WANTED TO BE HERE."
TO BE CONTINUED

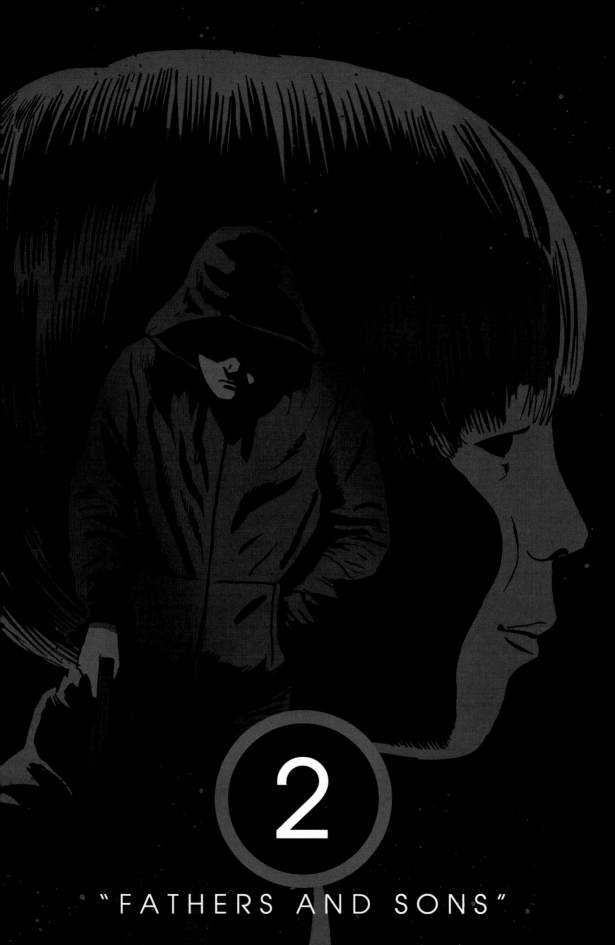

2

"FATHERS AND SONS"

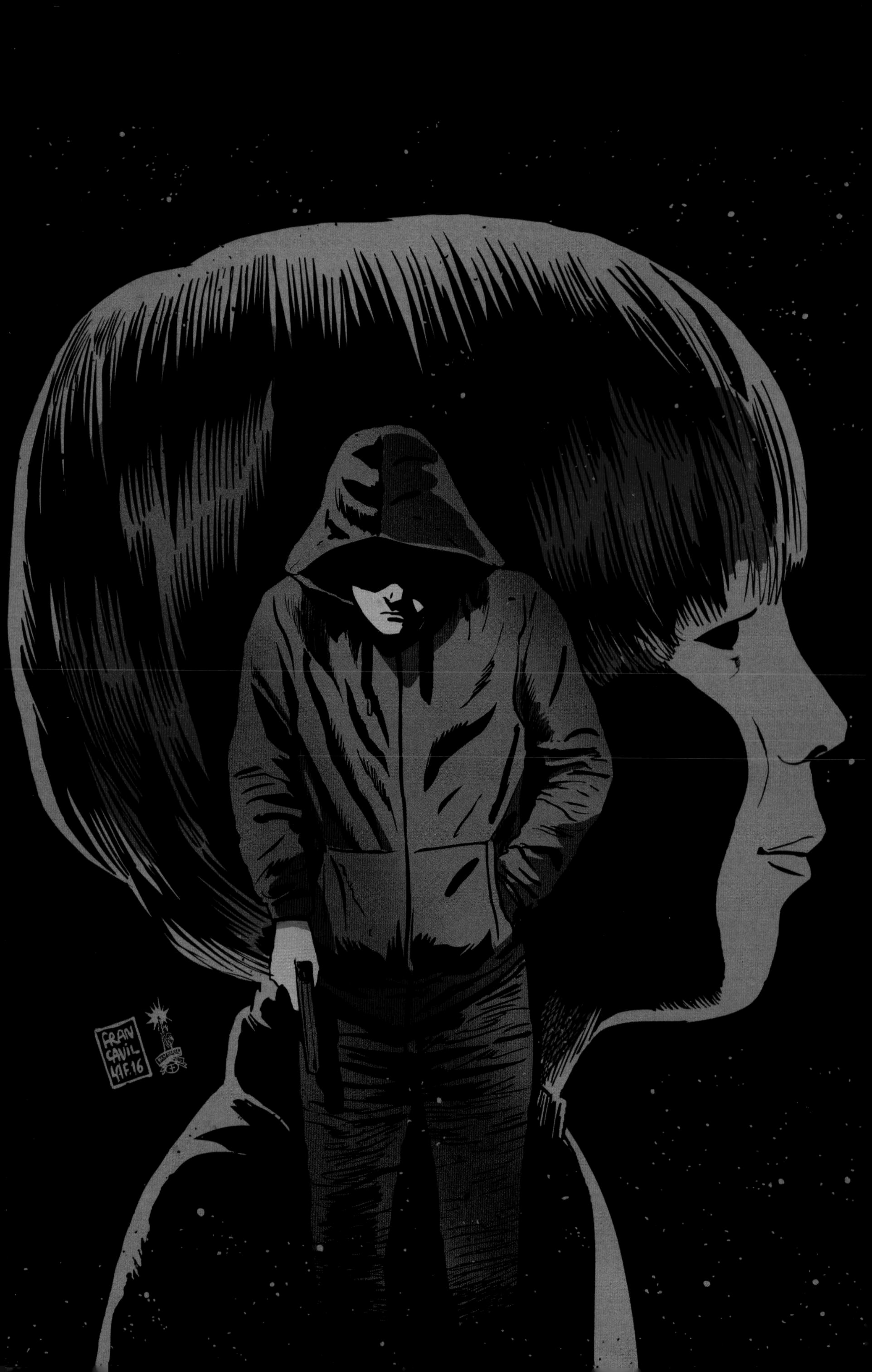
FRAN
CAVIL
LAF.16

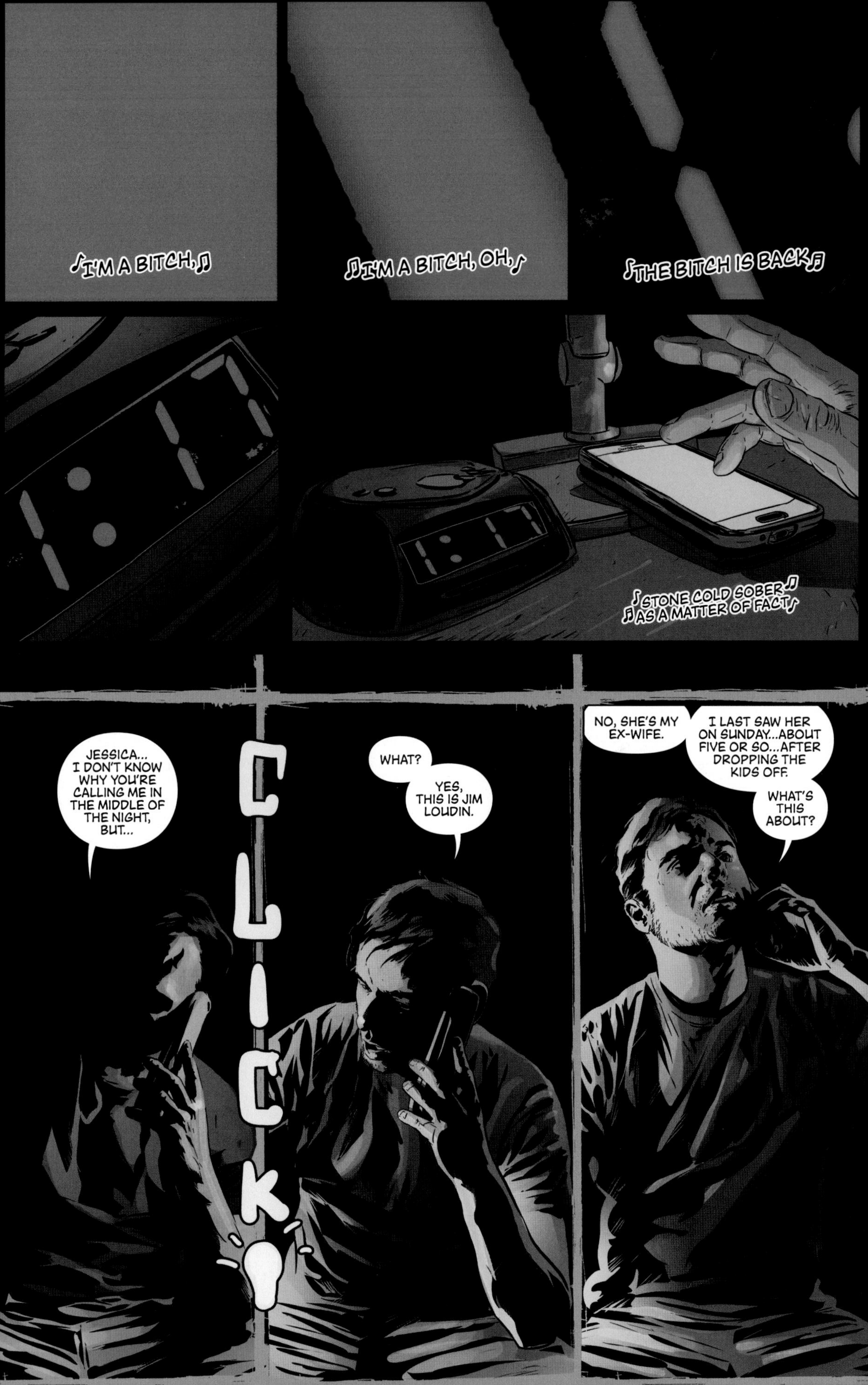
♪I'M A BITCH,♫
♫I'M A BITCH, OH,♪
♪THE BITCH IS BACK♫
♪STONE COLD SOBER♫
♫AS A MATTER OF FACT♪
JESSICA... I DON'T KNOW WHY YOU'RE CALLING ME IN THE MIDDLE OF THE NIGHT, BUT...
CLICK
WHAT?
YES, THIS IS JIM LOUDIN.
NO, SHE'S MY EX-WIFE.
I LAST SAW HER ON SUNDAY...ABOUT FIVE OR SO...AFTER DROPPING THE KIDS OFF.
WHAT'S THIS ABOUT?

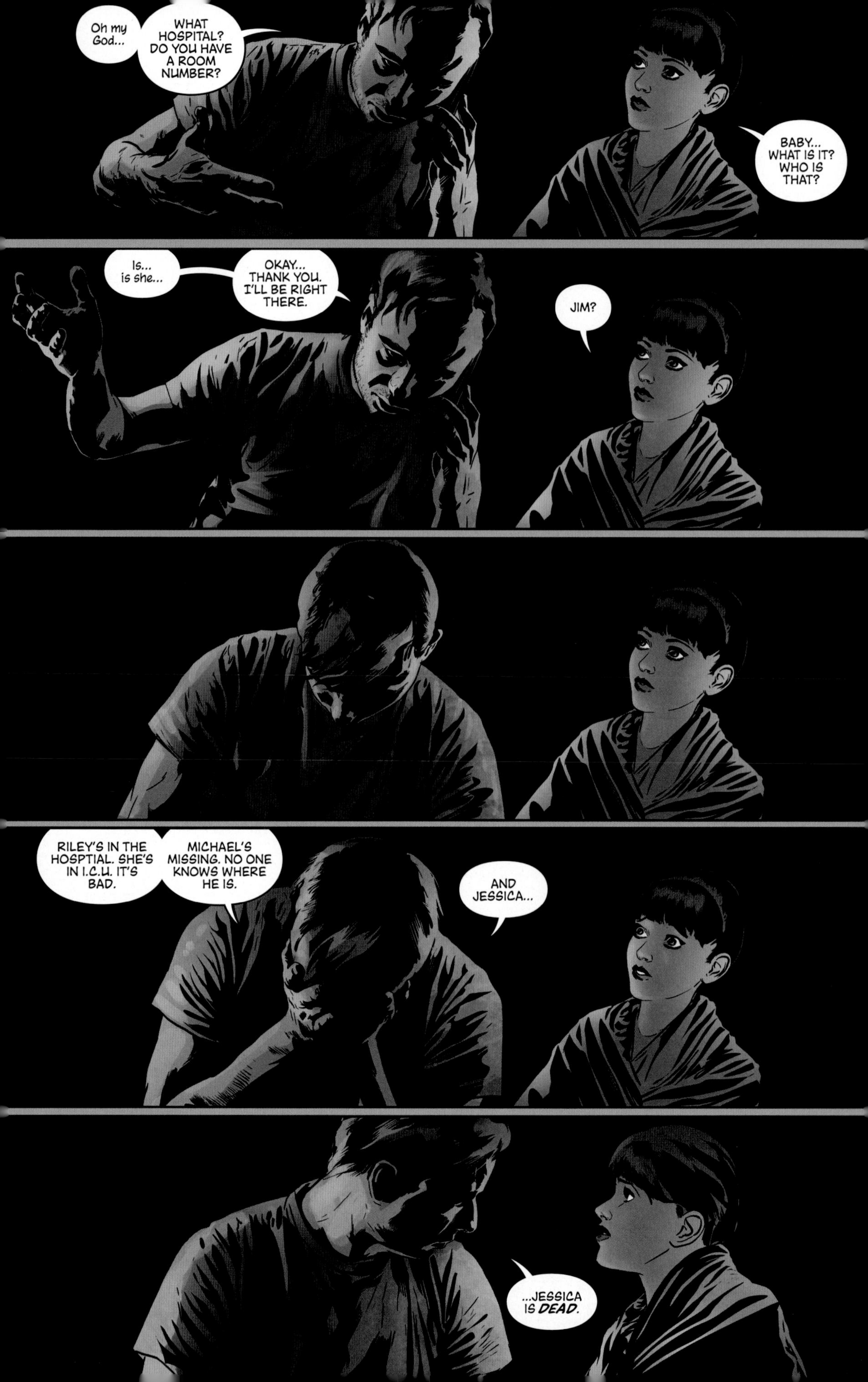
Oh my God...
WHAT HOSPITAL? DO YOU HAVE A ROOM NUMBER?
BABY... WHAT IS IT? WHO IS THAT?
Is... is she...
OKAY... THANK YOU. I'LL BE RIGHT THERE.
JIM?
RILEY'S IN THE HOSPTIAL. SHE'S IN I.C.U. IT'S BAD.
MICHAEL'S MISSING. NO ONE KNOWS WHERE HE IS.
AND JESSICA...
...JESSICA IS *DEAD*.

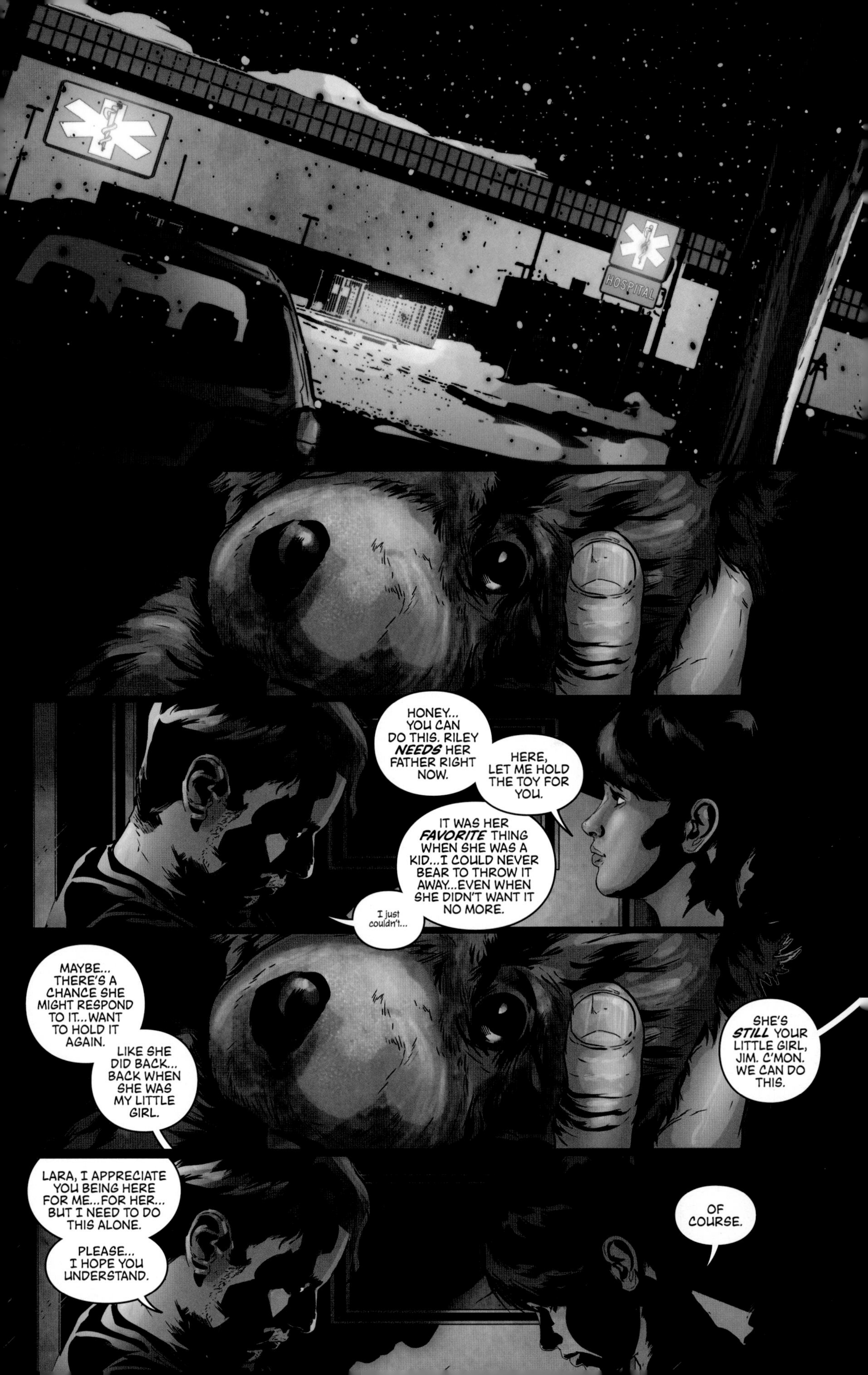
HOSPITAL
HONEY... YOU CAN DO THIS. RILEY NEEDS HER FATHER RIGHT NOW.
HERE, LET ME HOLD THE TOY FOR YOU.
IT WAS HER FAVORITE THING WHEN SHE WAS A KID...I COULD NEVER BEAR TO THROW IT AWAY...EVEN WHEN SHE DIDN'T WANT IT NO MORE.
I just couldn't...
MAYBE... THERE'S A CHANCE SHE MIGHT RESPOND TO IT...WANT TO HOLD IT AGAIN.
LIKE SHE DID BACK... BACK WHEN SHE WAS MY LITTLE GIRL.
SHE'S STILL YOUR LITTLE GIRL, JIM. C'MON. WE CAN DO THIS.
LARA, I APPRECIATE YOU BEING HERE FOR ME...FOR HER... BUT I NEED TO DO THIS ALONE.
PLEASE... I HOPE YOU UNDERSTAND.
OF COURSE.

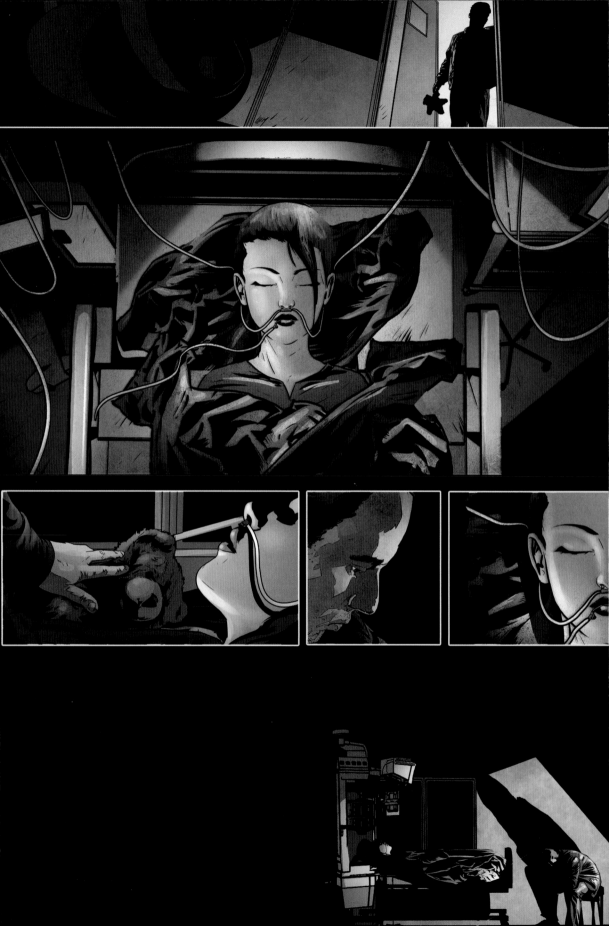

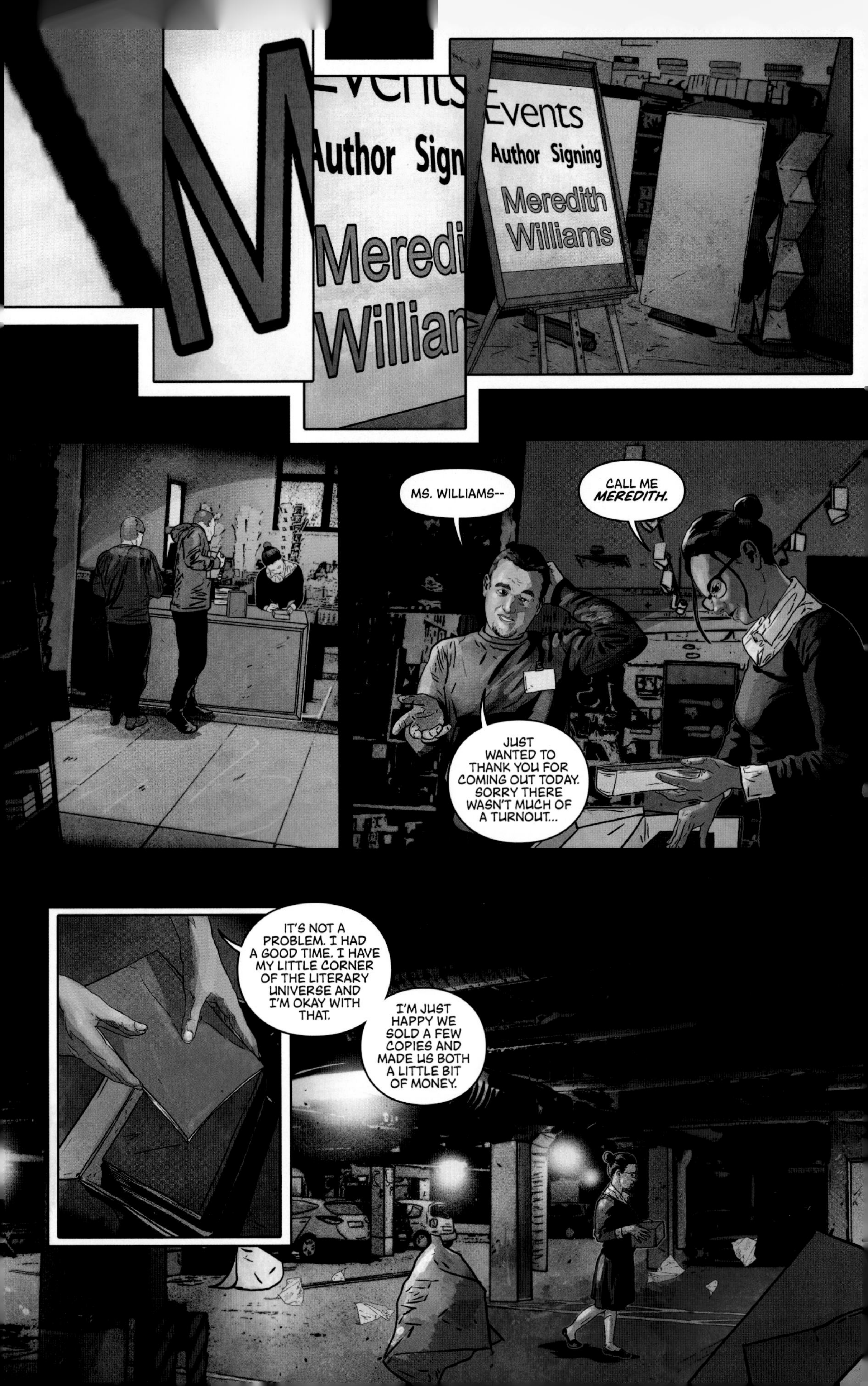
Events
Author Signing
Meredith Williams
MS. WILLIAMS--
CALL ME MEREDITH.
JUST WANTED TO THANK YOU FOR COMING OUT TODAY. SORRY THERE WASN'T MUCH OF A TURNOUT...
IT'S NOT A PROBLEM. I HAD A GOOD TIME. I HAVE MY LITTLE CORNER OF THE LITERARY UNIVERSE AND I'M OKAY WITH THAT.
I'M JUST HAPPY WE SOLD A FEW COPIES AND MADE US BOTH A LITTLE BIT OF MONEY.

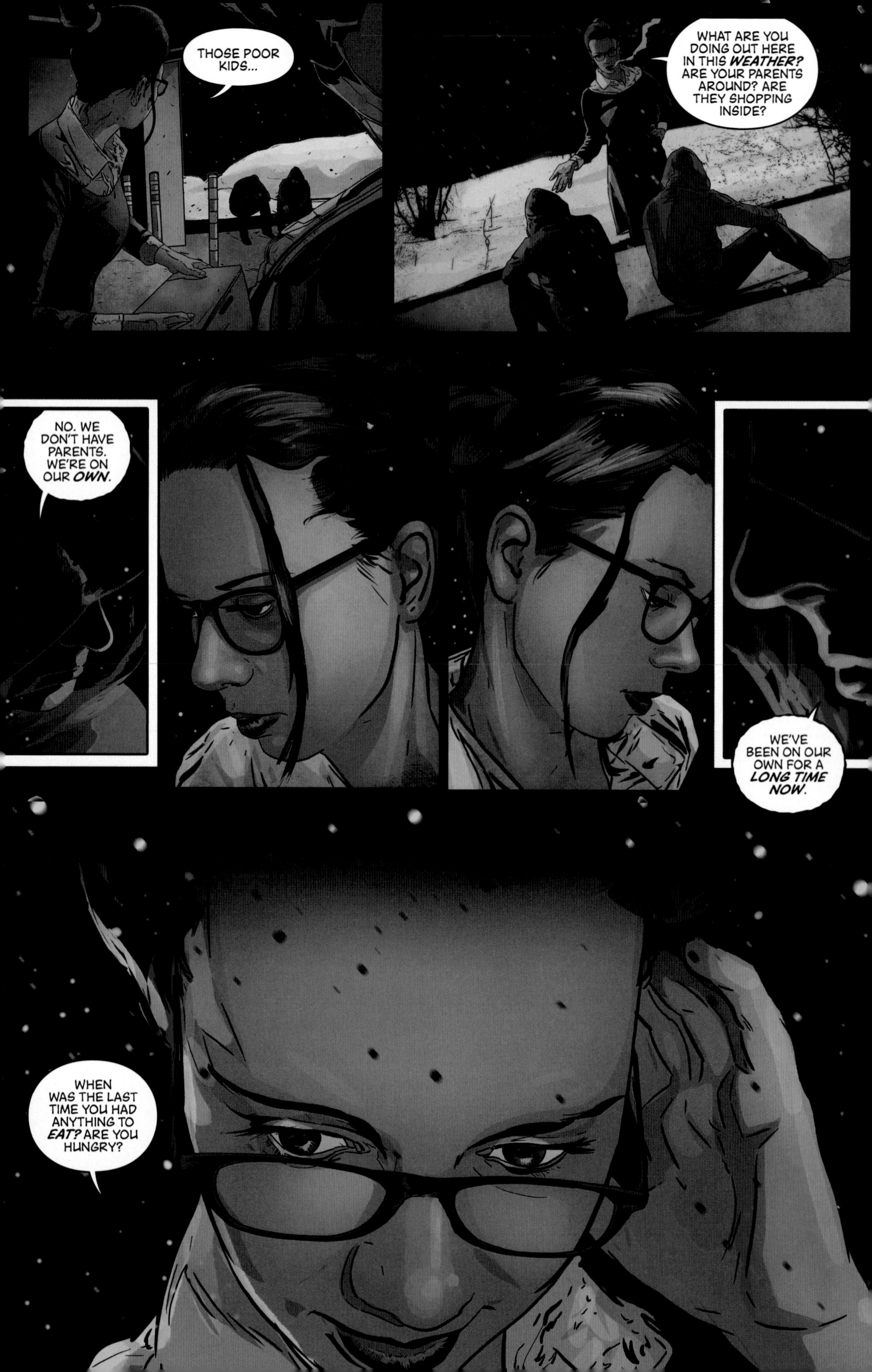
THOSE POOR KIDS...
WHAT ARE YOU DOING OUT HERE IN THIS *WEATHER?* ARE YOUR PARENTS AROUND? ARE THEY SHOPPING INSIDE?
NO. WE DON'T HAVE PARENTS. WE'RE ON OUR *OWN*.
WE'VE BEEN ON OUR OWN FOR A *LONG TIME NOW*.
WHEN WAS THE LAST TIME YOU HAD ANYTHING TO *EAT?* ARE YOU HUNGRY?

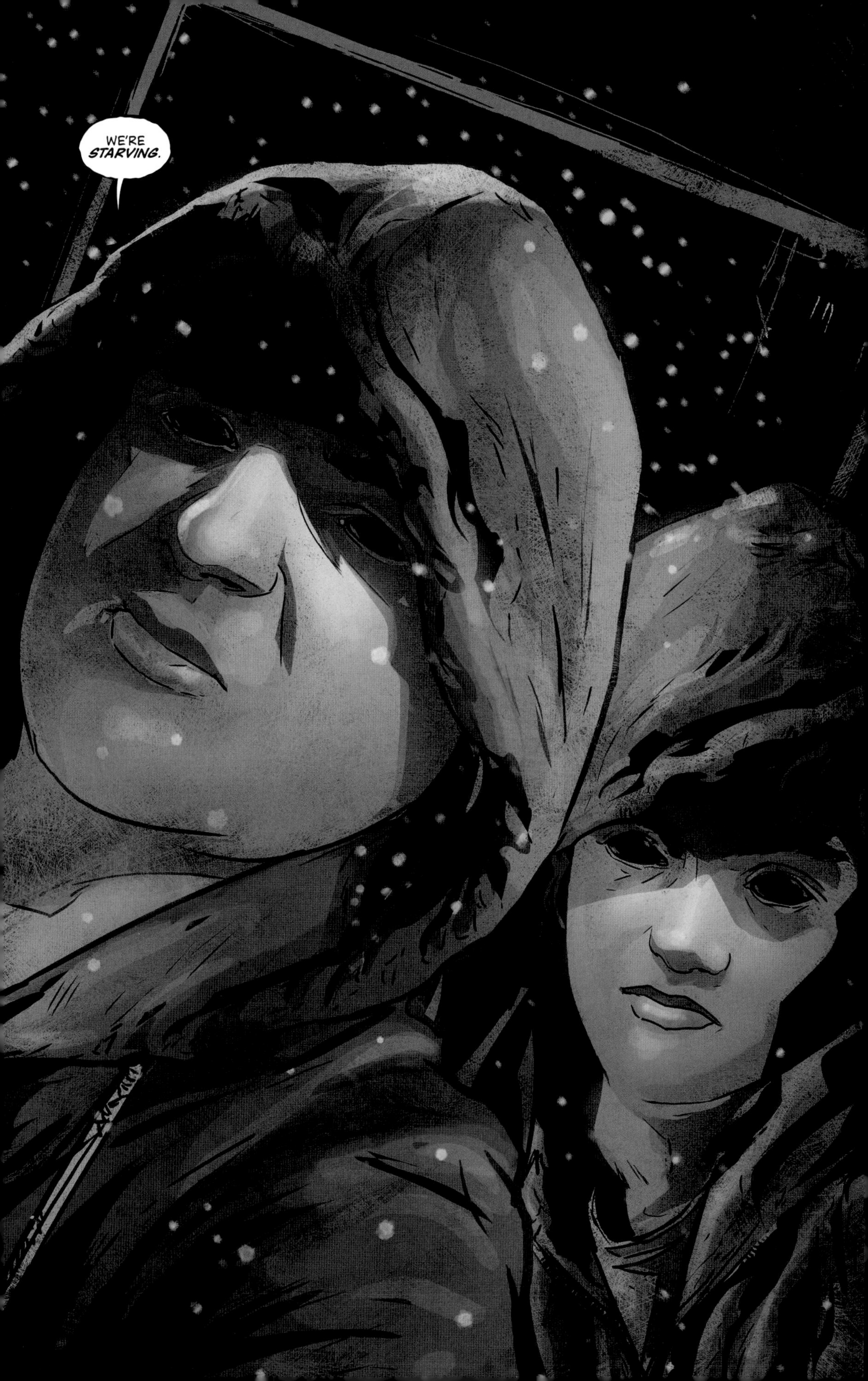
WE'RE STARVING.

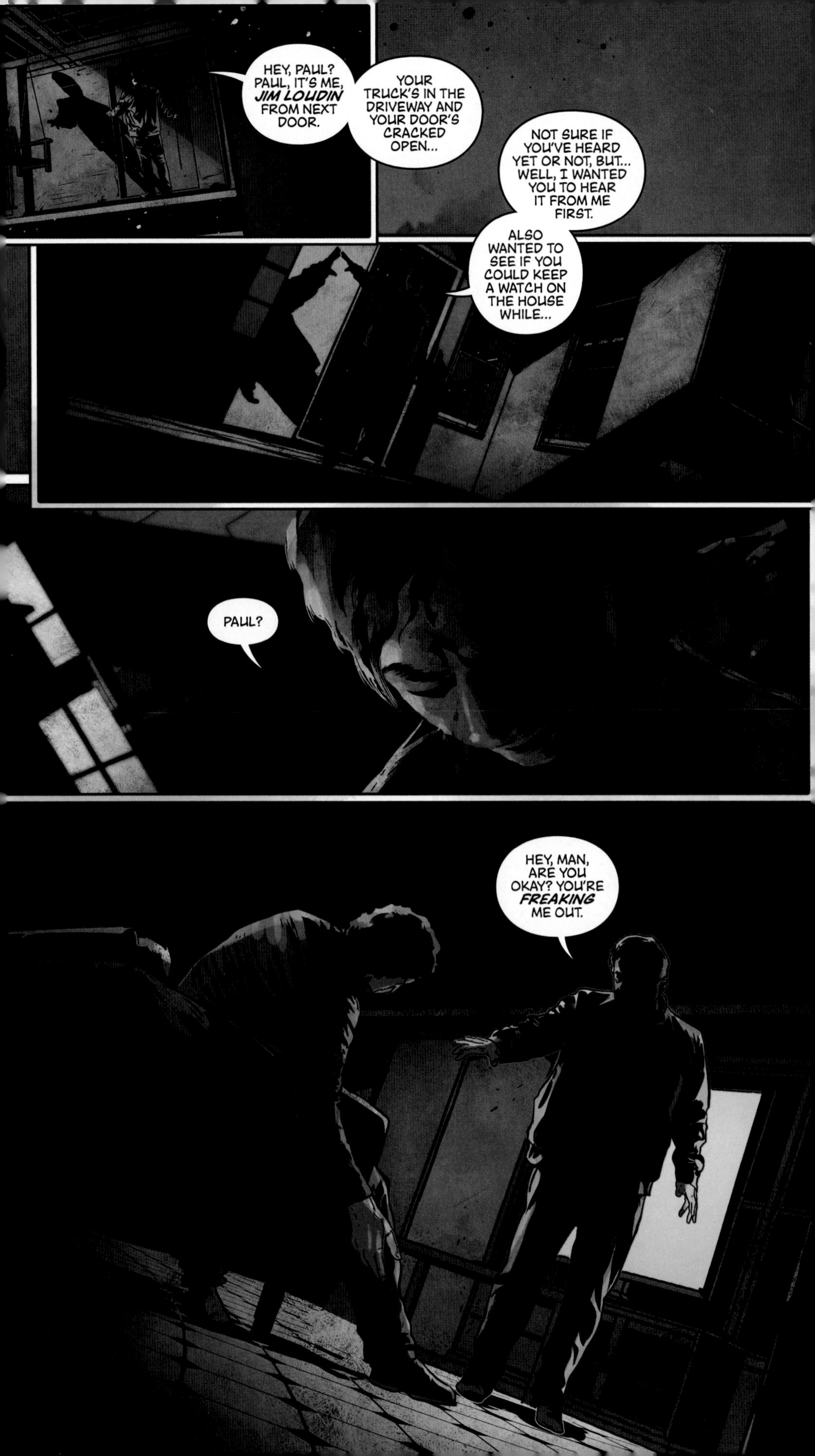
HEY, PAUL? PAUL, IT'S ME, JIM LOUDIN FROM NEXT DOOR.
YOUR TRUCK'S IN THE DRIVEWAY AND YOUR DOOR'S CRACKED OPEN...
NOT SURE IF YOU'VE HEARD YET OR NOT, BUT... WELL, I WANTED YOU TO HEAR IT FROM ME FIRST.
ALSO WANTED TO SEE IF YOU COULD KEEP A WATCH ON THE HOUSE WHILE...
PAUL?
HEY, MAN, ARE YOU OKAY? YOU'RE FREAKING ME OUT.

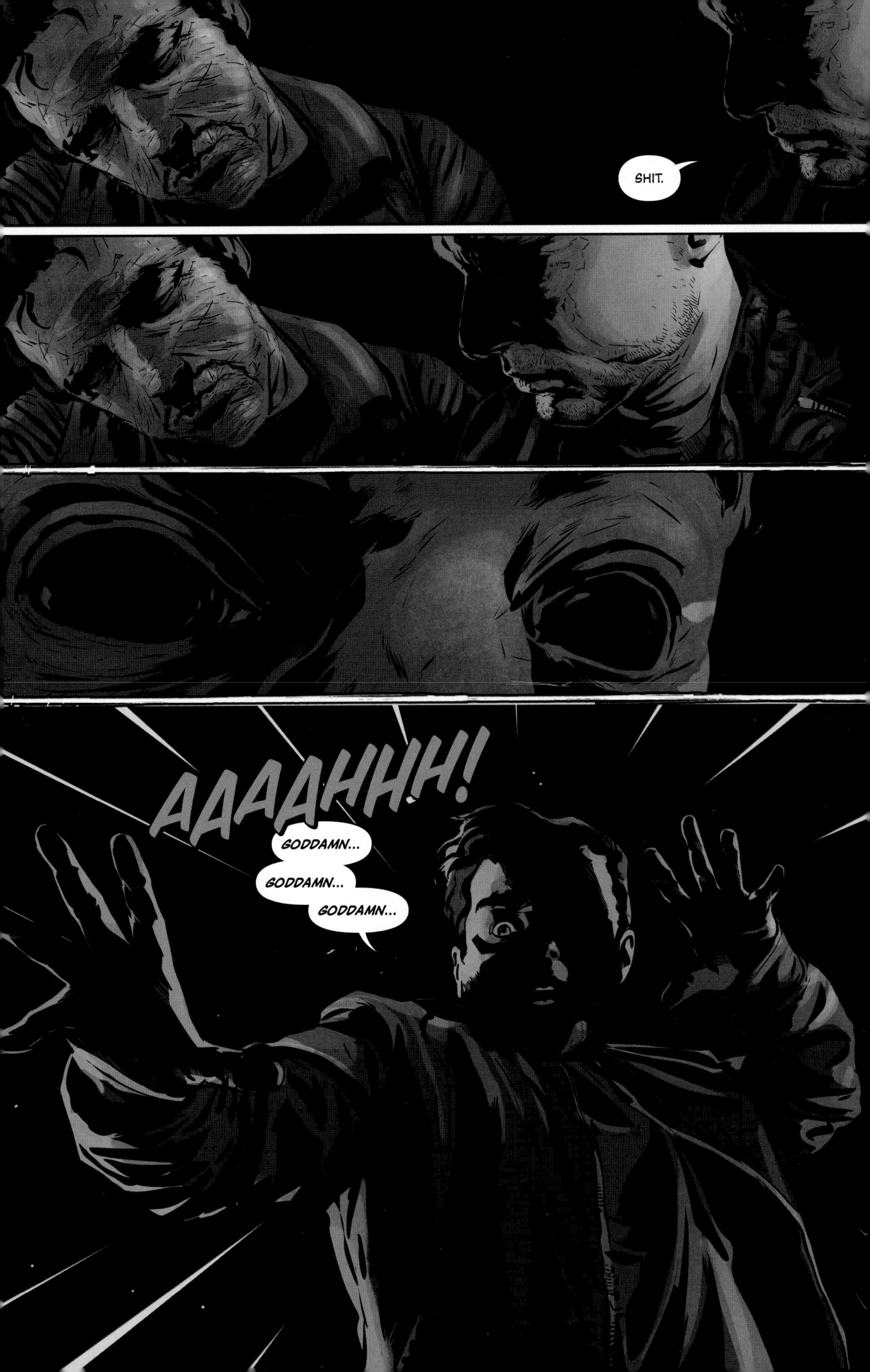
SHIT.
AAAAHHH!
GODDAMN...
GODDAMN...
GODDAMN...

KNOCK
KNOCK

MICHAEL...?

OH MY GOD, WE'VE BEEN SO *WORRIED* ABOUT YOU! WE DIDN'T KNOW WHAT HAPPENED TO YOU WHEN YOUR MOM--

YOUR DAD WILL BE SO *RELIEVED*...

MICHAEL... WHERE HAVE YOU *BEEN*? WHAT *HAPPENED* AT YOUR HOUSE?

AND-- WHO ARE THESE *BOYS* YOU'RE WITH?

I'LL TELL YOU EVERYTHING. BUT FIRST...

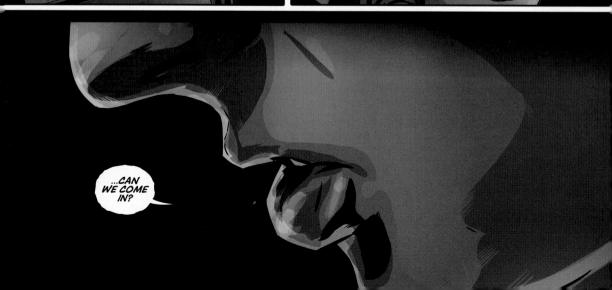

...CAN WE COME IN?

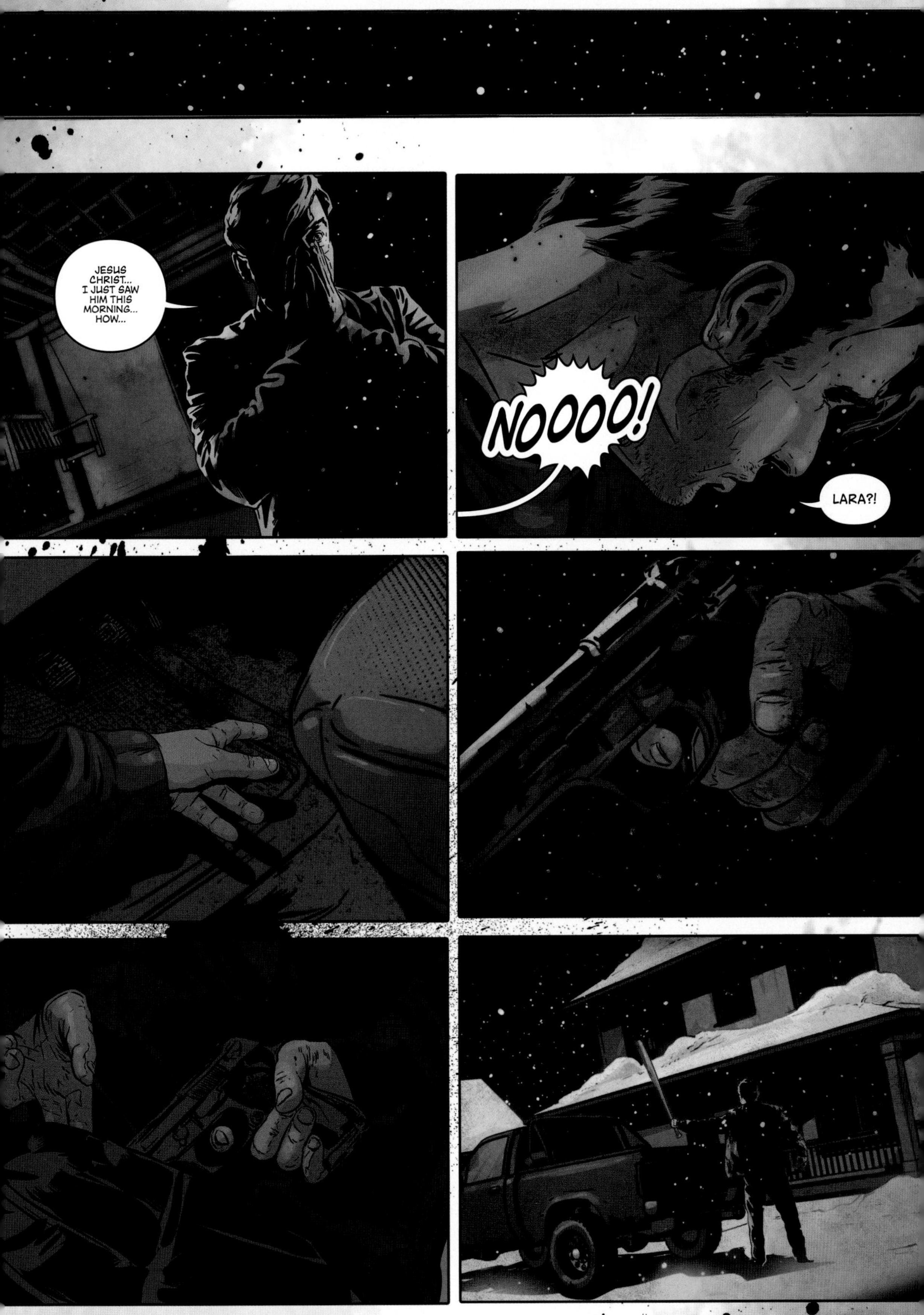
JESUS CHRIST... I JUST SAW HIM THIS MORNING... HOW...
NOOOO!
LARA?!

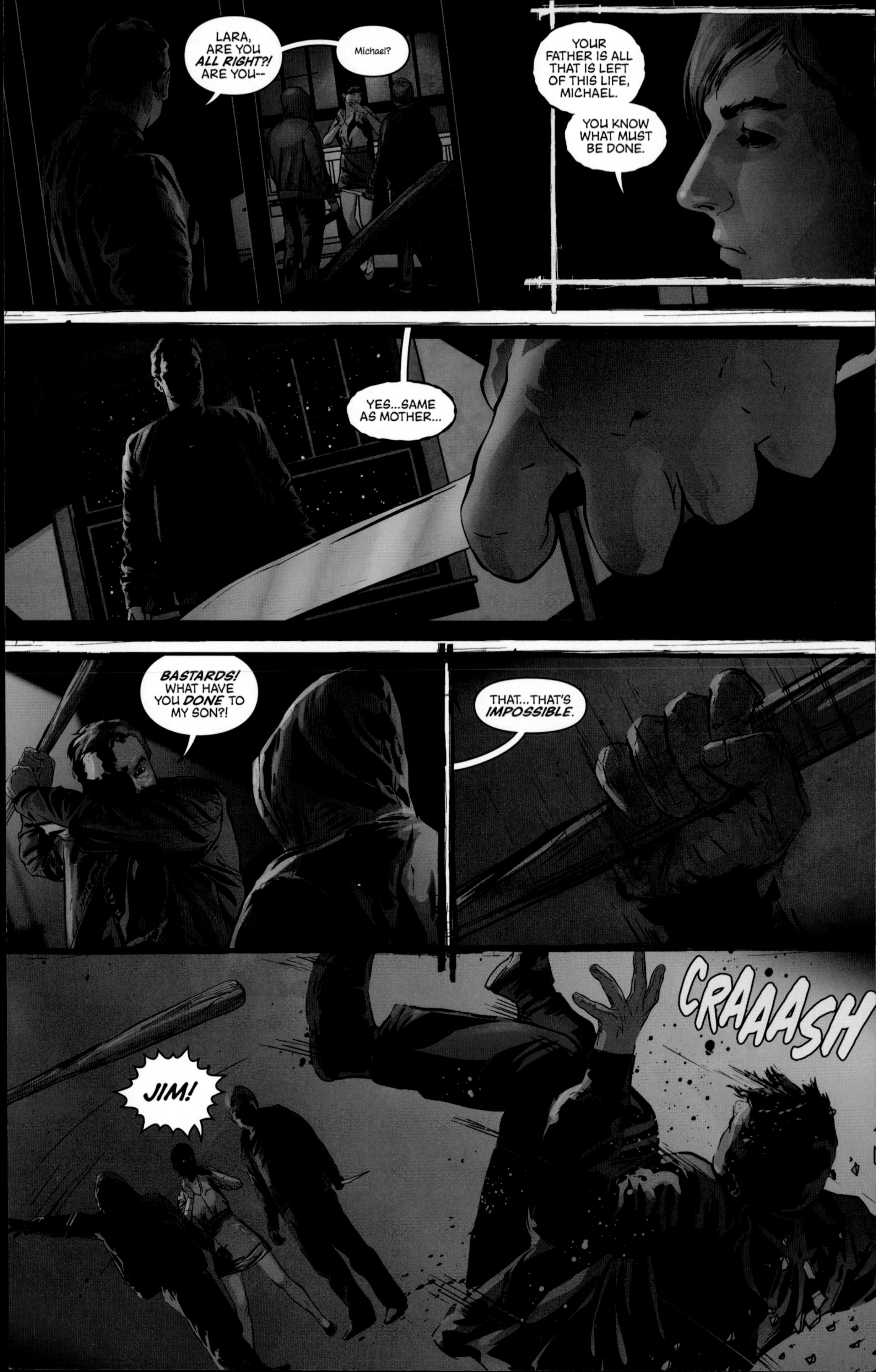
LARA, ARE YOU ***ALL RIGHT?!*** ARE YOU--
Michael?
YOUR FATHER IS ALL THAT IS LEFT OF THIS LIFE, MICHAEL.
YOU KNOW WHAT MUST BE DONE.
YES...SAME AS MOTHER...
BASTARDS! WHAT HAVE YOU ***DONE*** TO MY SON?!
THAT...THAT'S ***IMPOSSIBLE***.
CRAAASH
JIM!

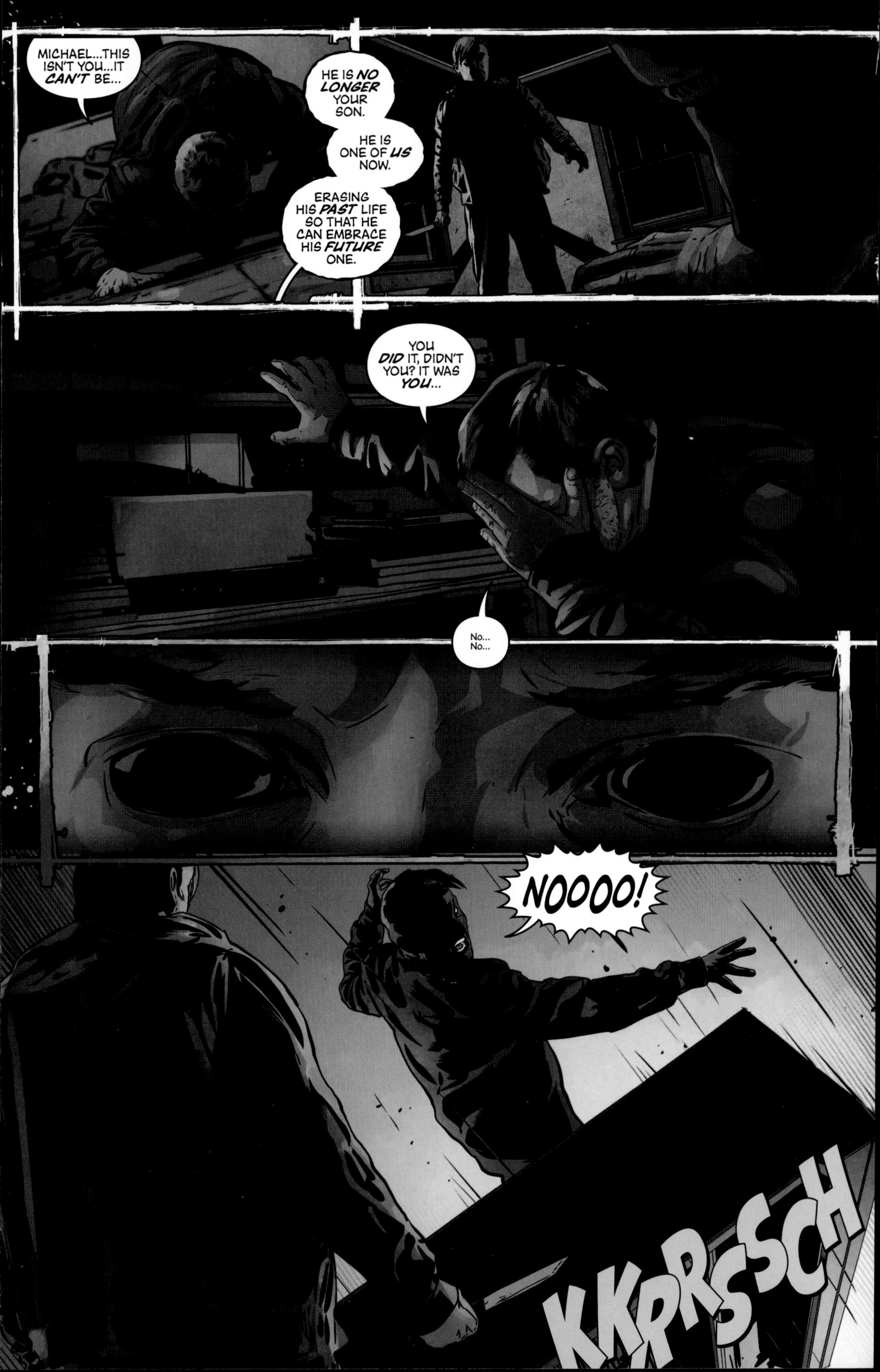
MICHAEL...THIS ISN'T YOU...IT CAN'T BE...
HE IS NO LONGER YOUR SON.
HE IS ONE OF US NOW.
ERASING HIS PAST LIFE SO THAT HE CAN EMBRACE HIS FUTURE ONE.
YOU DID IT, DIDN'T YOU? IT WAS YOU...
No... No...
NOOOO!
KKPRSSCH

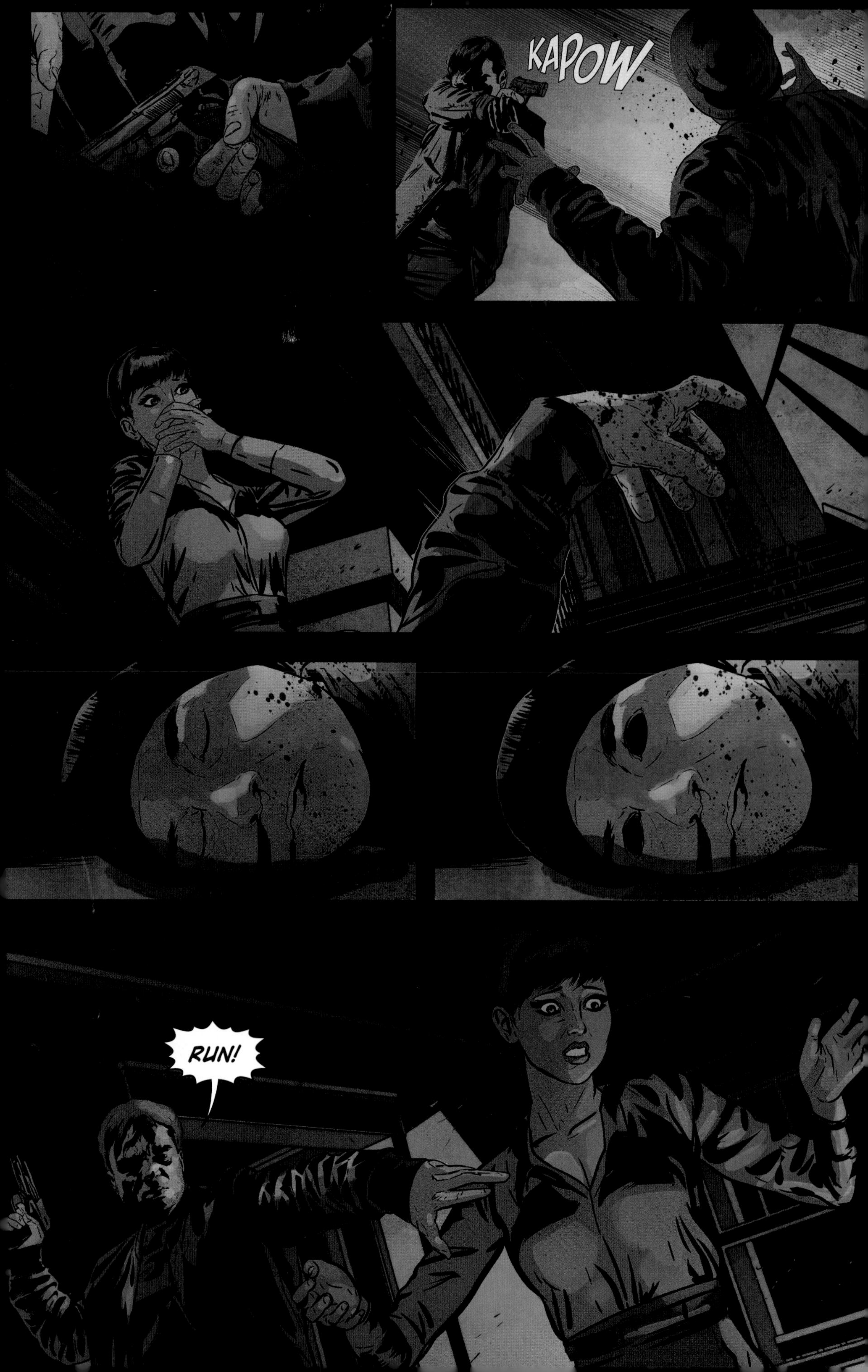
KAPOW
RUN!

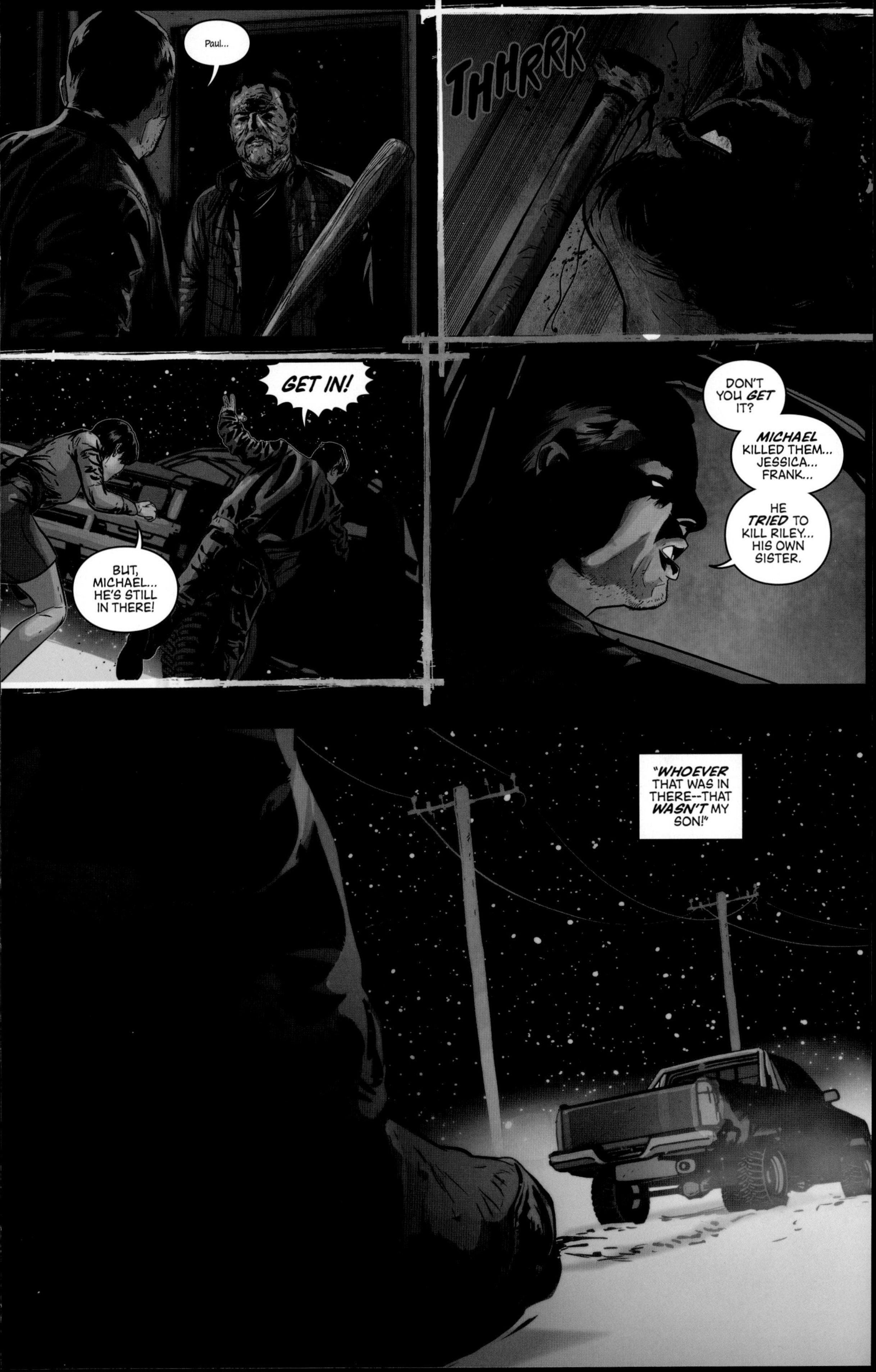
Paul...
THHRRK
GET IN!
BUT, MICHAEL... HE'S STILL IN THERE!
DON'T YOU GET IT?
MICHAEL KILLED THEM... JESSICA... FRANK...
HE TRIED TO KILL RILEY... HIS OWN SISTER.
"WHOEVER THAT WAS IN THERE--THAT WASN'T MY SON!"

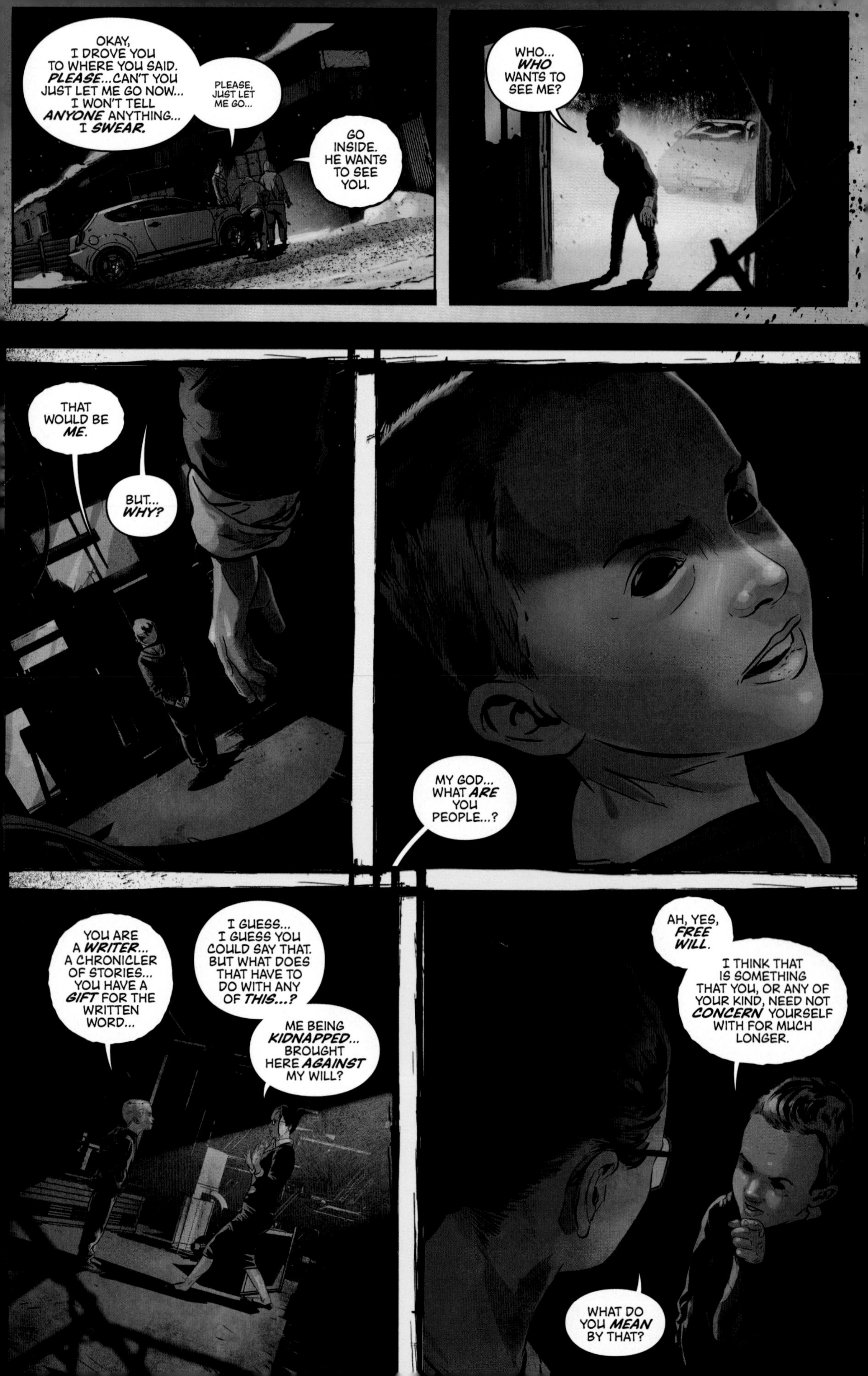
OKAY, I DROVE YOU TO WHERE YOU SAID. PLEASE...CAN'T YOU JUST LET ME GO NOW... I WON'T TELL ANYONE ANYTHING... I SWEAR.
PLEASE, JUST LET ME GO...
GO INSIDE. HE WANTS TO SEE YOU.
WHO... WHO WANTS TO SEE ME?
THAT WOULD BE ME.
BUT... WHY?
MY GOD... WHAT ARE YOU PEOPLE...?
YOU ARE A WRITER... A CHRONICLER OF STORIES... YOU HAVE A GIFT FOR THE WRITTEN WORD...
I GUESS... I GUESS YOU COULD SAY THAT. BUT WHAT DOES THAT HAVE TO DO WITH ANY OF THIS...?
ME BEING KIDNAPPED... BROUGHT HERE AGAINST MY WILL?
AH, YES, FREE WILL.
I THINK THAT IS SOMETHING THAT YOU, OR ANY OF YOUR KIND, NEED NOT CONCERN YOURSELF WITH FOR MUCH LONGER.
WHAT DO YOU MEAN BY THAT?

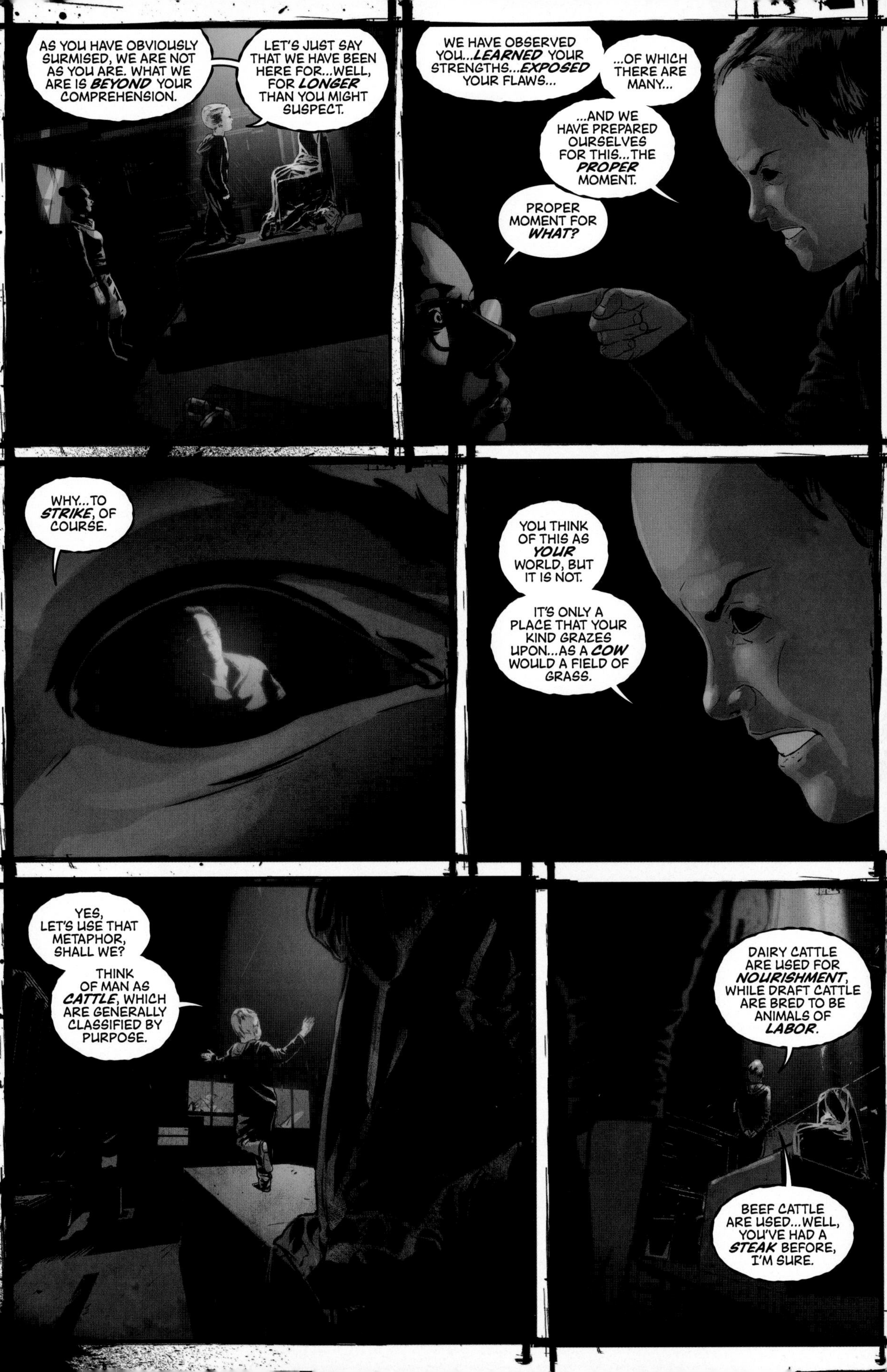
AS YOU HAVE OBVIOUSLY SURMISED, WE ARE NOT AS YOU ARE. WHAT WE ARE IS BEYOND YOUR COMPREHENSION.
LET'S JUST SAY THAT WE HAVE BEEN HERE FOR...WELL, FOR LONGER THAN YOU MIGHT SUSPECT.
WE HAVE OBSERVED YOU...LEARNED YOUR STRENGTHS...EXPOSED YOUR FLAWS...
...OF WHICH THERE ARE MANY...
...AND WE HAVE PREPARED OURSELVES FOR THIS...THE PROPER MOMENT.
PROPER MOMENT FOR WHAT?
WHY...TO STRIKE, OF COURSE.
YOU THINK OF THIS AS YOUR WORLD, BUT IT IS NOT.
IT'S ONLY A PLACE THAT YOUR KIND GRAZES UPON...AS A COW WOULD A FIELD OF GRASS.
YES, LET'S USE THAT METAPHOR, SHALL WE?
THINK OF MAN AS CATTLE, WHICH ARE GENERALLY CLASSIFIED BY PURPOSE.
DAIRY CATTLE ARE USED FOR NOURISHMENT, WHILE DRAFT CATTLE ARE BRED TO BE ANIMALS OF LABOR.
BEEF CATTLE ARE USED...WELL, YOU'VE HAD A STEAK BEFORE, I'M SURE.

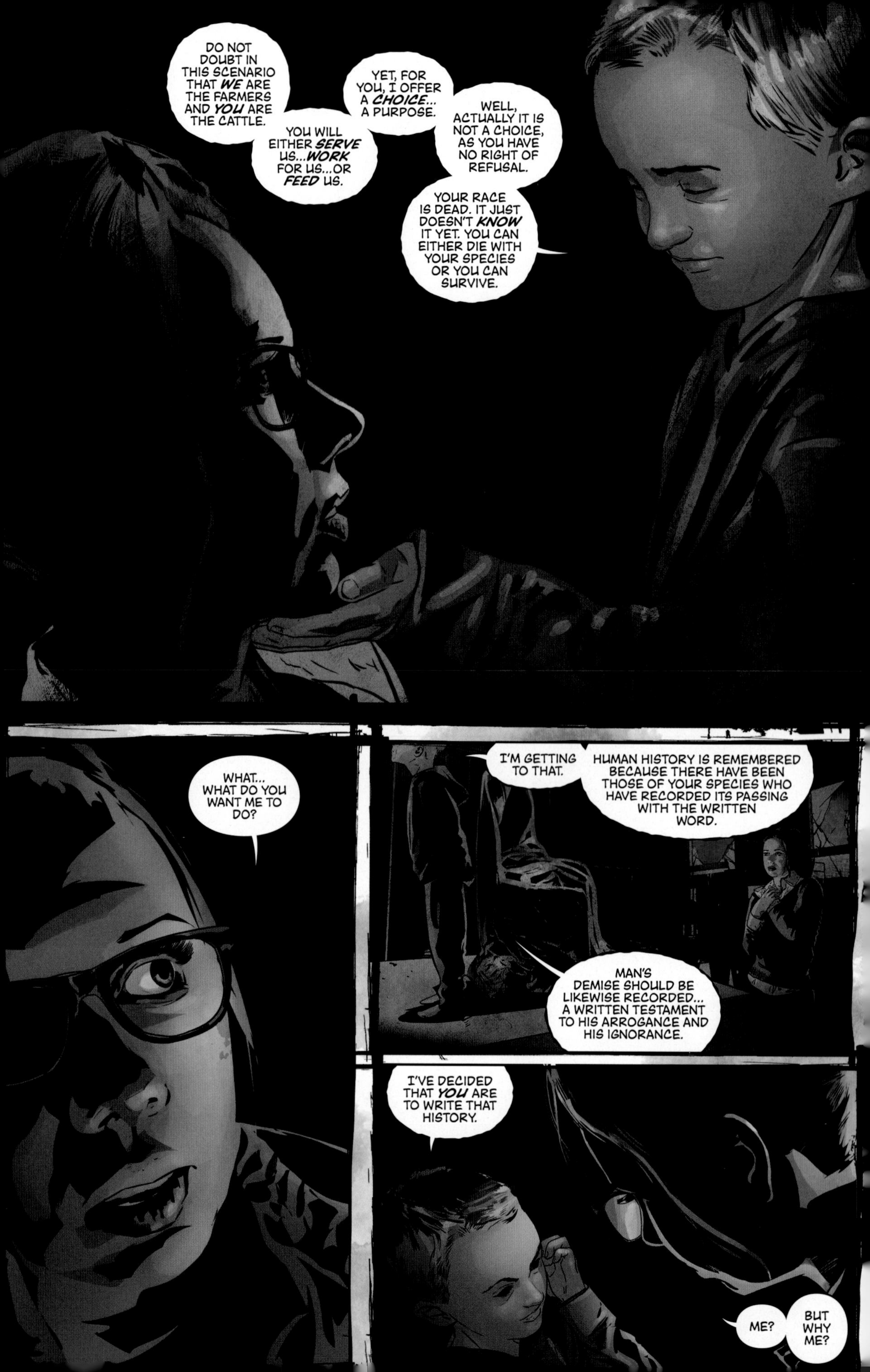

DO NOT DOUBT IN THIS SCENARIO THAT WE ARE THE FARMERS AND YOU ARE THE CATTLE.
YOU WILL EITHER SERVE US...WORK FOR US...OR FEED US.
YET, FOR YOU, I OFFER A CHOICE... A PURPOSE.
WELL, ACTUALLY IT IS NOT A CHOICE, AS YOU HAVE NO RIGHT OF REFUSAL.
YOUR RACE IS DEAD. IT JUST DOESN'T KNOW IT YET. YOU CAN EITHER DIE WITH YOUR SPECIES OR YOU CAN SURVIVE.
WHAT... WHAT DO YOU WANT ME TO DO?
I'M GETTING TO THAT.
HUMAN HISTORY IS REMEMBERED BECAUSE THERE HAVE BEEN THOSE OF YOUR SPECIES WHO HAVE RECORDED ITS PASSING WITH THE WRITTEN WORD.
MAN'S DEMISE SHOULD BE LIKEWISE RECORDED... A WRITTEN TESTAMENT TO HIS ARROGANCE AND HIS IGNORANCE.
I'VE DECIDED THAT YOU ARE TO WRITE THAT HISTORY.
ME?
BUT WHY ME?

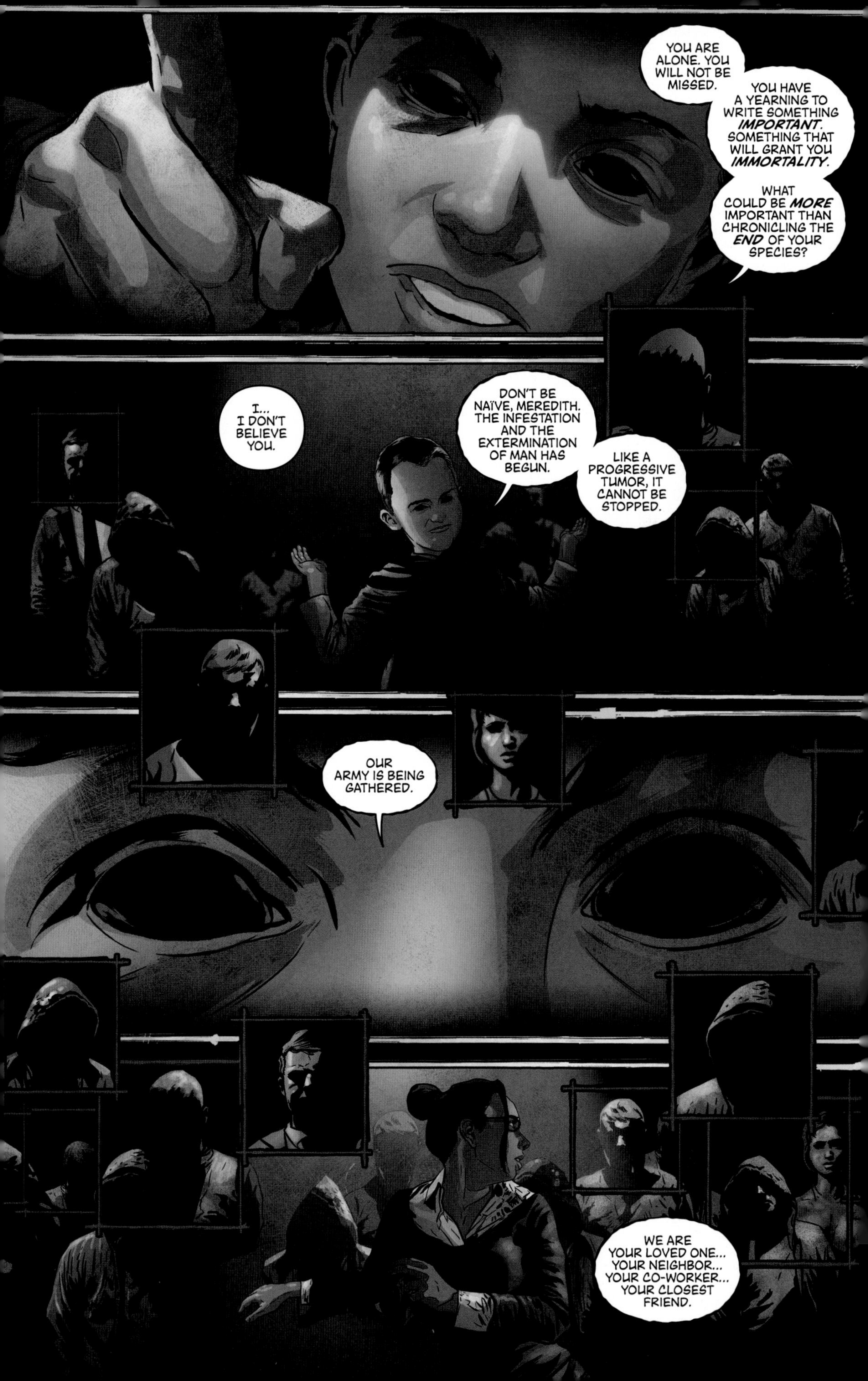
YOU ARE ALONE. YOU WILL NOT BE MISSED.
YOU HAVE A YEARNING TO WRITE SOMETHING *IMPORTANT*. SOMETHING THAT WILL GRANT YOU *IMMORTALITY*.
WHAT COULD BE *MORE* IMPORTANT THAN CHRONICLING THE *END* OF YOUR SPECIES?
I... I DON'T BELIEVE YOU.
DON'T BE NAÏVE, MEREDITH. THE INFESTATION AND THE EXTERMINATION OF MAN HAS BEGUN.
LIKE A PROGRESSIVE TUMOR, IT CANNOT BE STOPPED.
OUR ARMY IS BEING GATHERED.
WE ARE YOUR LOVED ONE... YOUR NEIGHBOR... YOUR CO-WORKER... YOUR CLOSEST FRIEND.

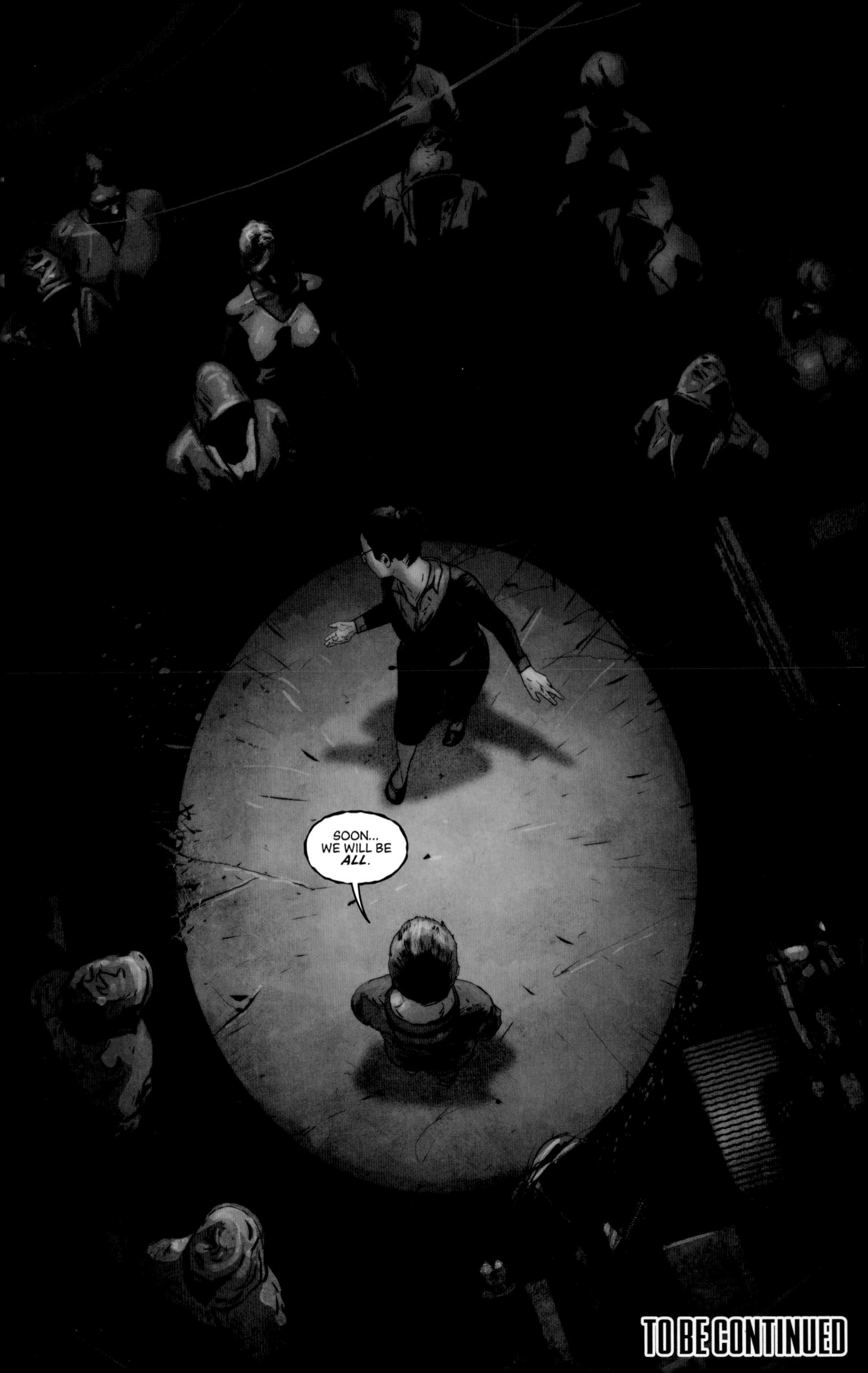
SOON... WE WILL BE ALL.
TO BE CONTINUED

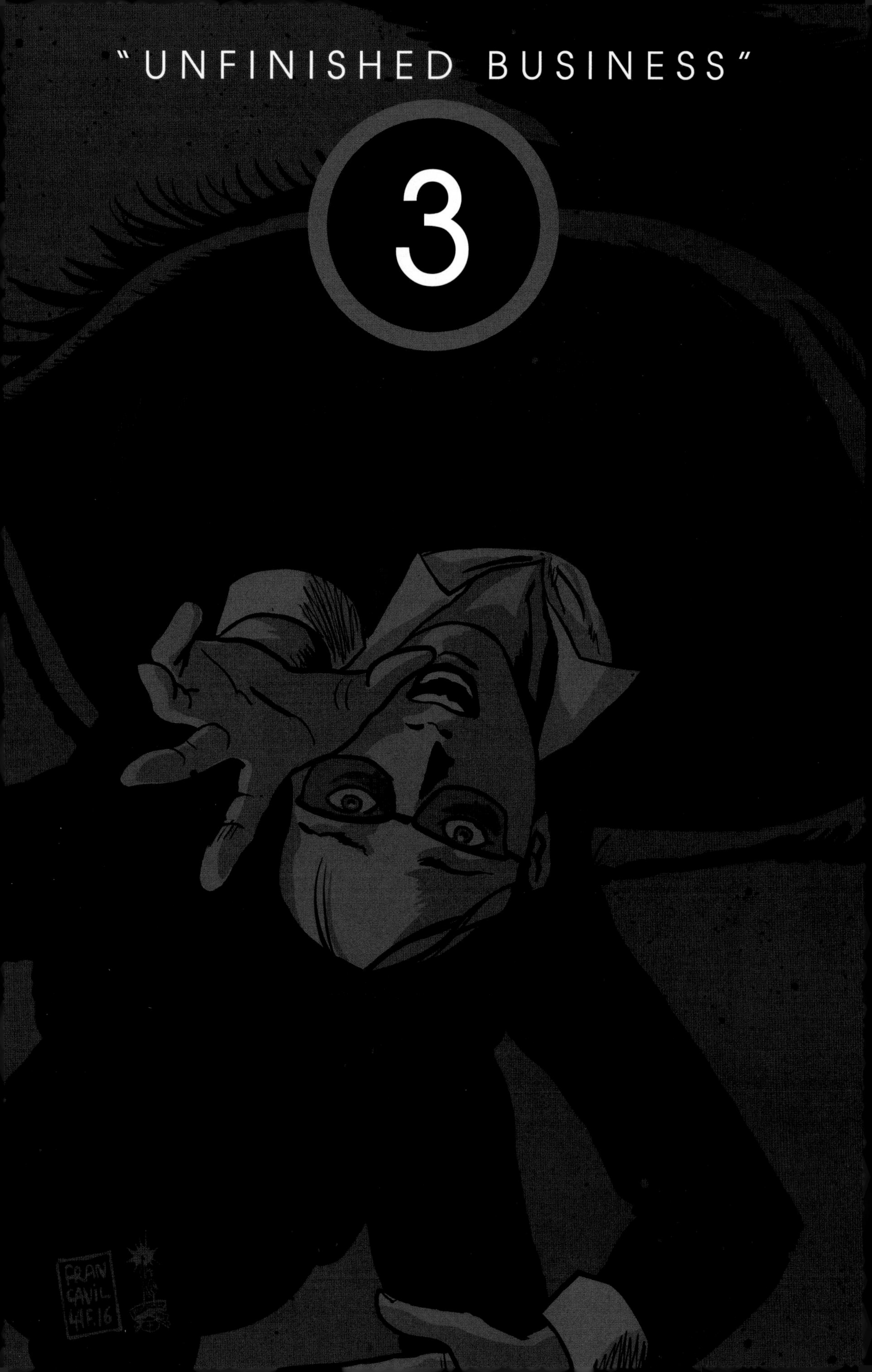
"UNFINISHED BUSINESS"
3

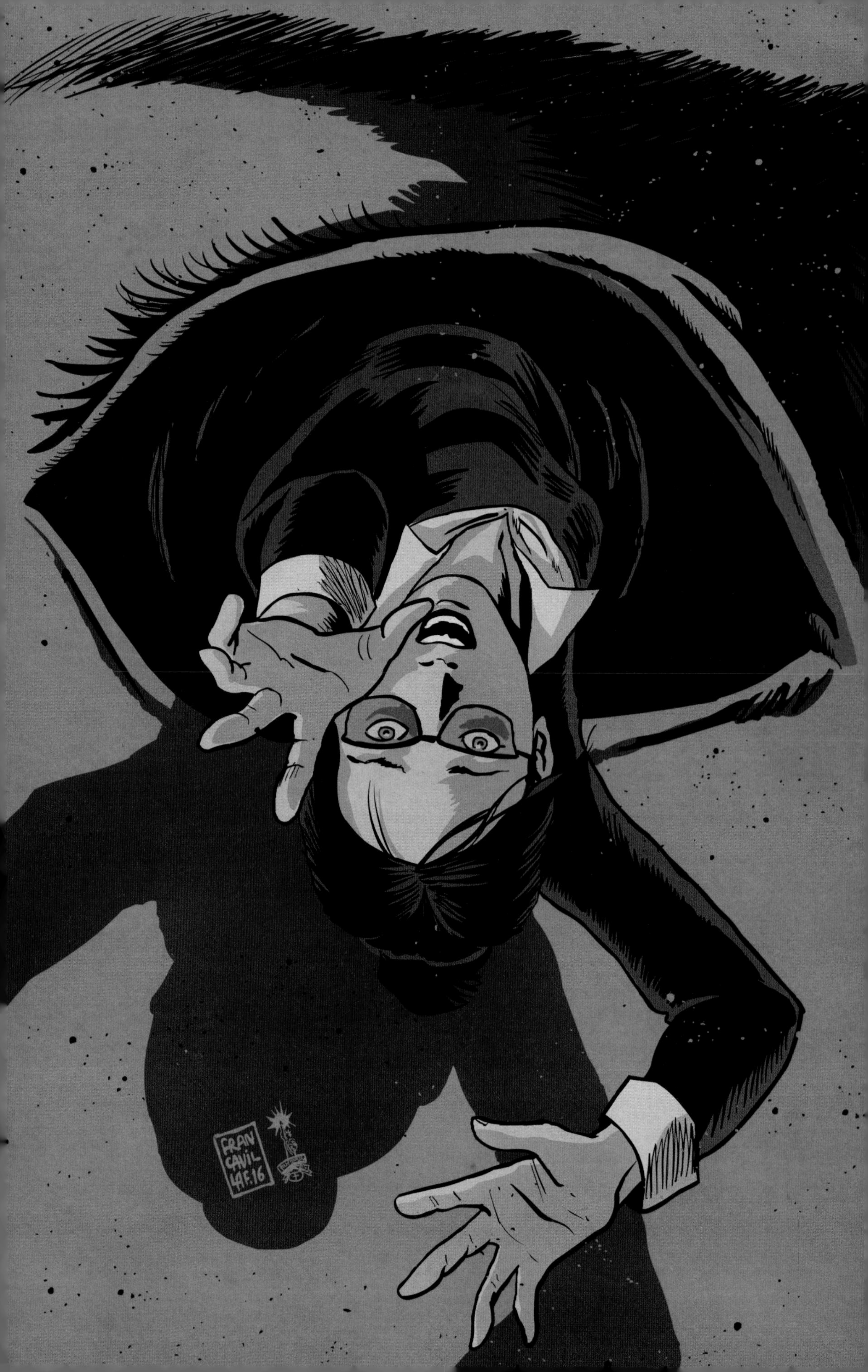

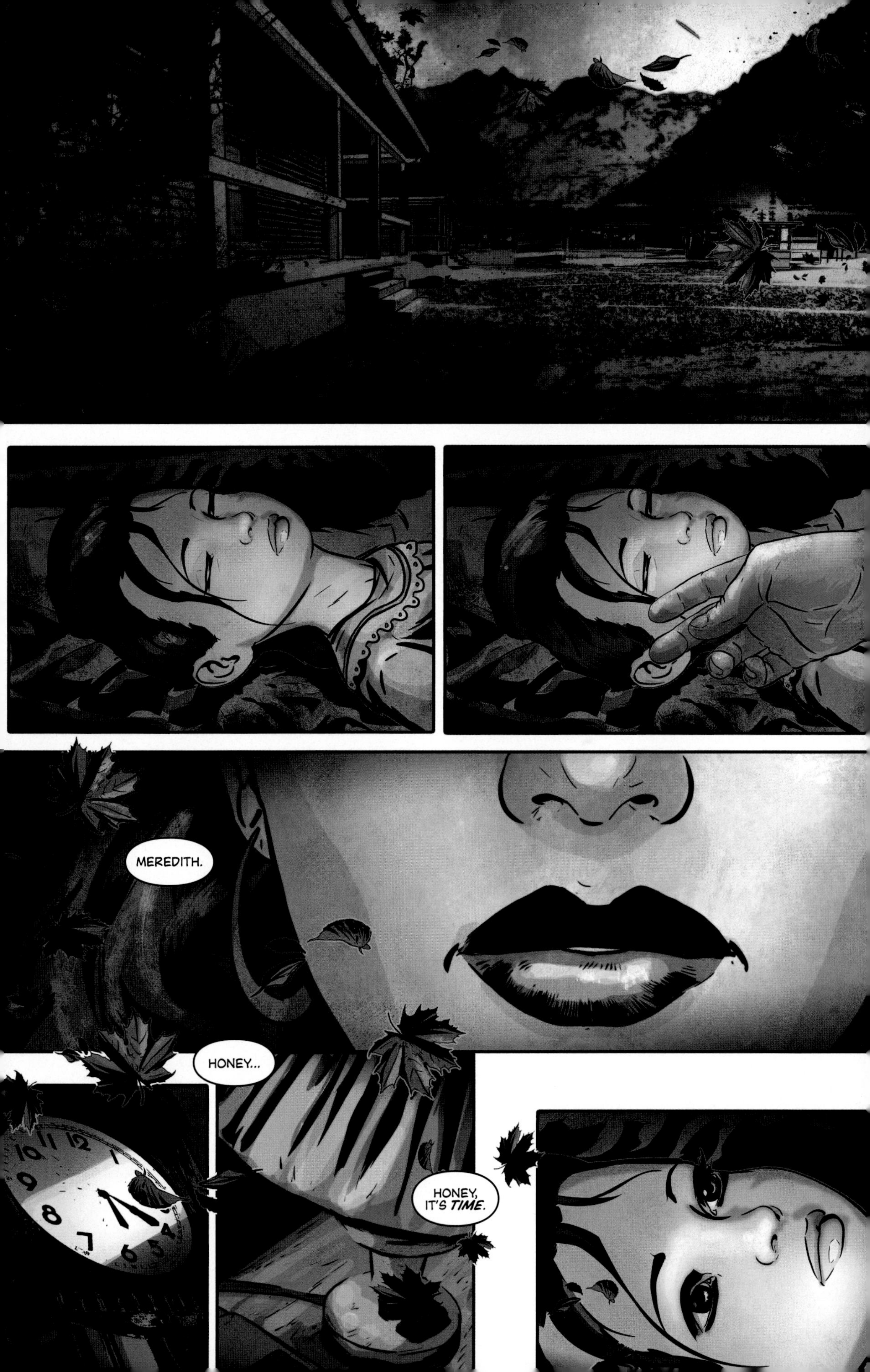

MEREDITH.
HONEY...
HONEY, IT'S *TIME*.

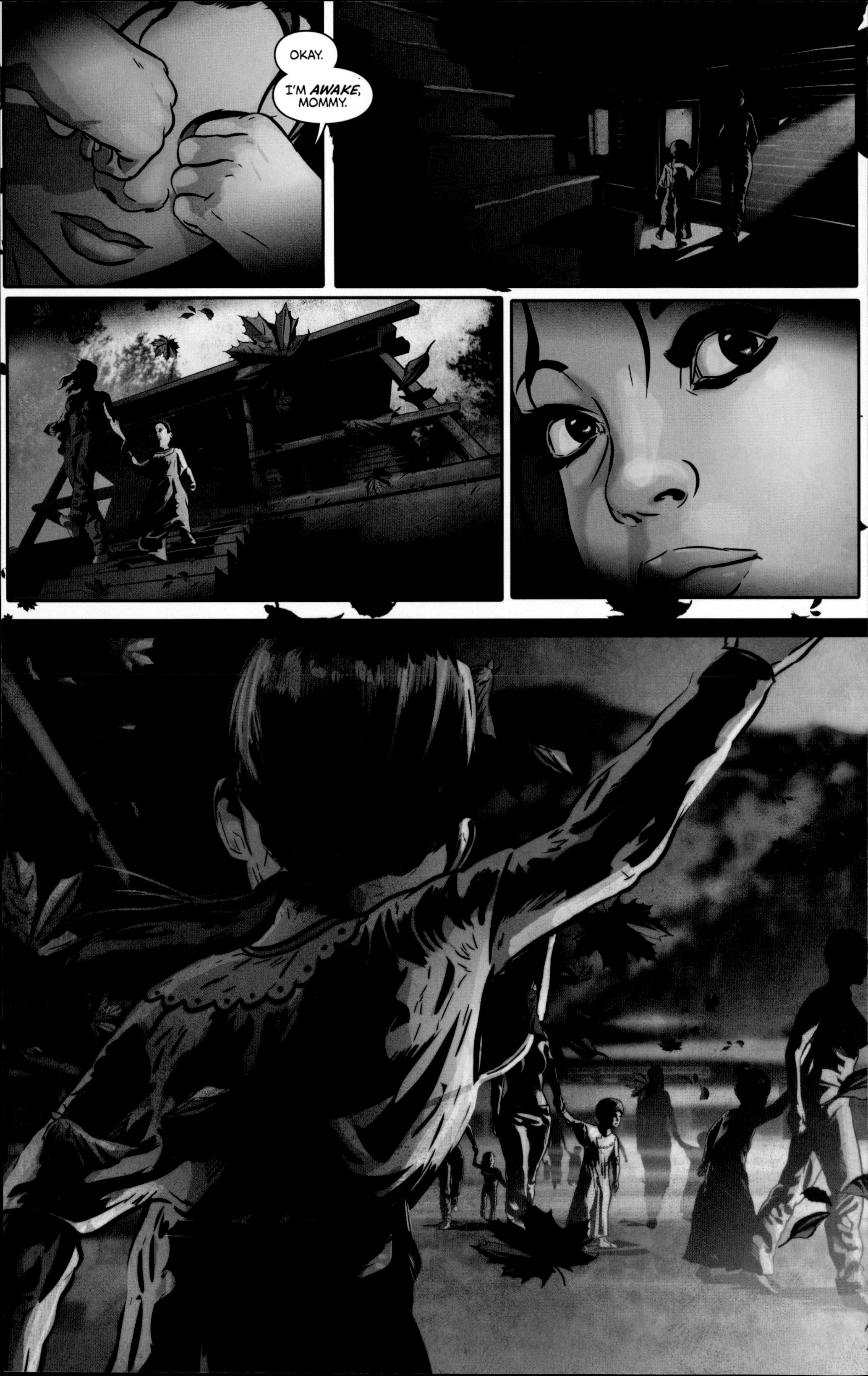
OKAY.
I'M *AWAKE*, MOMMY.

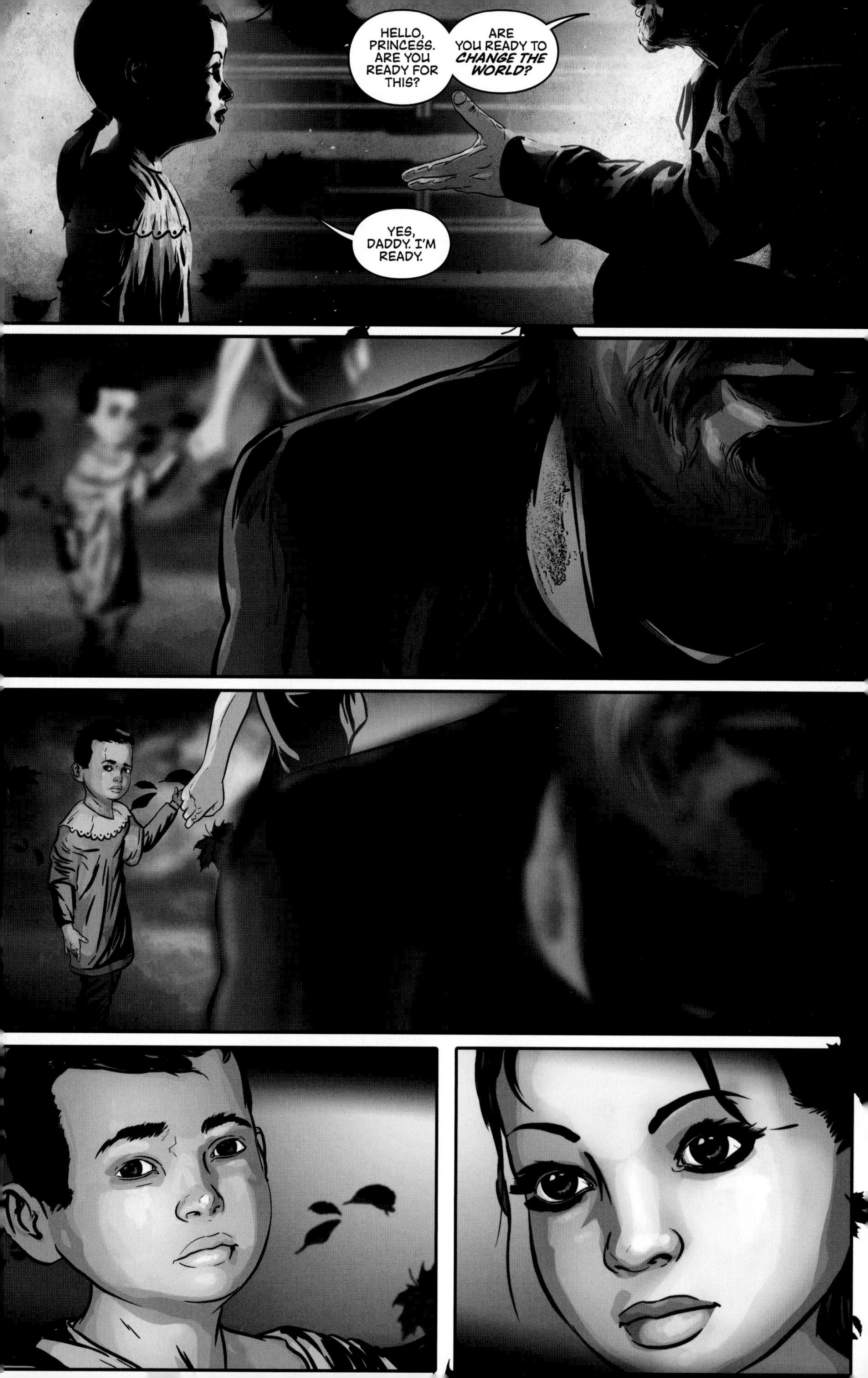
HELLO, PRINCESS. ARE YOU READY FOR THIS?
ARE YOU READY TO *CHANGE THE WORLD?*
YES, DADDY. I'M READY.

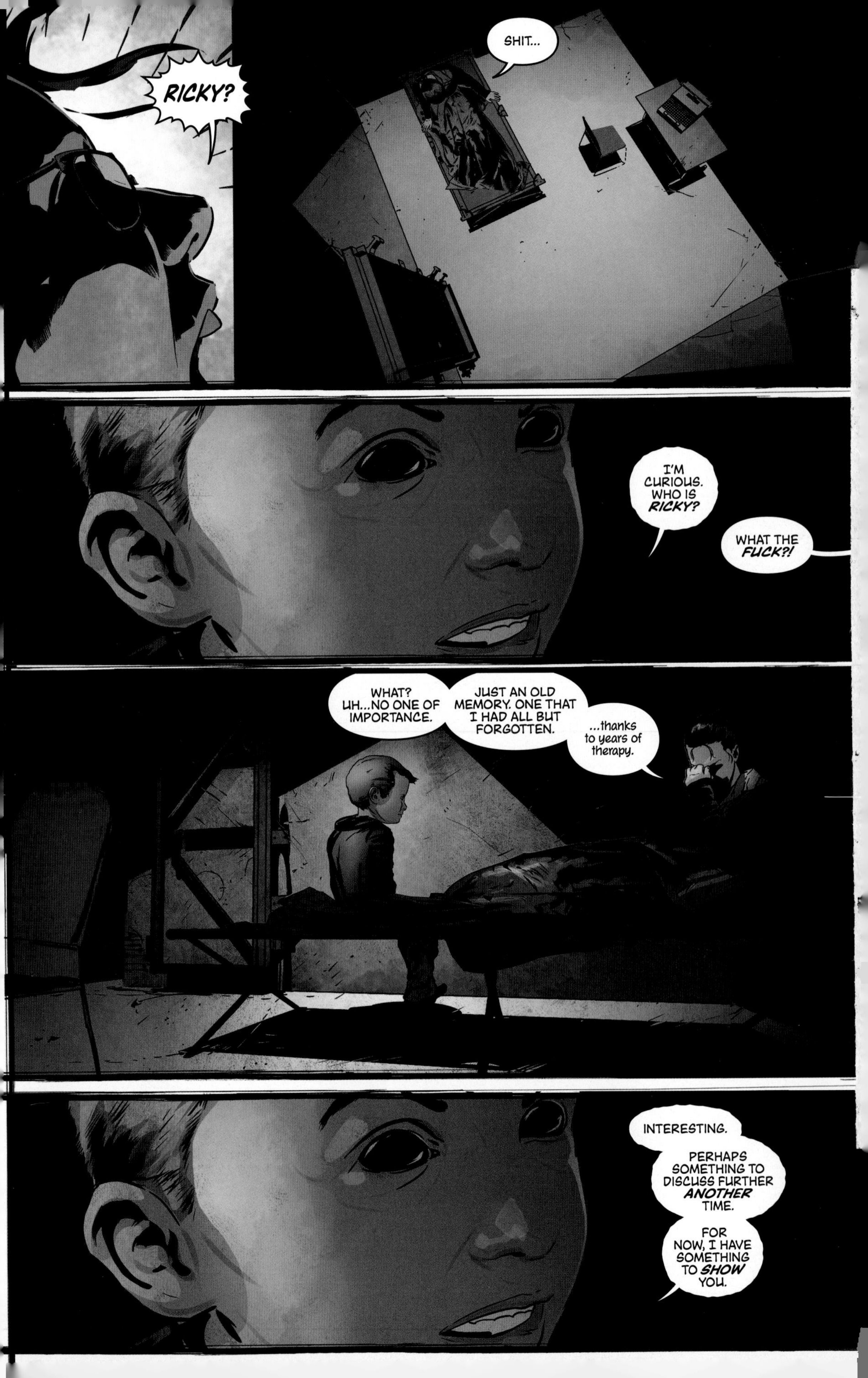
RICKY?
SHIT...
I'M CURIOUS. WHO IS RICKY?
WHAT THE FUCK?!
WHAT? UH...NO ONE OF IMPORTANCE.
JUST AN OLD MEMORY. ONE THAT I HAD ALL BUT FORGOTTEN.
...thanks to years of therapy.
INTERESTING.
PERHAPS SOMETHING TO DISCUSS FURTHER ANOTHER TIME.
FOR NOW, I HAVE SOMETHING TO SHOW YOU.

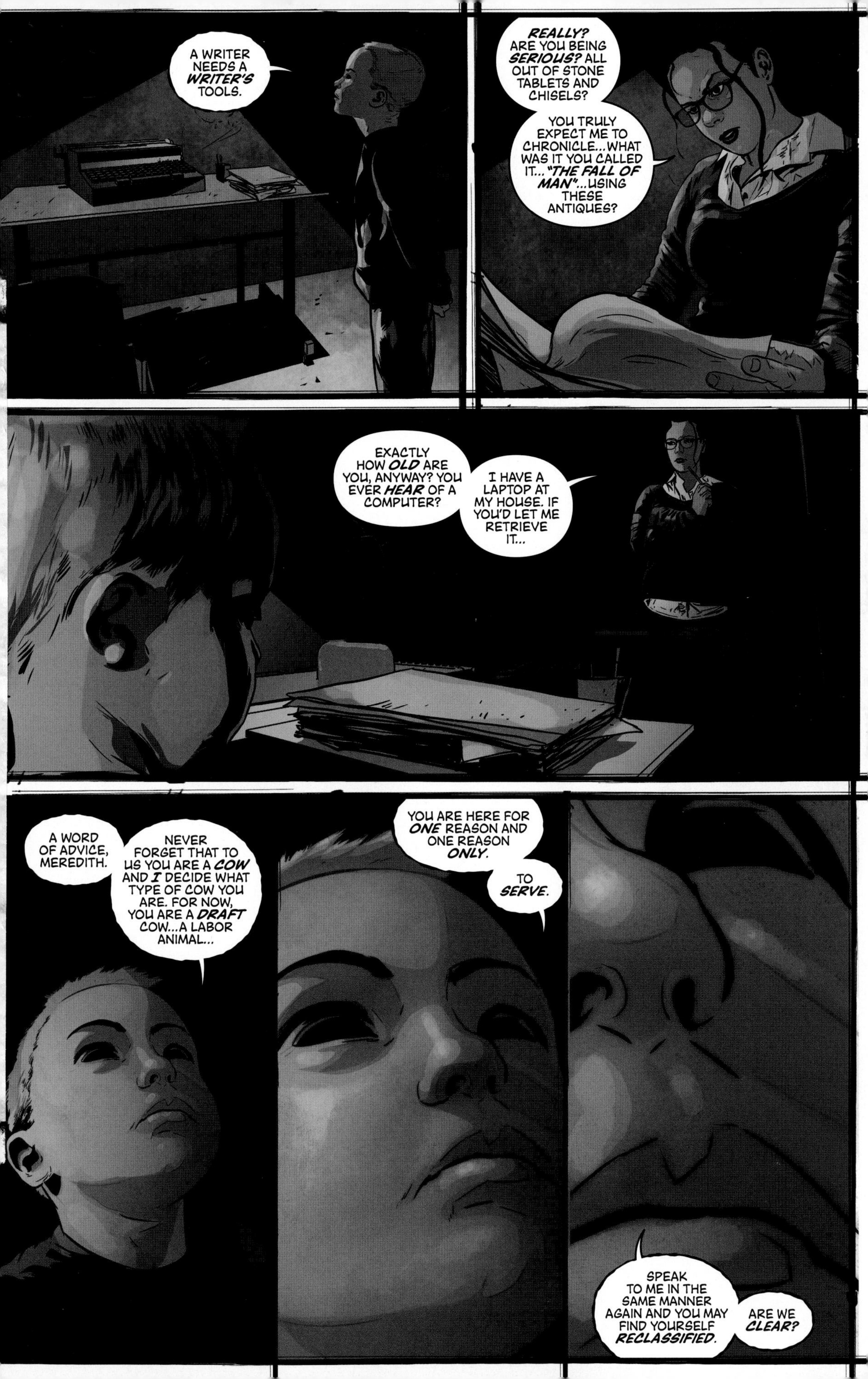
A WRITER NEEDS A WRITER'S TOOLS.
REALLY? ARE YOU BEING SERIOUS? ALL OUT OF STONE TABLETS AND CHISELS?
YOU TRULY EXPECT ME TO CHRONICLE...WHAT WAS IT YOU CALLED IT... "THE FALL OF MAN"...USING THESE ANTIQUES?
EXACTLY HOW OLD ARE YOU, ANYWAY? YOU EVER HEAR OF A COMPUTER?
I HAVE A LAPTOP AT MY HOUSE. IF YOU'D LET ME RETRIEVE IT...
A WORD OF ADVICE, MEREDITH.
NEVER FORGET THAT TO US YOU ARE A COW AND I DECIDE WHAT TYPE OF COW YOU ARE. FOR NOW, YOU ARE A DRAFT COW...A LABOR ANIMAL...
YOU ARE HERE FOR ONE REASON AND ONE REASON ONLY.
TO SERVE.
SPEAK TO ME IN THE SAME MANNER AGAIN AND YOU MAY FIND YOURSELF RECLASSIFIED.
ARE WE CLEAR?

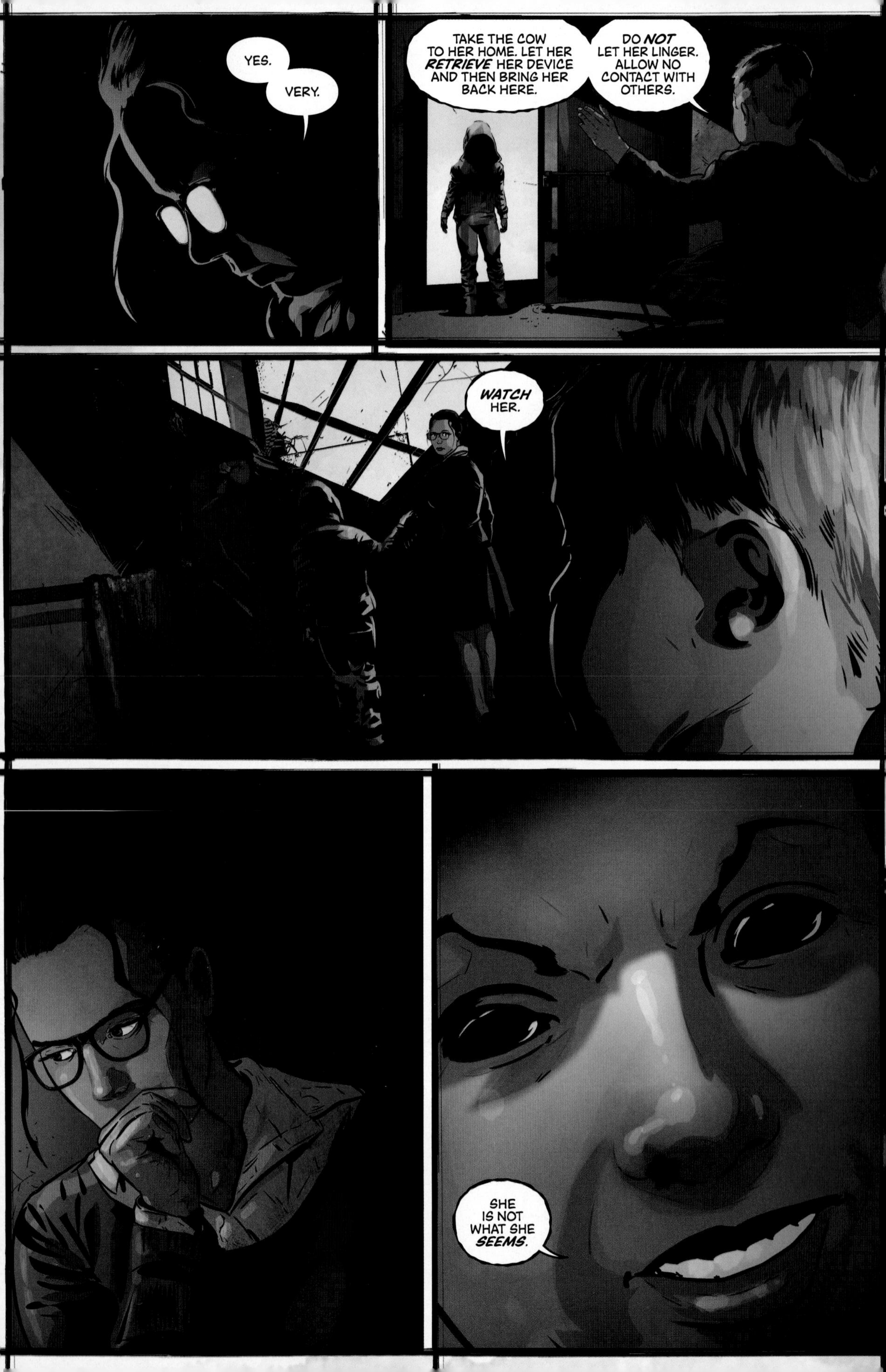
YES.
VERY.
TAKE THE COW TO HER HOME. LET HER *RETRIEVE* HER DEVICE AND THEN BRING HER BACK HERE.
DO *NOT* LET HER LINGER. ALLOW NO CONTACT WITH OTHERS.
WATCH HER.
SHE IS NOT WHAT SHE *SEEMS*.

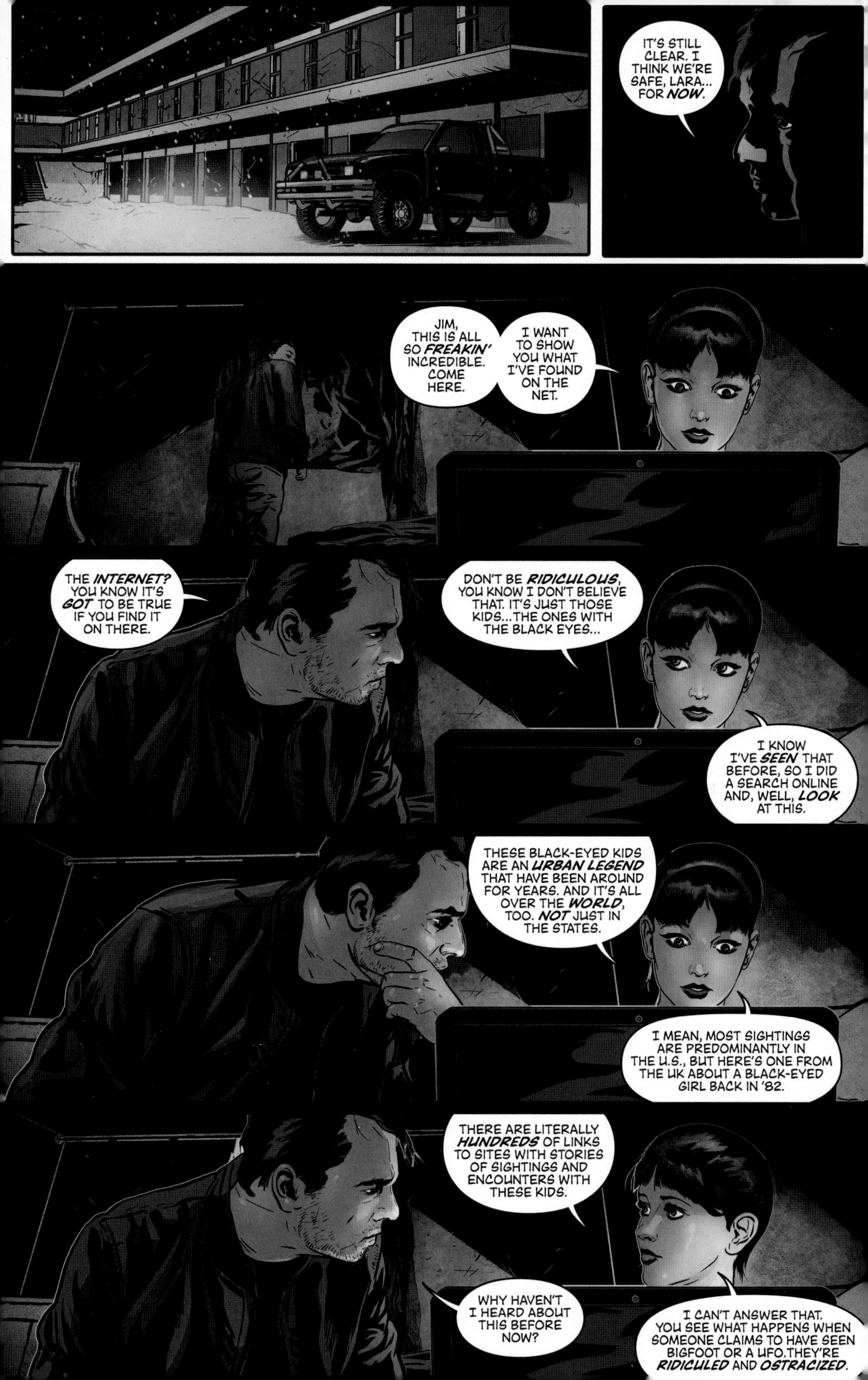
IT'S STILL CLEAR. I THINK WE'RE SAFE, LARA... FOR NOW.
JIM, THIS IS ALL SO FREAKIN' INCREDIBLE. COME HERE.
I WANT TO SHOW YOU WHAT I'VE FOUND ON THE NET.
THE INTERNET? YOU KNOW IT'S GOT TO BE TRUE IF YOU FIND IT ON THERE.
DON'T BE RIDICULOUS, YOU KNOW I DON'T BELIEVE THAT. IT'S JUST THOSE KIDS...THE ONES WITH THE BLACK EYES...
I KNOW I'VE SEEN THAT BEFORE, SO I DID A SEARCH ONLINE AND, WELL, LOOK AT THIS.
THESE BLACK-EYED KIDS ARE AN URBAN LEGEND THAT HAVE BEEN AROUND FOR YEARS. AND IT'S ALL OVER THE WORLD, TOO. NOT JUST IN THE STATES.
I MEAN, MOST SIGHTINGS ARE PREDOMINANTLY IN THE U.S., BUT HERE'S ONE FROM THE UK ABOUT A BLACK-EYED GIRL BACK IN '82.
THERE ARE LITERALLY HUNDREDS OF LINKS TO SITES WITH STORIES OF SIGHTINGS AND ENCOUNTERS WITH THESE KIDS.
WHY HAVEN'T I HEARD ABOUT THIS BEFORE NOW?
I CAN'T ANSWER THAT. YOU SEE WHAT HAPPENS WHEN SOMEONE CLAIMS TO HAVE SEEN BIGFOOT OR A UFO.THEY'RE RIDICULED AND OSTRACIZED.

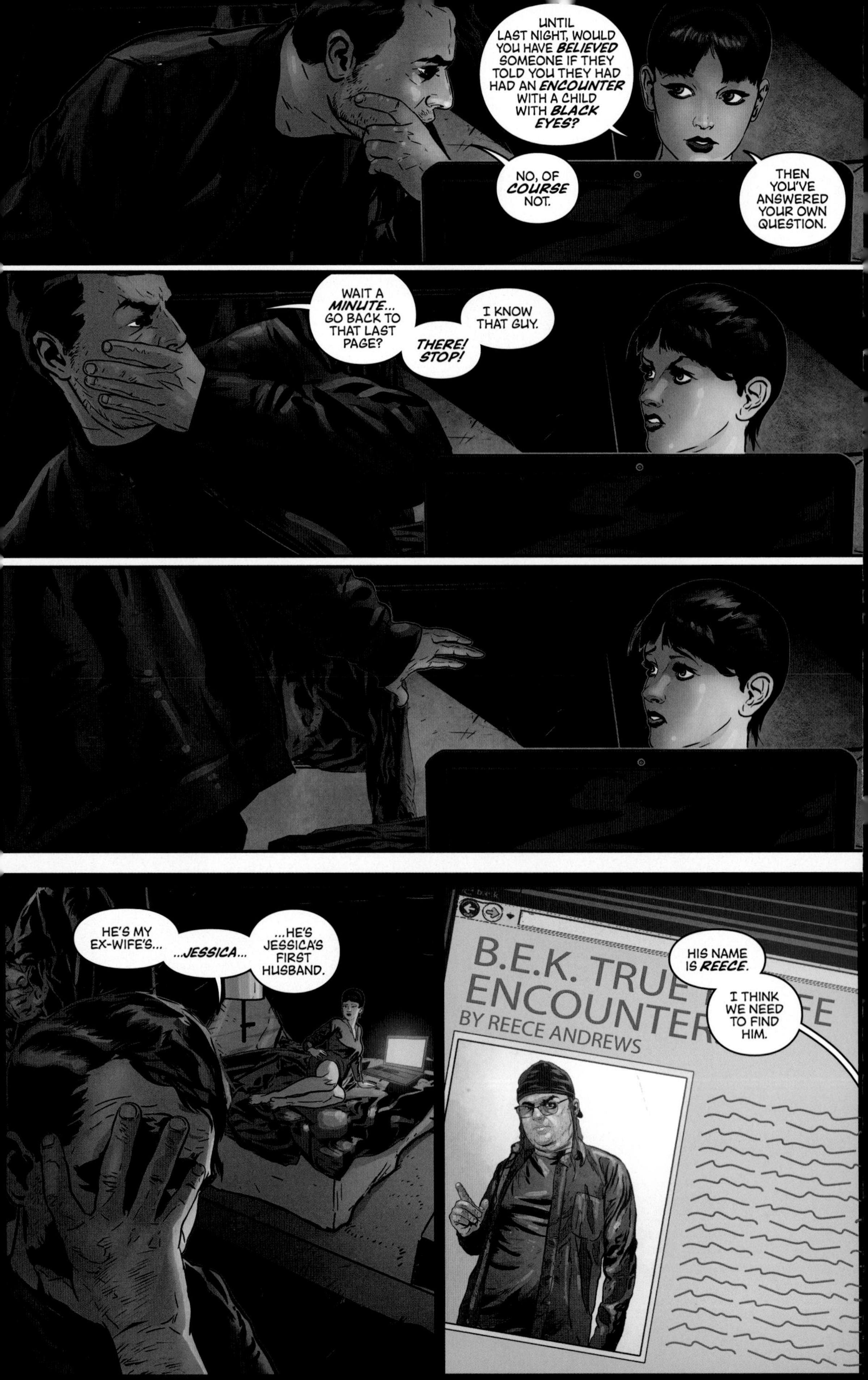
UNTIL LAST NIGHT, WOULD YOU HAVE BELIEVED SOMEONE IF THEY TOLD YOU THEY HAD HAD AN ENCOUNTER WITH A CHILD WITH BLACK EYES?
NO, OF COURSE NOT.
THEN YOU'VE ANSWERED YOUR OWN QUESTION.
WAIT A MINUTE... GO BACK TO THAT LAST PAGE?
THERE! STOP!
I KNOW THAT GUY.
HE'S MY EX-WIFE'S...
...JESSICA...
...HE'S JESSICA'S FIRST HUSBAND.
B.E.K. TRUE
ENCOUNTER
BY REECE ANDREWS
HIS NAME IS REECE.
I THINK WE NEED TO FIND HIM.

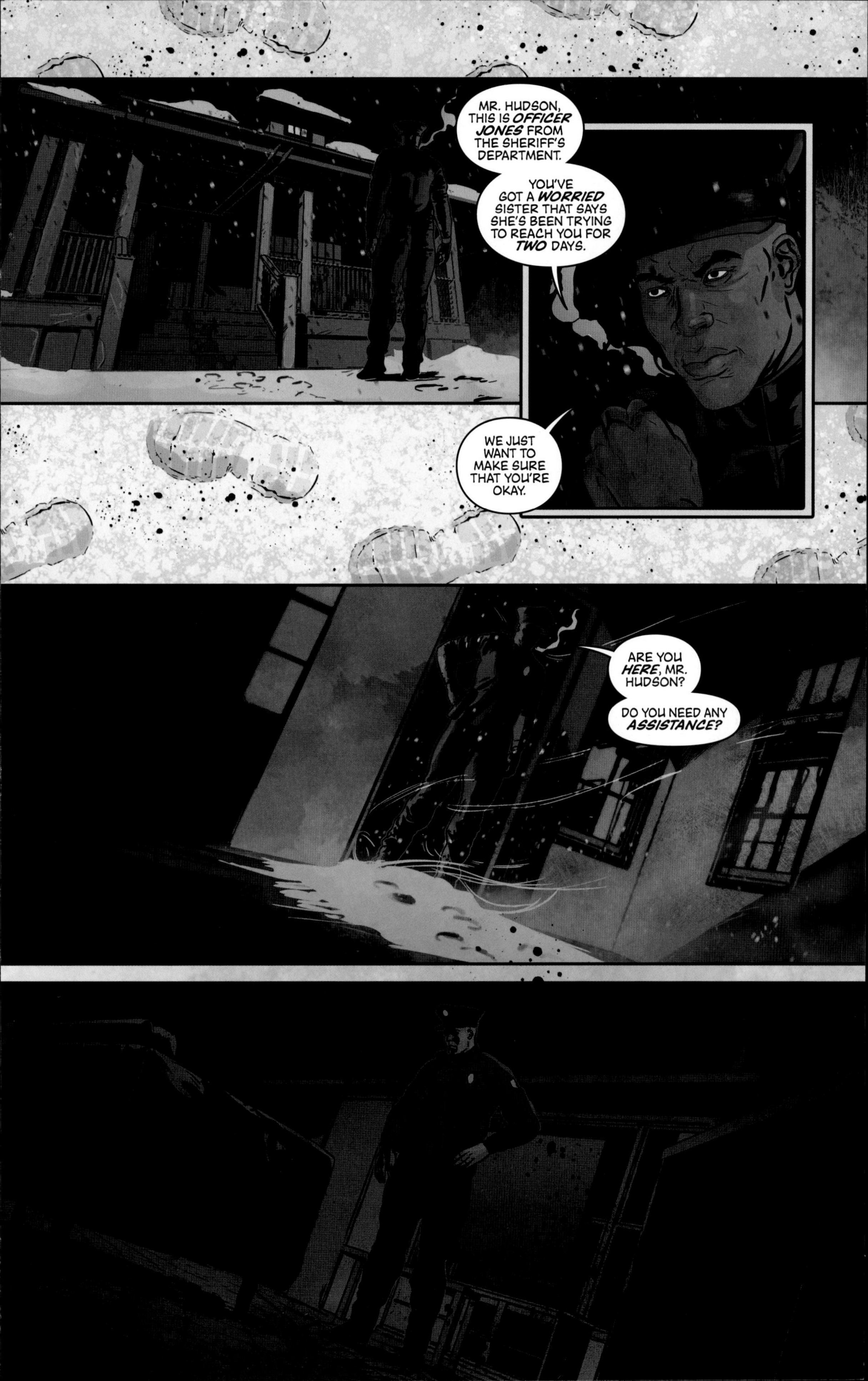
MR. HUDSON, THIS IS OFFICER JONES FROM THE SHERIFF'S DEPARTMENT.
YOU'VE GOT A WORRIED SISTER THAT SAYS SHE'S BEEN TRYING TO REACH YOU FOR TWO DAYS.
WE JUST WANT TO MAKE SURE THAT YOU'RE OKAY.
ARE YOU HERE, MR. HUDSON?
DO YOU NEED ANY ASSISTANCE?

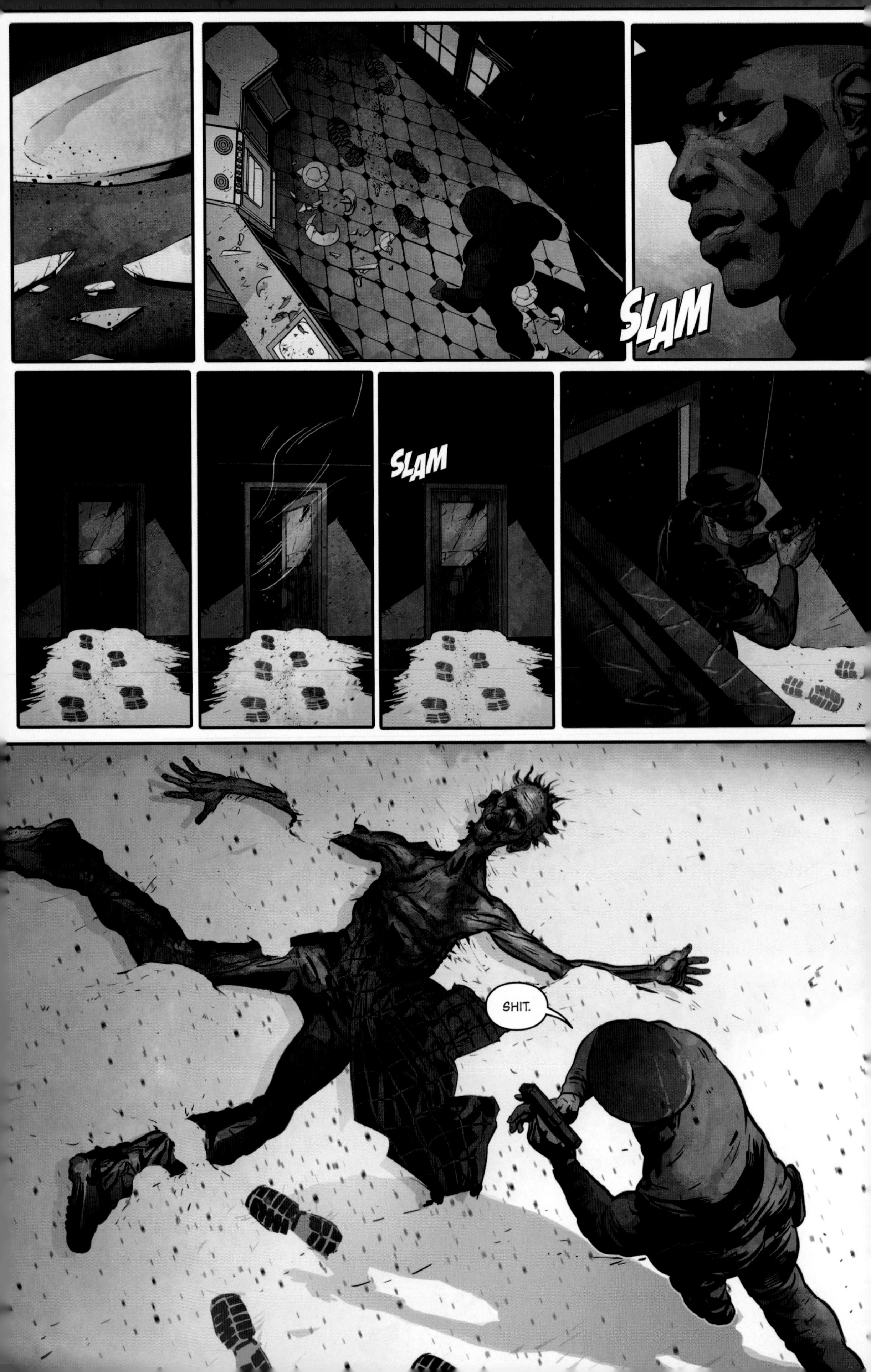

SLAM
SLAM
SHIT.

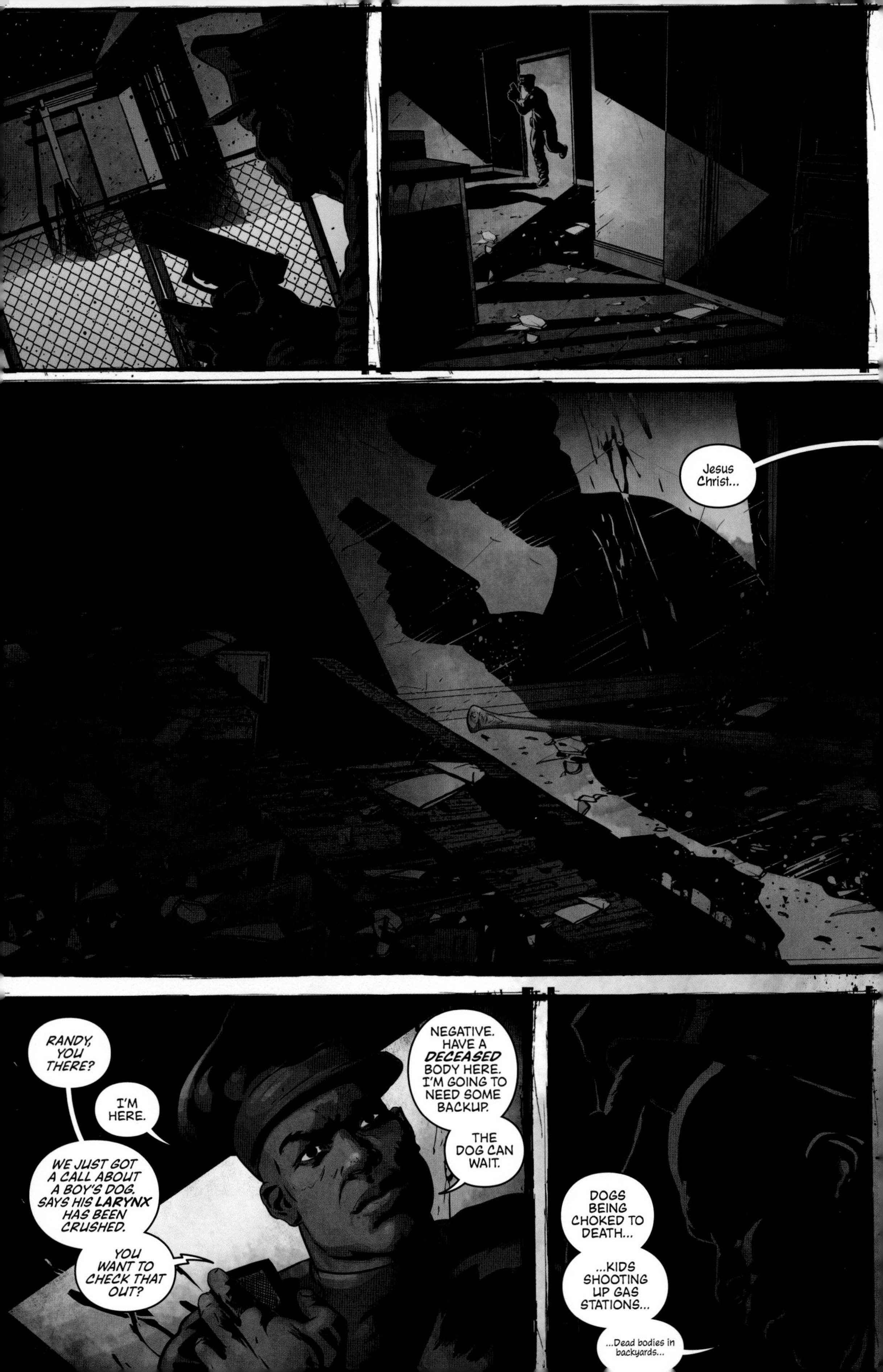
Jesus Christ...
RANDY, YOU THERE?
I'M HERE.
WE JUST GOT A CALL ABOUT A BOY'S DOG. SAYS HIS LARYNX HAS BEEN CRUSHED.
YOU WANT TO CHECK THAT OUT?
NEGATIVE. HAVE A DECEASED BODY HERE. I'M GOING TO NEED SOME BACKUP.
THE DOG CAN WAIT.
DOGS BEING CHOKED TO DEATH...
...KIDS SHOOTING UP GAS STATIONS...
...Dead bodies in backyards...

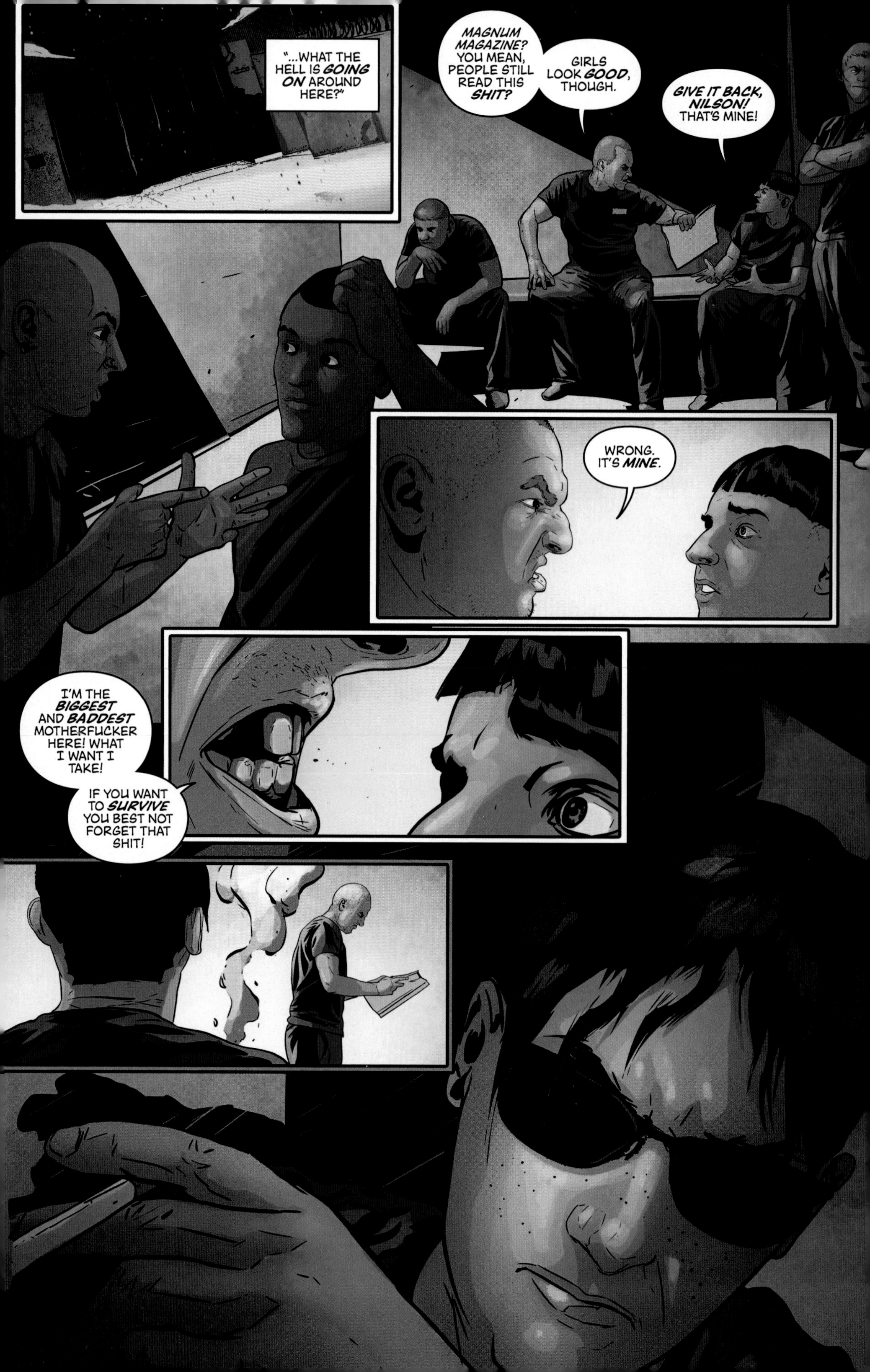
"...WHAT THE HELL IS GOING ON AROUND HERE?"
MAGNUM MAGAZINE? YOU MEAN, PEOPLE STILL READ THIS SHIT?
GIRLS LOOK GOOD, THOUGH.
GIVE IT BACK, NILSON! THAT'S MINE!
WRONG. IT'S MINE.
I'M THE BIGGEST AND BADDEST MOTHERFUCKER HERE! WHAT I WANT I TAKE!
IF YOU WANT TO SURVIVE YOU BEST NOT FORGET THAT SHIT!

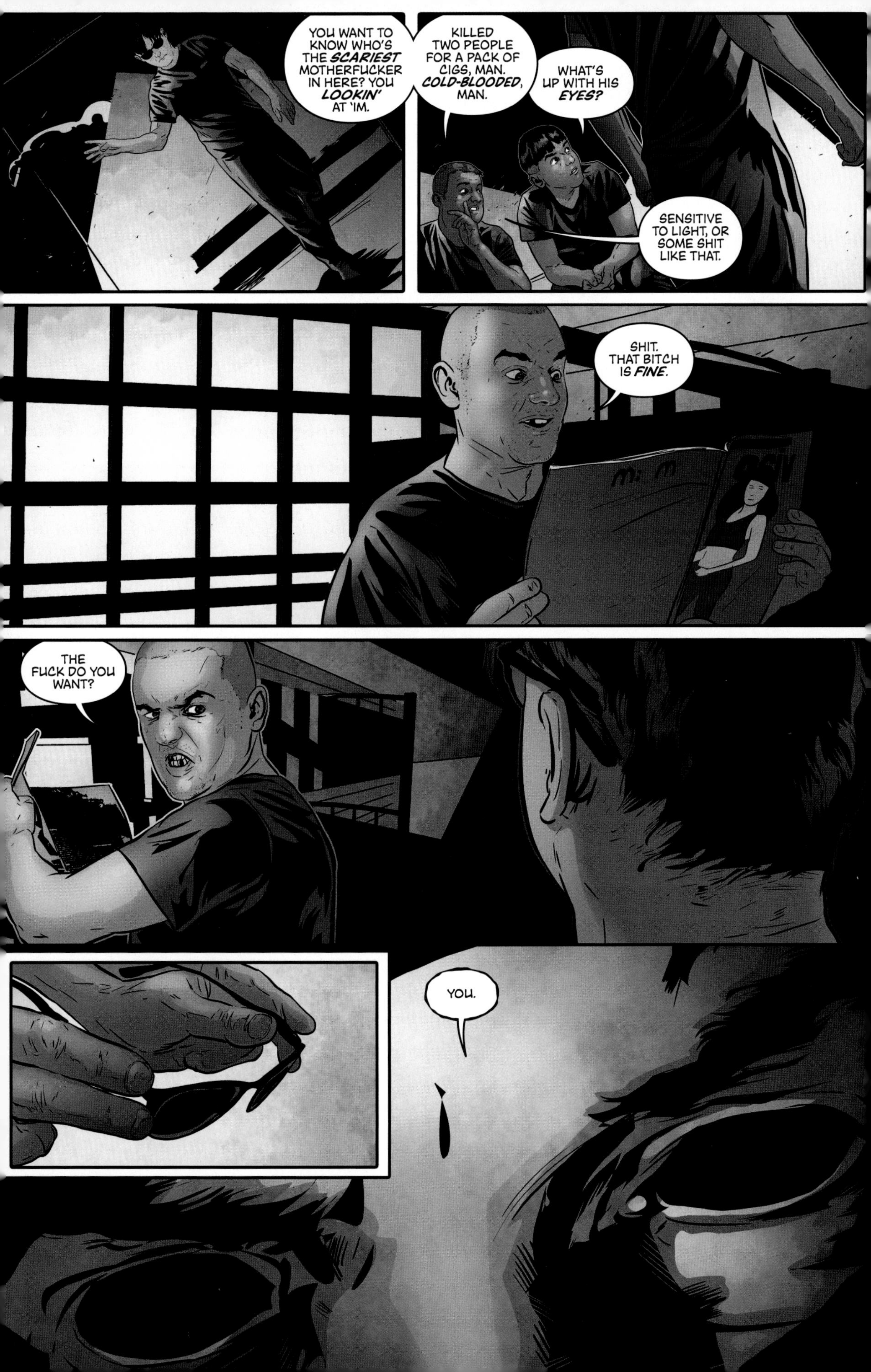
YOU WANT TO KNOW WHO'S THE SCARIEST MOTHERFUCKER IN HERE? YOU LOOKIN' AT 'IM.
KILLED TWO PEOPLE FOR A PACK OF CIGS, MAN. COLD-BLOODED, MAN.
WHAT'S UP WITH HIS EYES?
SENSITIVE TO LIGHT, OR SOME SHIT LIKE THAT.
SHIT. THAT BITCH IS FINE.
THE FUCK DO YOU WANT?
YOU.

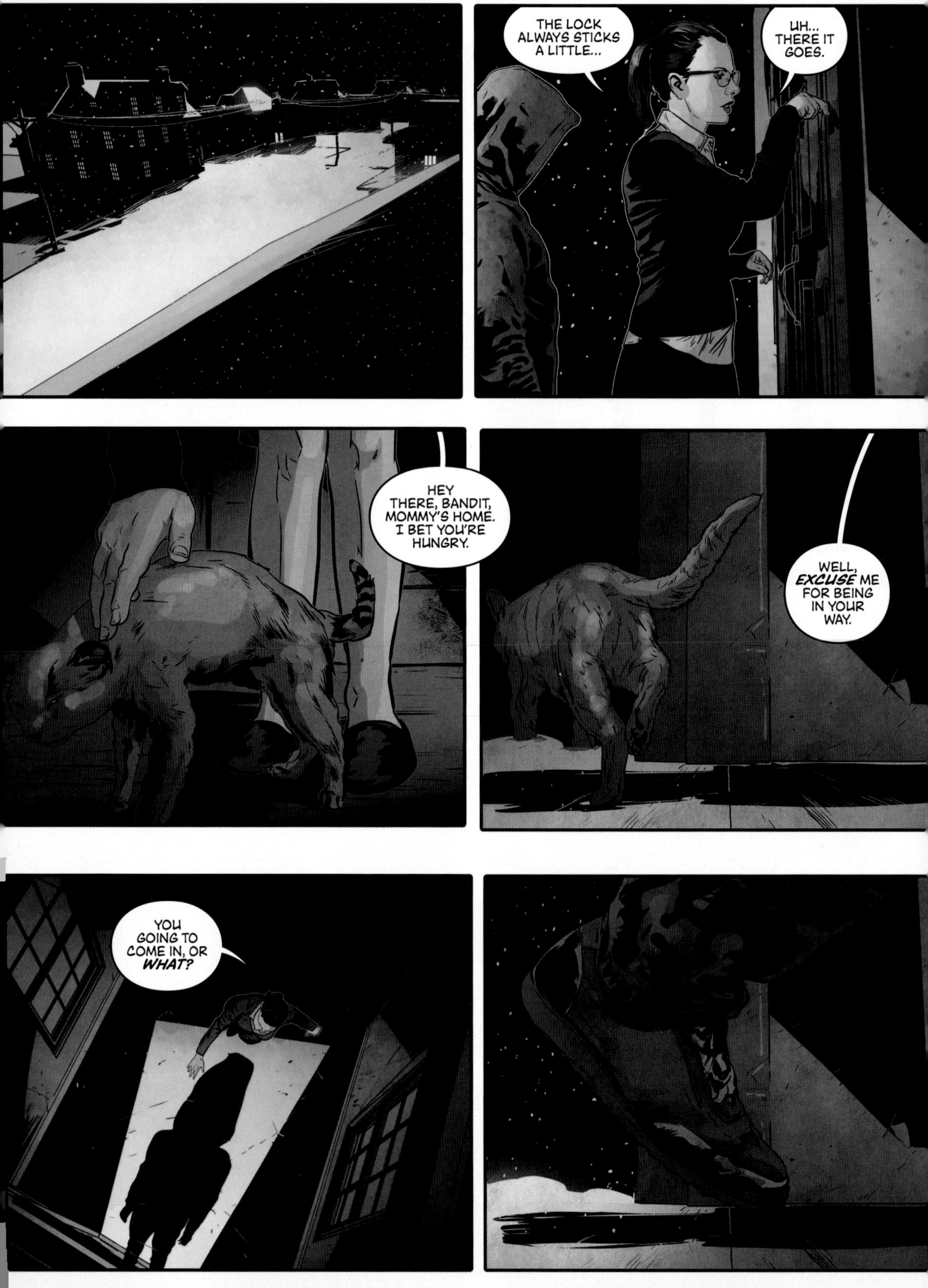
THE LOCK ALWAYS STICKS A LITTLE...
UH... THERE IT GOES.
HEY THERE, BANDIT, MOMMY'S HOME. I BET YOU'RE HUNGRY.
WELL, *EXCUSE* ME FOR BEING IN YOUR WAY.
YOU GOING TO COME IN, OR *WHAT?*

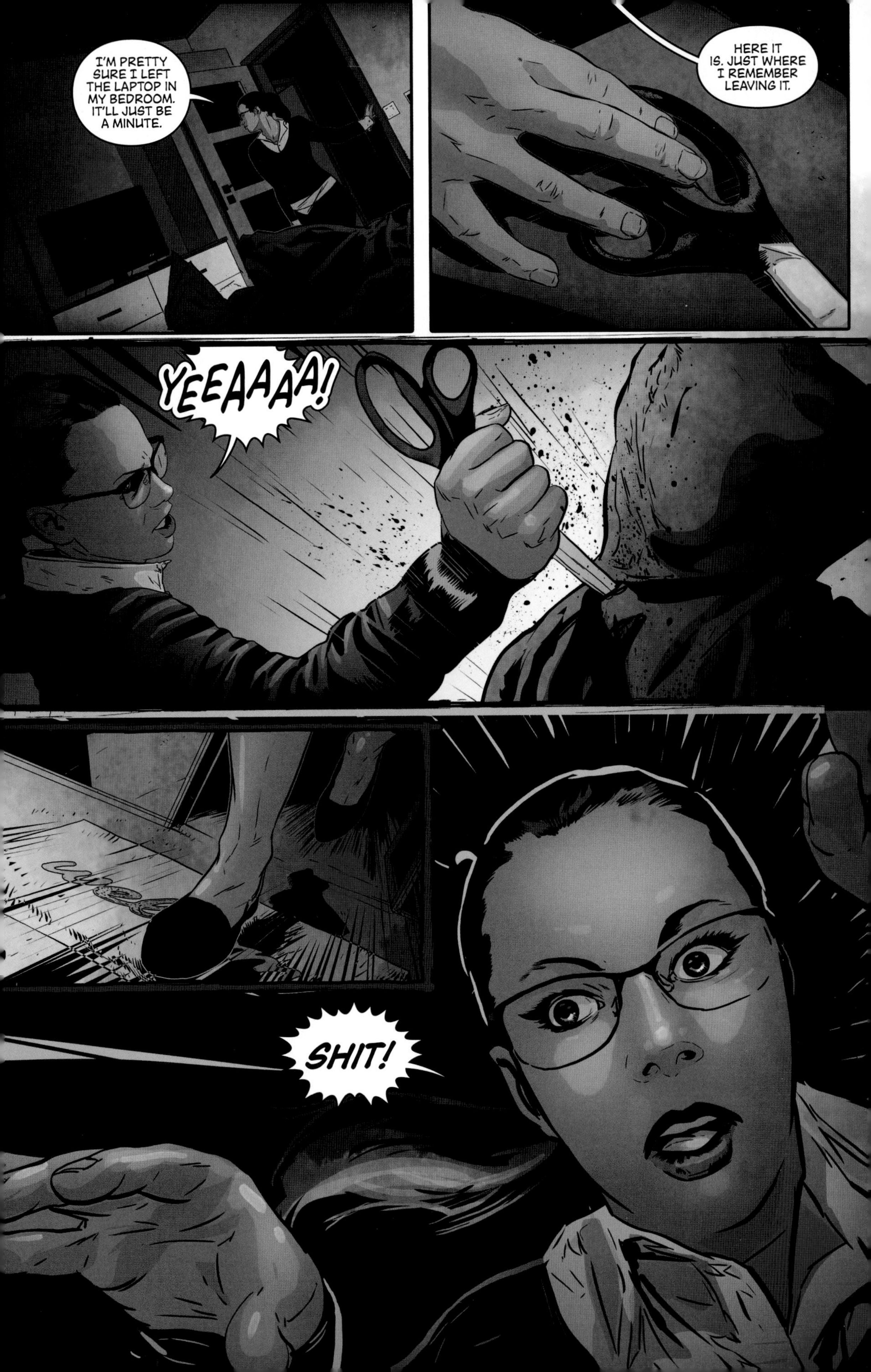
I'M PRETTY SURE I LEFT THE LAPTOP IN MY BEDROOM. IT'LL JUST BE A MINUTE.
HERE IT IS. JUST WHERE I REMEMBER LEAVING IT.
YEEAAAAA!
SHIT!

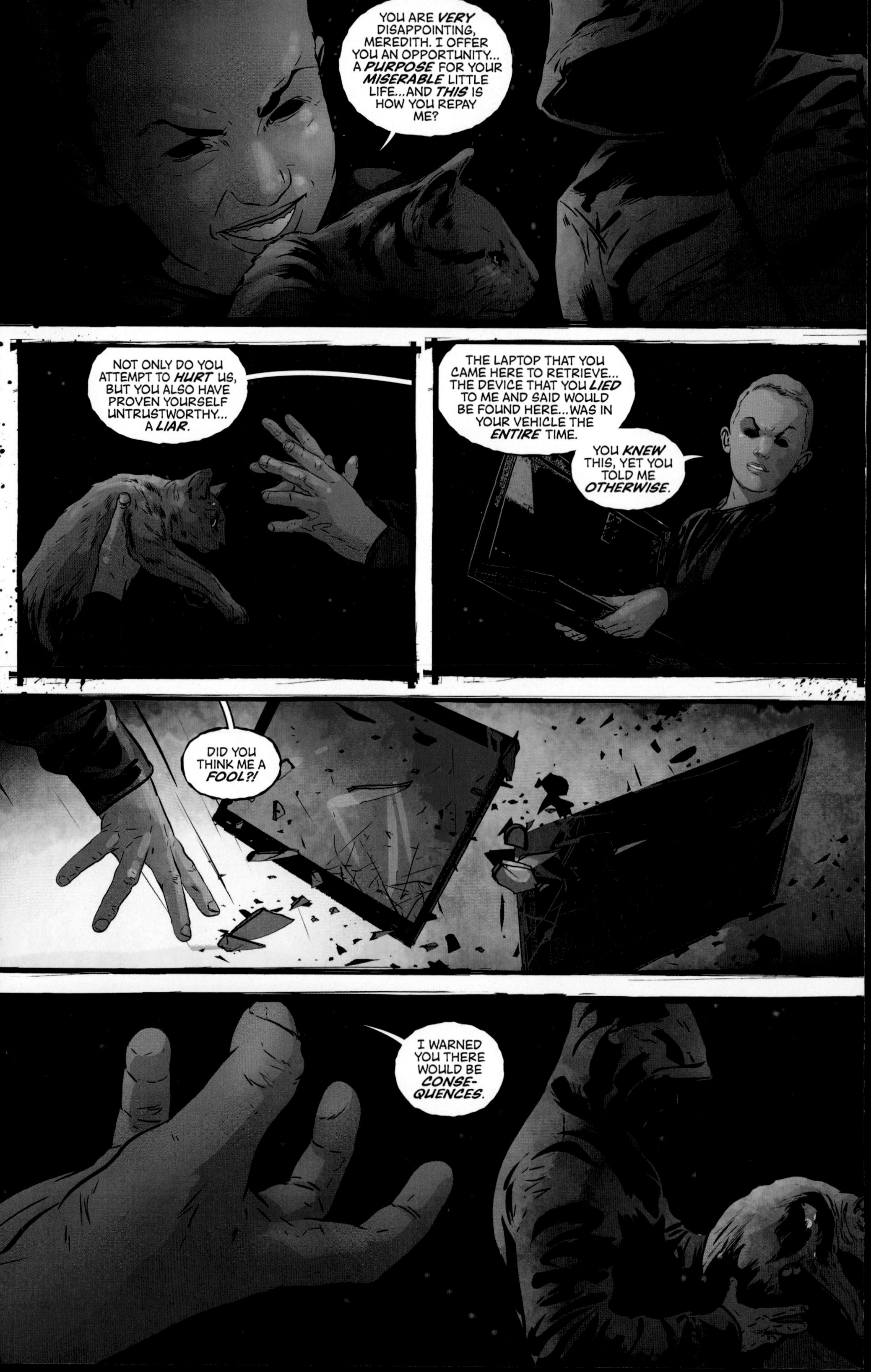
YOU ARE VERY DISAPPOINTING, MEREDITH. I OFFER YOU AN OPPORTUNITY... A PURPOSE FOR YOUR MISERABLE LITTLE LIFE...AND THIS IS HOW YOU REPAY ME?
NOT ONLY DO YOU ATTEMPT TO HURT US, BUT YOU ALSO HAVE PROVEN YOURSELF UNTRUSTWORTHY... A LIAR.
THE LAPTOP THAT YOU CAME HERE TO RETRIEVE... THE DEVICE THAT YOU LIED TO ME AND SAID WOULD BE FOUND HERE...WAS IN YOUR VEHICLE THE ENTIRE TIME.
YOU KNEW THIS, YET YOU TOLD ME OTHERWISE.
DID YOU THINK ME A FOOL?!
I WARNED YOU THERE WOULD BE CONSE-QUENCES.

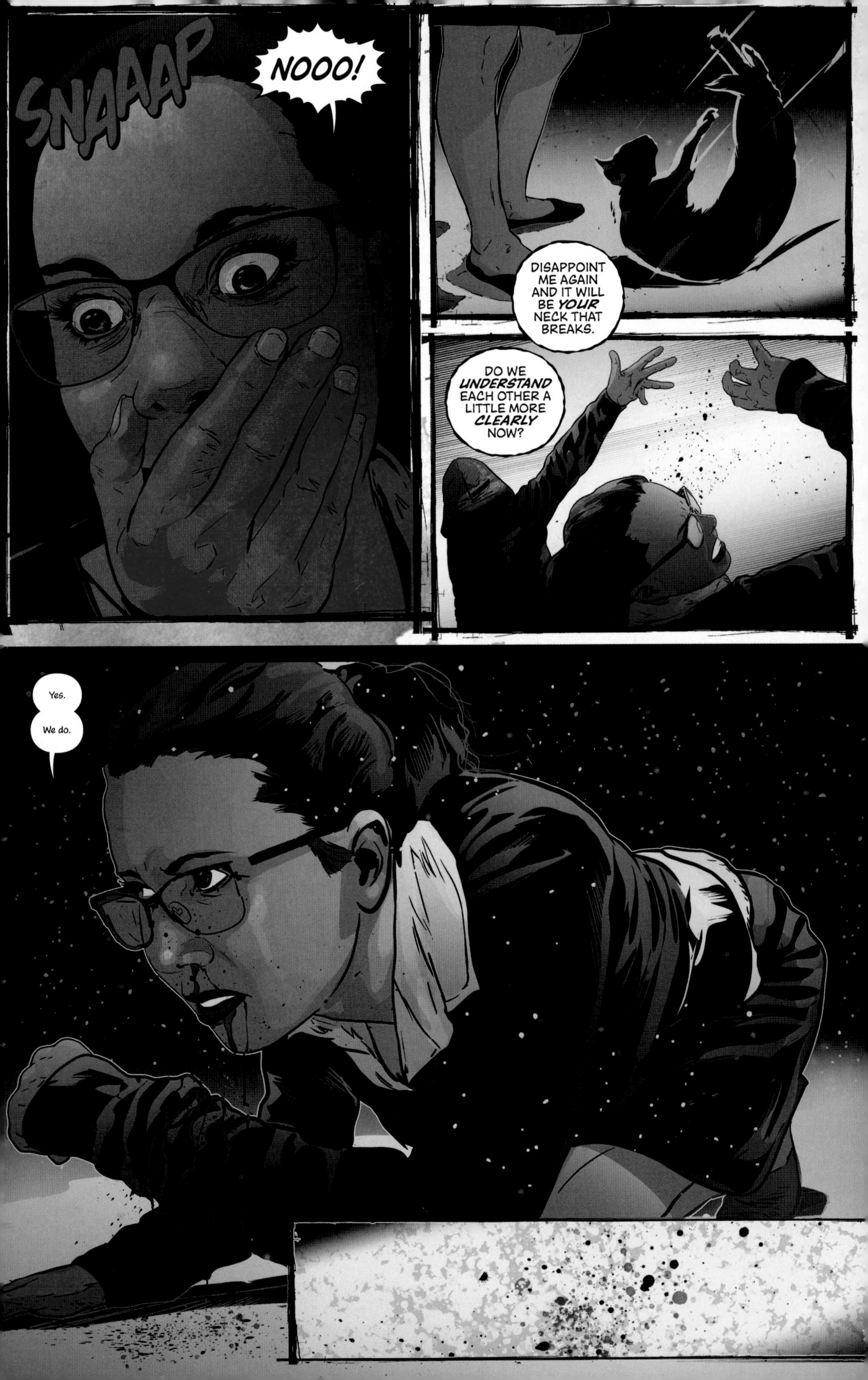
SNAAAP
NOOO!
DISAPPOINT ME AGAIN AND IT WILL BE YOUR NECK THAT BREAKS.
DO WE UNDERSTAND EACH OTHER A LITTLE MORE CLEARLY NOW?
Yes.
We do.

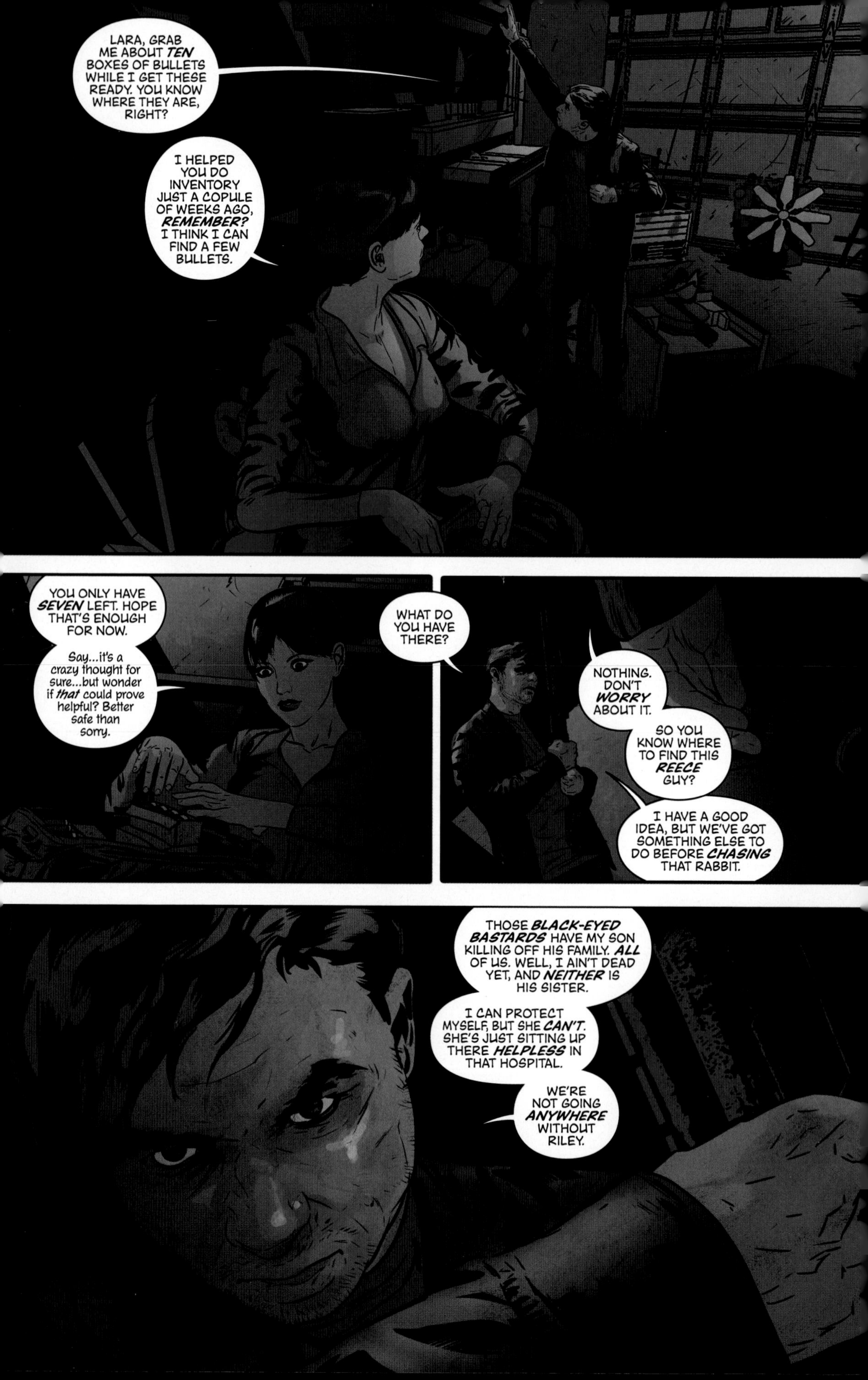
LARA, GRAB ME ABOUT *TEN* BOXES OF BULLETS WHILE I GET THESE READY. YOU KNOW WHERE THEY ARE, RIGHT?
I HELPED YOU DO INVENTORY JUST A COPULE OF WEEKS AGO, *REMEMBER?* I THINK I CAN FIND A FEW BULLETS.
YOU ONLY HAVE *SEVEN* LEFT. HOPE THAT'S ENOUGH FOR NOW.
Say...it's a crazy thought for sure...but wonder if *that* could prove helpful? Better safe than sorry.
WHAT DO YOU HAVE THERE?
NOTHING. DON'T *WORRY* ABOUT IT.
SO YOU KNOW WHERE TO FIND THIS *REECE* GUY?
I HAVE A GOOD IDEA, BUT WE'VE GOT SOMETHING ELSE TO DO BEFORE *CHASING* THAT RABBIT.
THOSE *BLACK-EYED BASTARDS* HAVE MY SON KILLING OFF HIS FAMILY. *ALL* OF US. WELL, I AIN'T DEAD YET, AND *NEITHER* IS HIS SISTER.
I CAN PROTECT MYSELF, BUT SHE *CAN'T*. SHE'S JUST SITTING UP THERE *HELPLESS* IN THAT HOSPITAL.
WE'RE NOT GOING *ANYWHERE* WITHOUT RILEY.

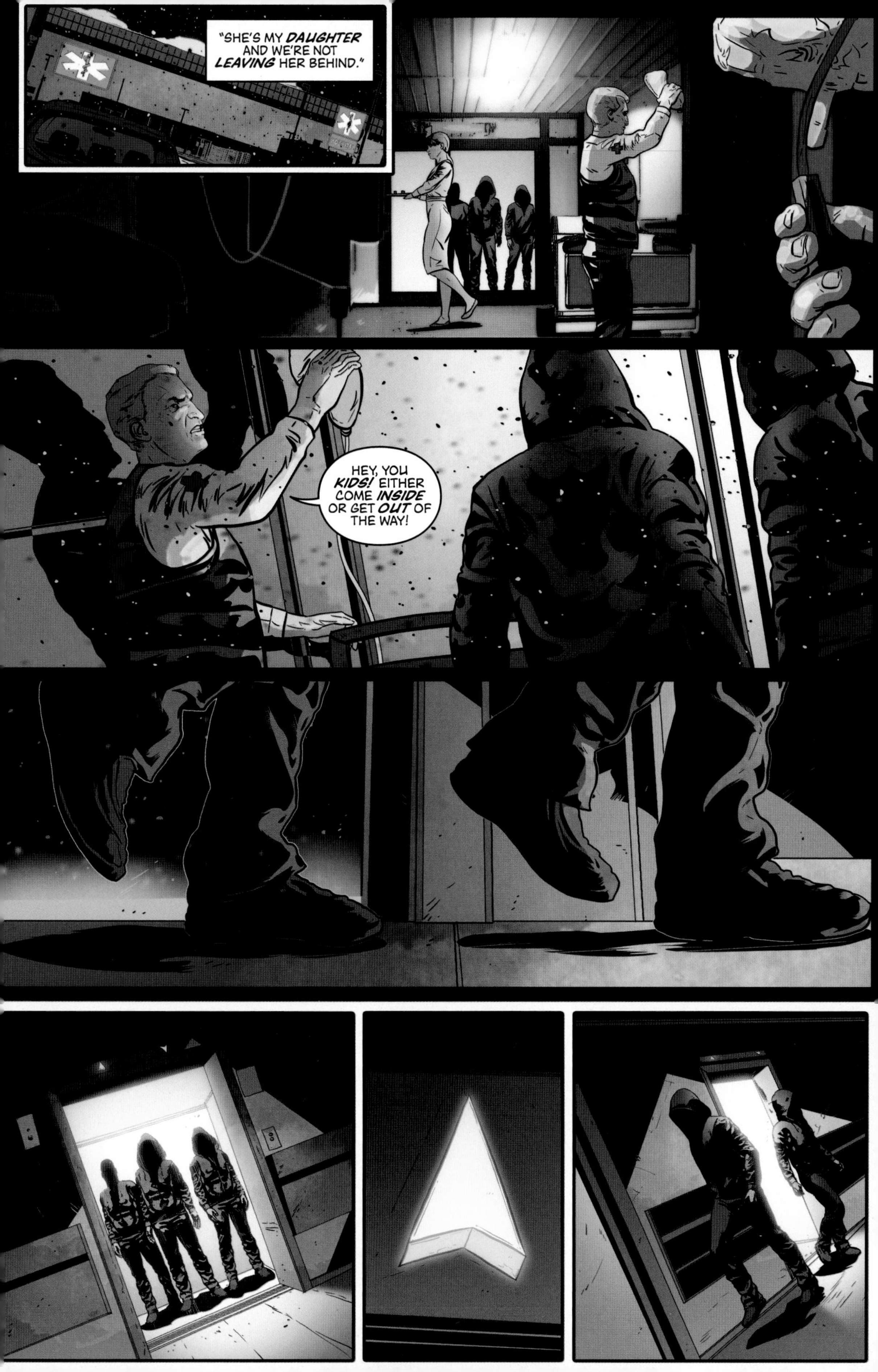

"SHE'S MY DAUGHTER AND WE'RE NOT LEAVING HER BEHIND."
HEY, YOU KIDS! EITHER COME INSIDE OR GET OUT OF THE WAY!

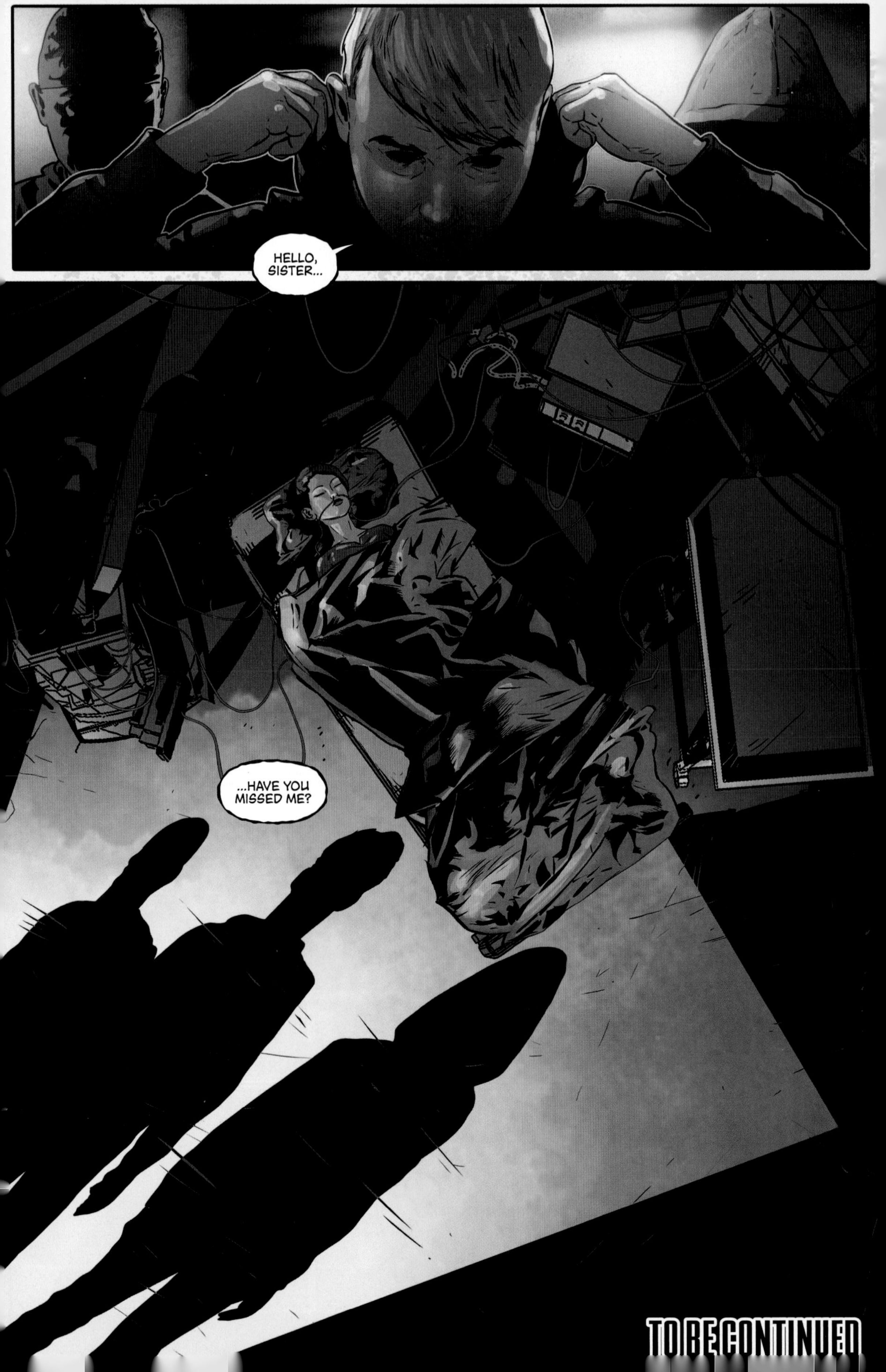
HELLO, SISTER...
...HAVE YOU MISSED ME?
TO BE CONTINUED

4

"URGENT CARE"

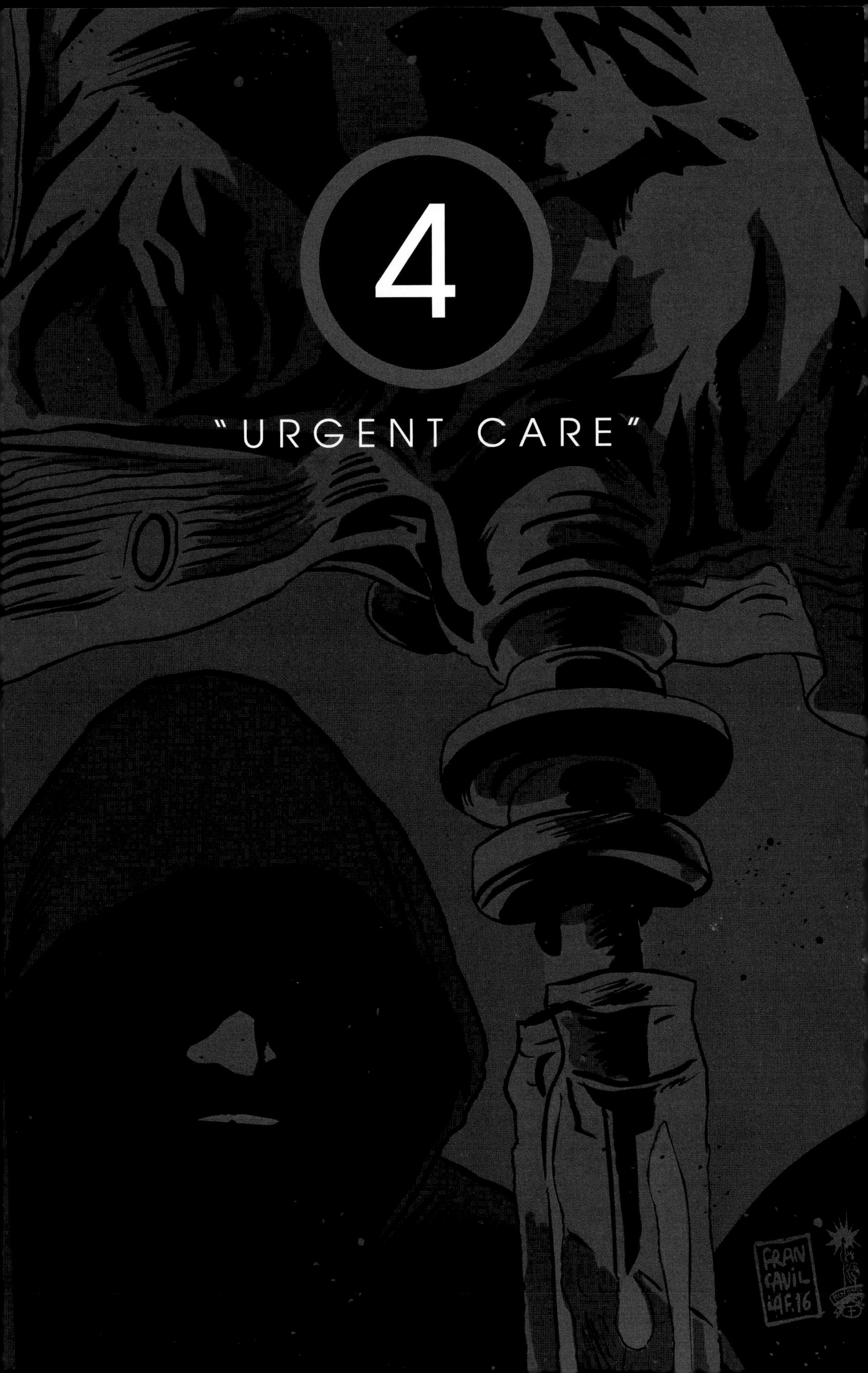

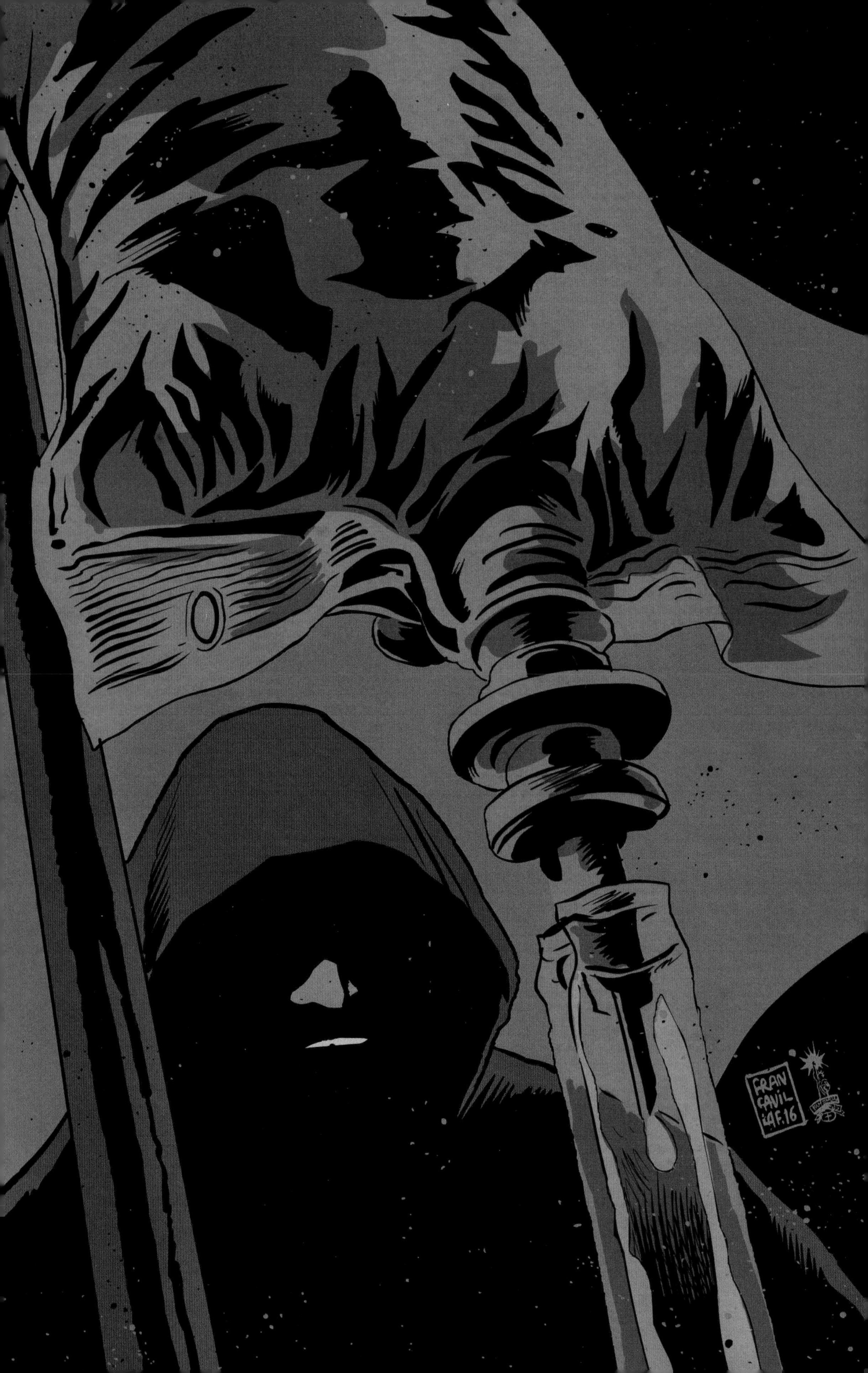

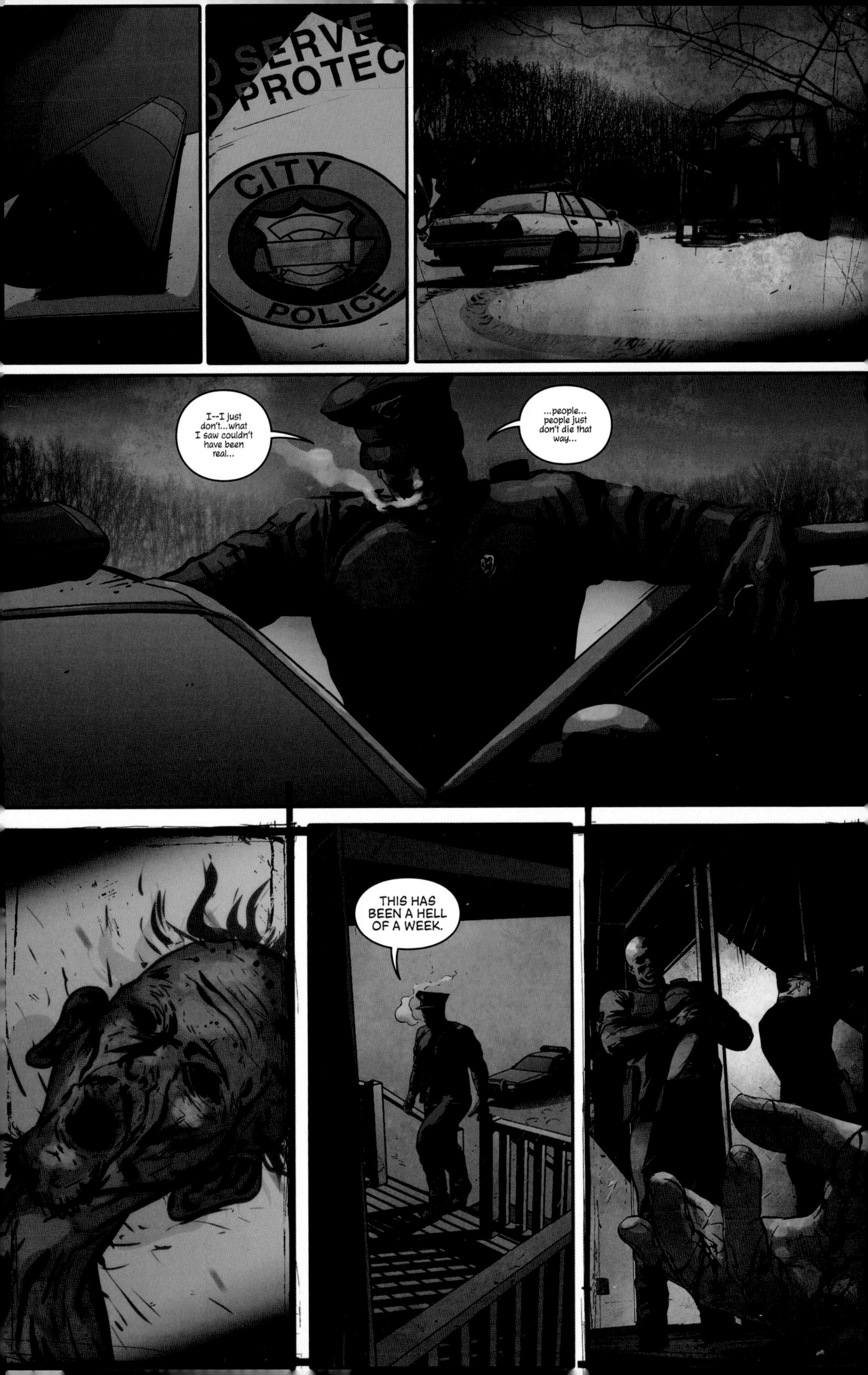
O SERVE
O PROTEC
CITY
POLICE
I--I just don't...what I saw couldn't have been real...
...people... people just don't die that way...
THIS HAS BEEN A HELL OF A WEEK.

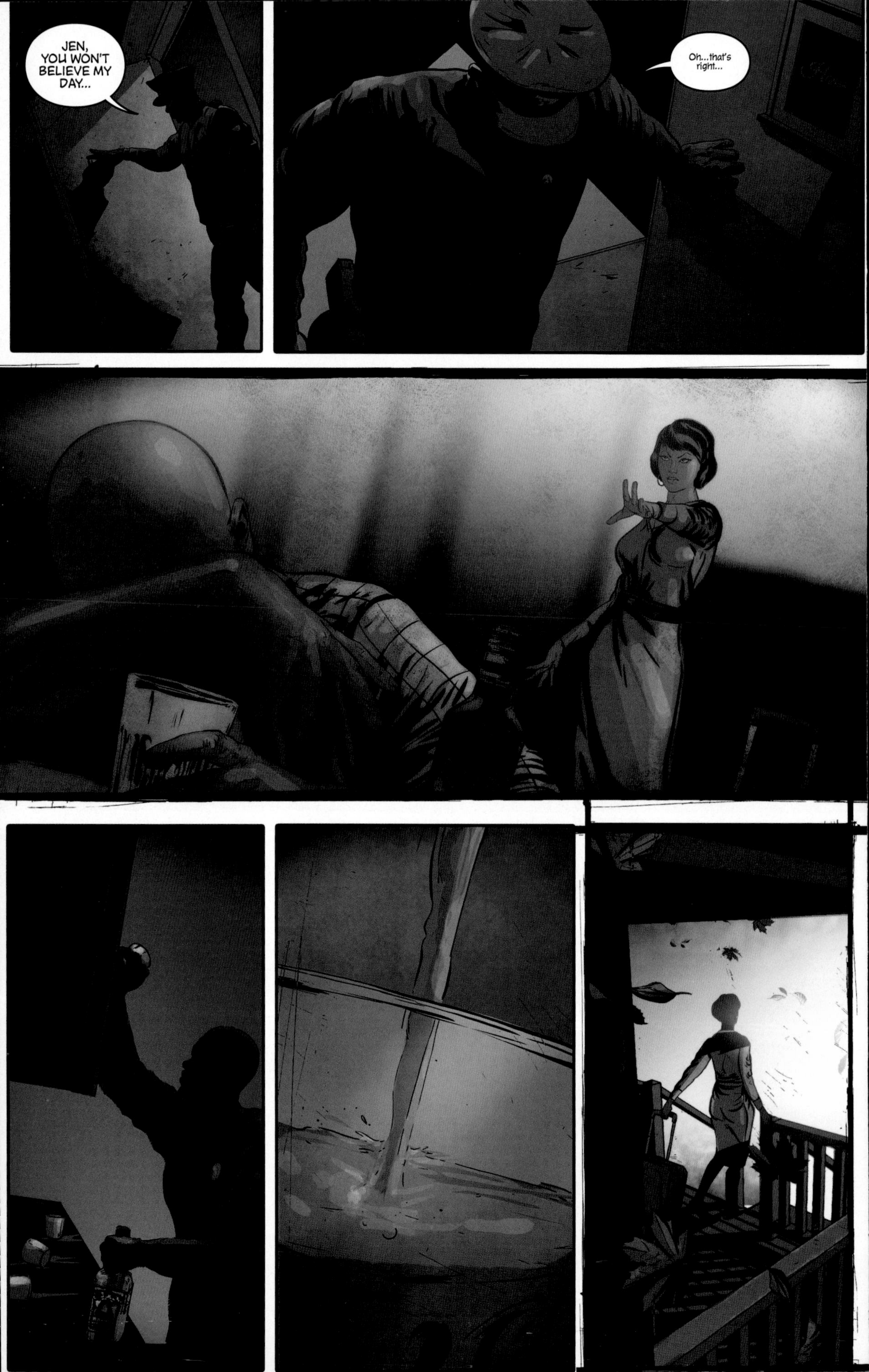
JEN, YOU WON'T BELIEVE MY DAY...
Oh...that's right...

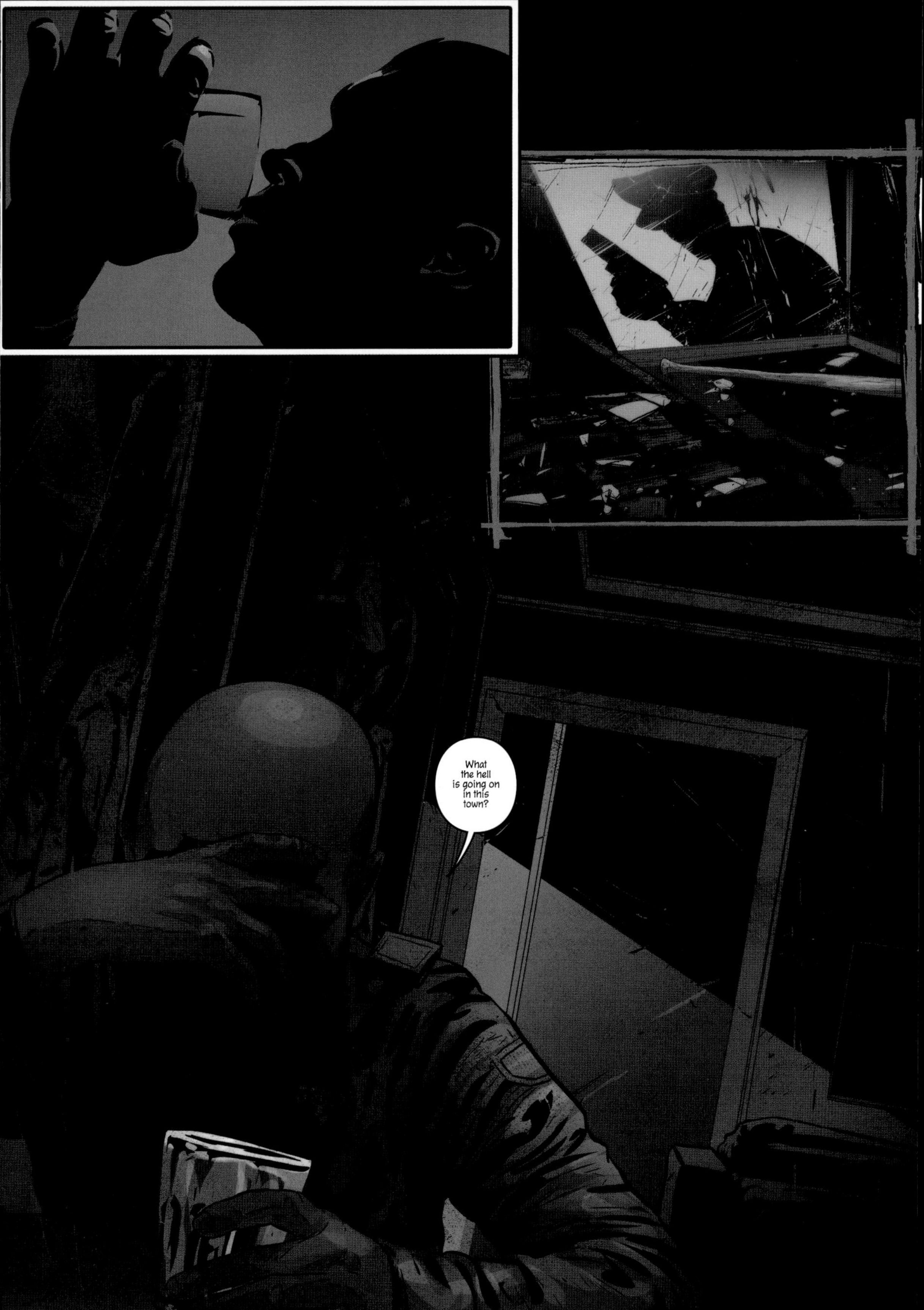
What the hell is going on in this town?

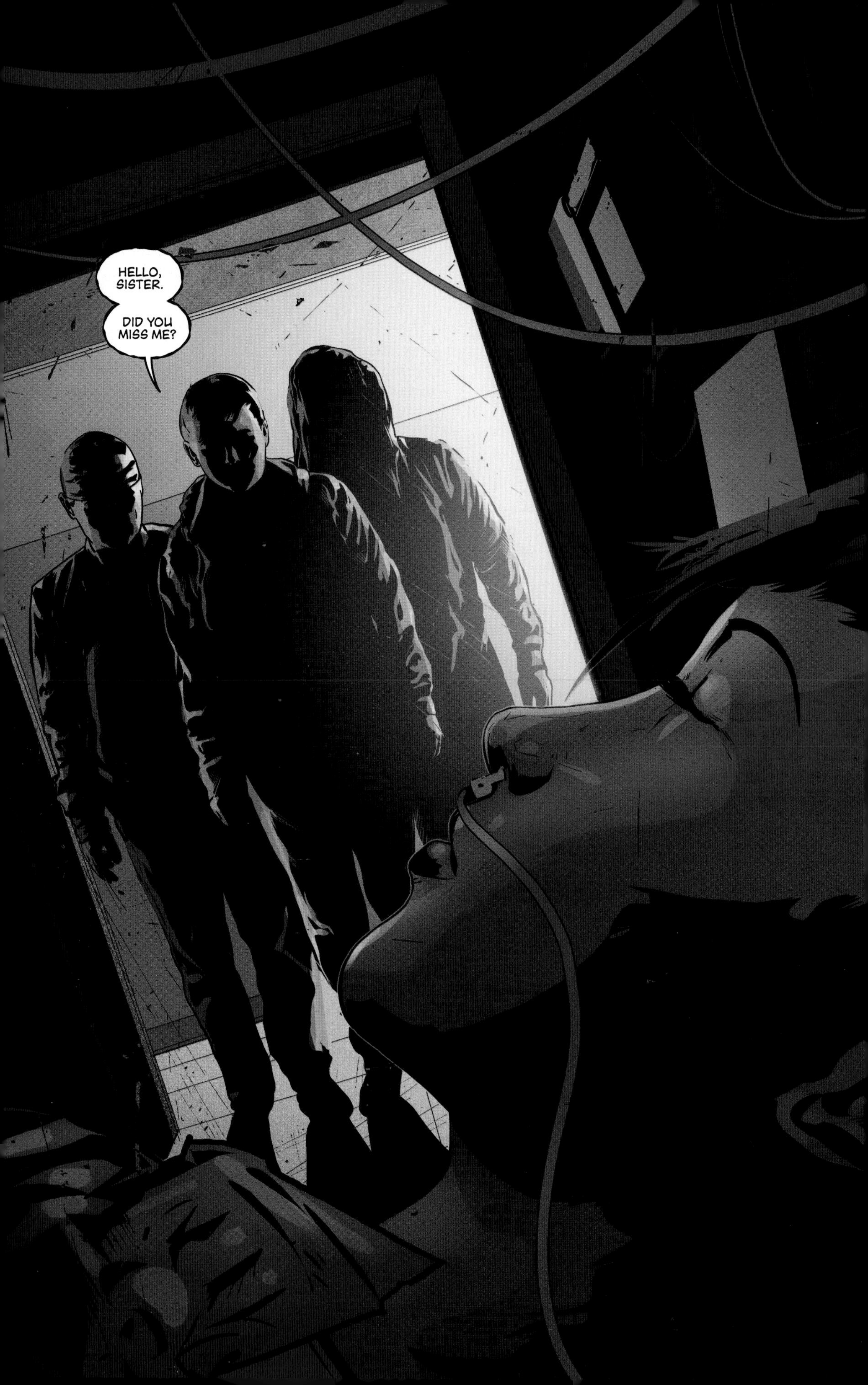
HELLO, SISTER.
DID YOU MISS ME?

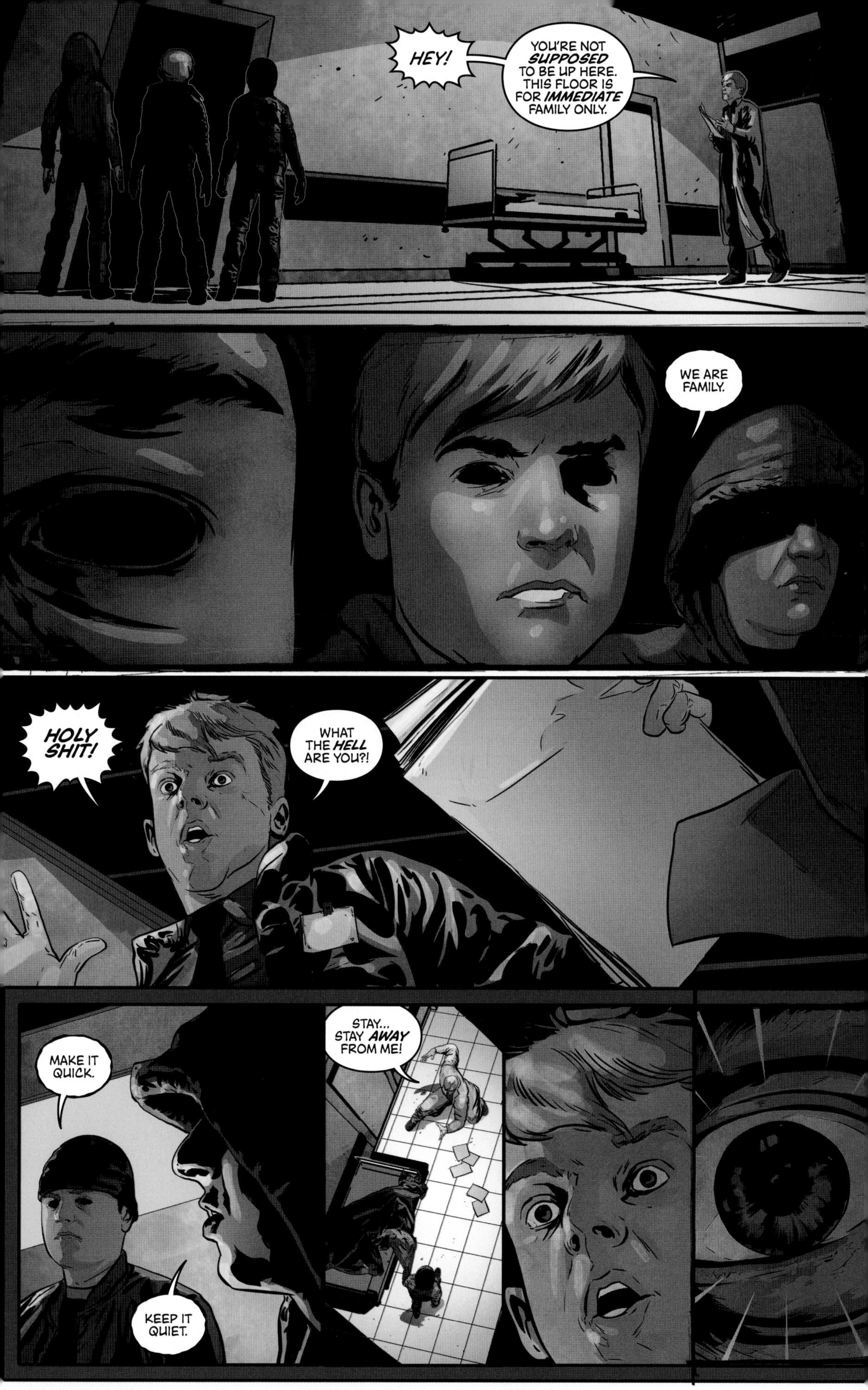
HEY!
YOU'RE NOT SUPPOSED TO BE UP HERE. THIS FLOOR IS FOR IMMEDIATE FAMILY ONLY.
WE ARE FAMILY.
HOLY SHIT!
WHAT THE HELL ARE YOU?!
MAKE IT QUICK.
KEEP IT QUIET.
STAY... STAY AWAY FROM ME!

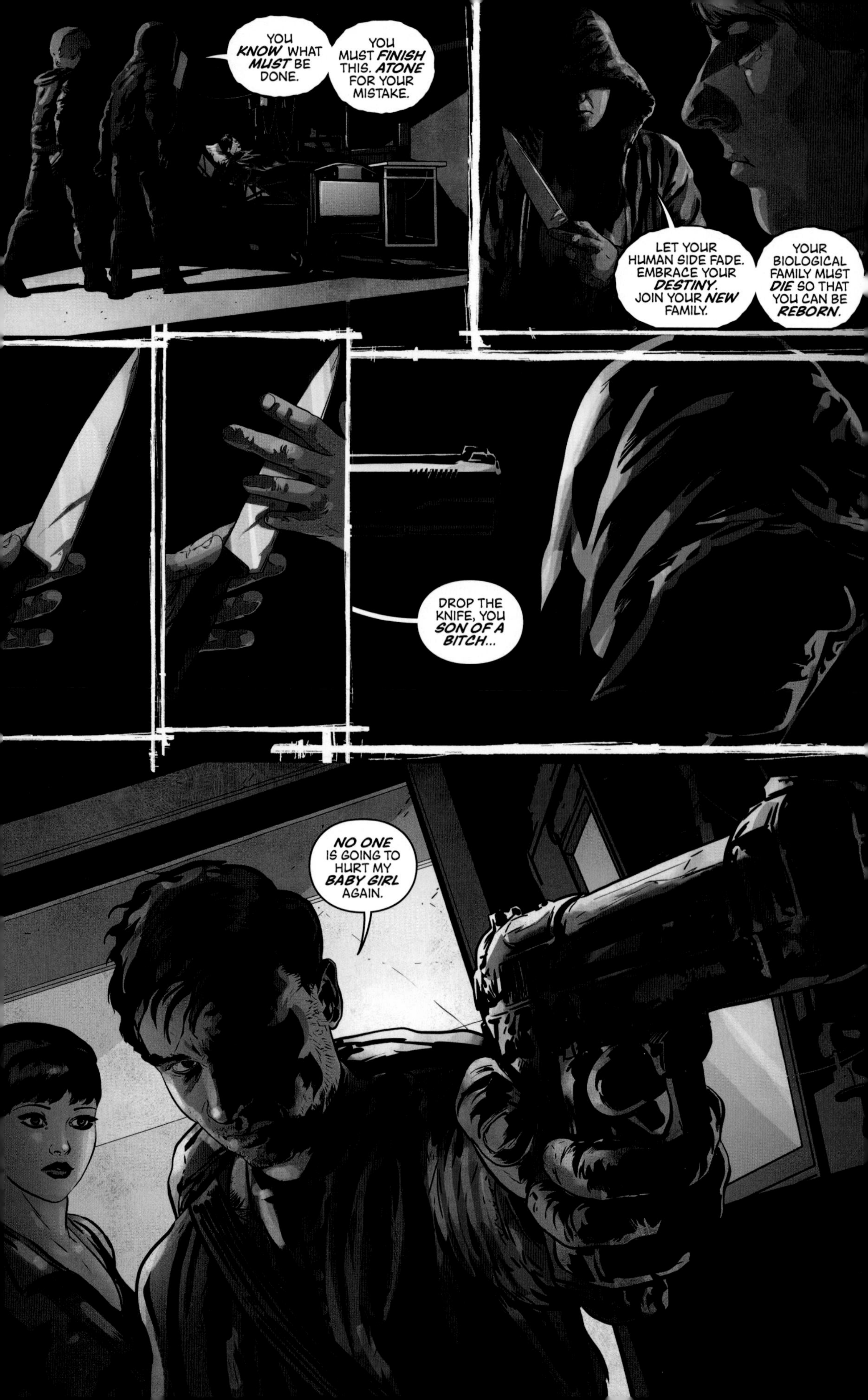
YOU KNOW WHAT MUST BE DONE.
YOU MUST FINISH THIS. ATONE FOR YOUR MISTAKE.
LET YOUR HUMAN SIDE FADE. EMBRACE YOUR DESTINY. JOIN YOUR NEW FAMILY.
YOUR BIOLOGICAL FAMILY MUST DIE SO THAT YOU CAN BE REBORN.
DROP THE KNIFE, YOU SON OF A BITCH...
NO ONE IS GOING TO HURT MY BABY GIRL AGAIN.

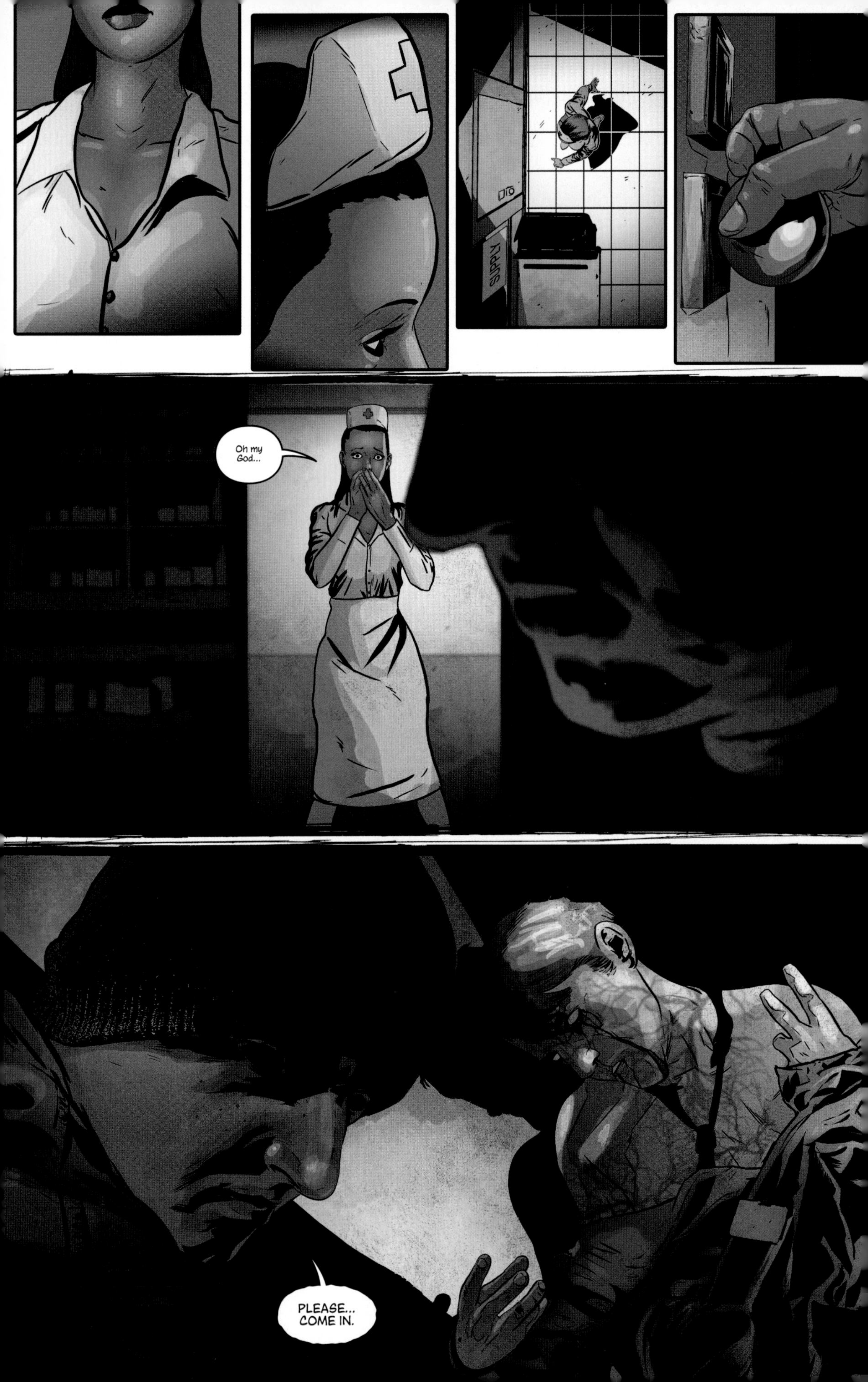
SUPPLY
Oh my God...
PLEASE... COME IN.

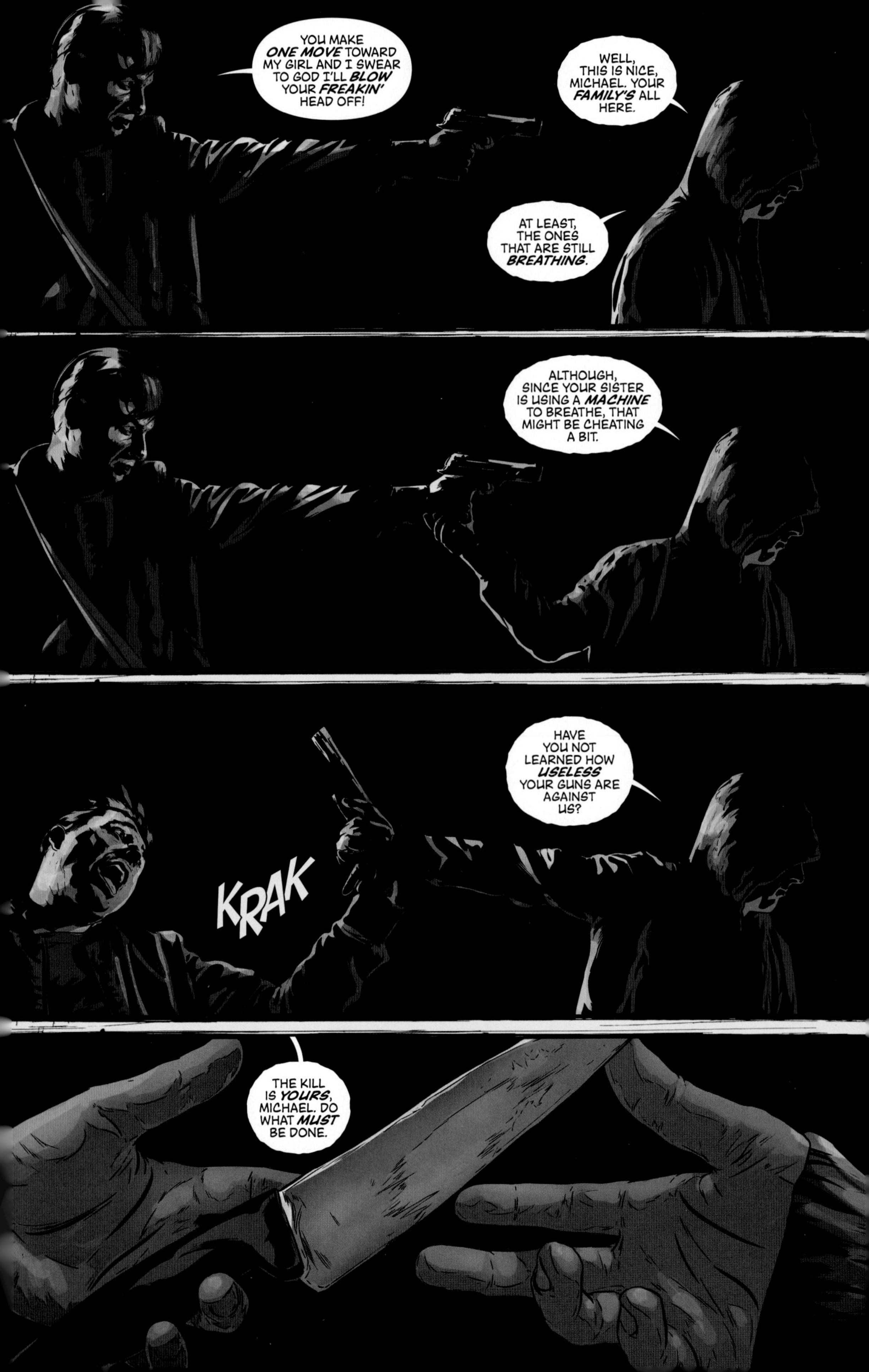
YOU MAKE ONE MOVE TOWARD MY GIRL AND I SWEAR TO GOD I'LL BLOW YOUR FREAKIN' HEAD OFF!
WELL, THIS IS NICE, MICHAEL. YOUR FAMILY'S ALL HERE.
AT LEAST, THE ONES THAT ARE STILL BREATHING.
ALTHOUGH, SINCE YOUR SISTER IS USING A MACHINE TO BREATHE, THAT MIGHT BE CHEATING A BIT.
HAVE YOU NOT LEARNED HOW USELESS YOUR GUNS ARE AGAINST US?
KRAK
THE KILL IS YOURS, MICHAEL. DO WHAT MUST BE DONE.

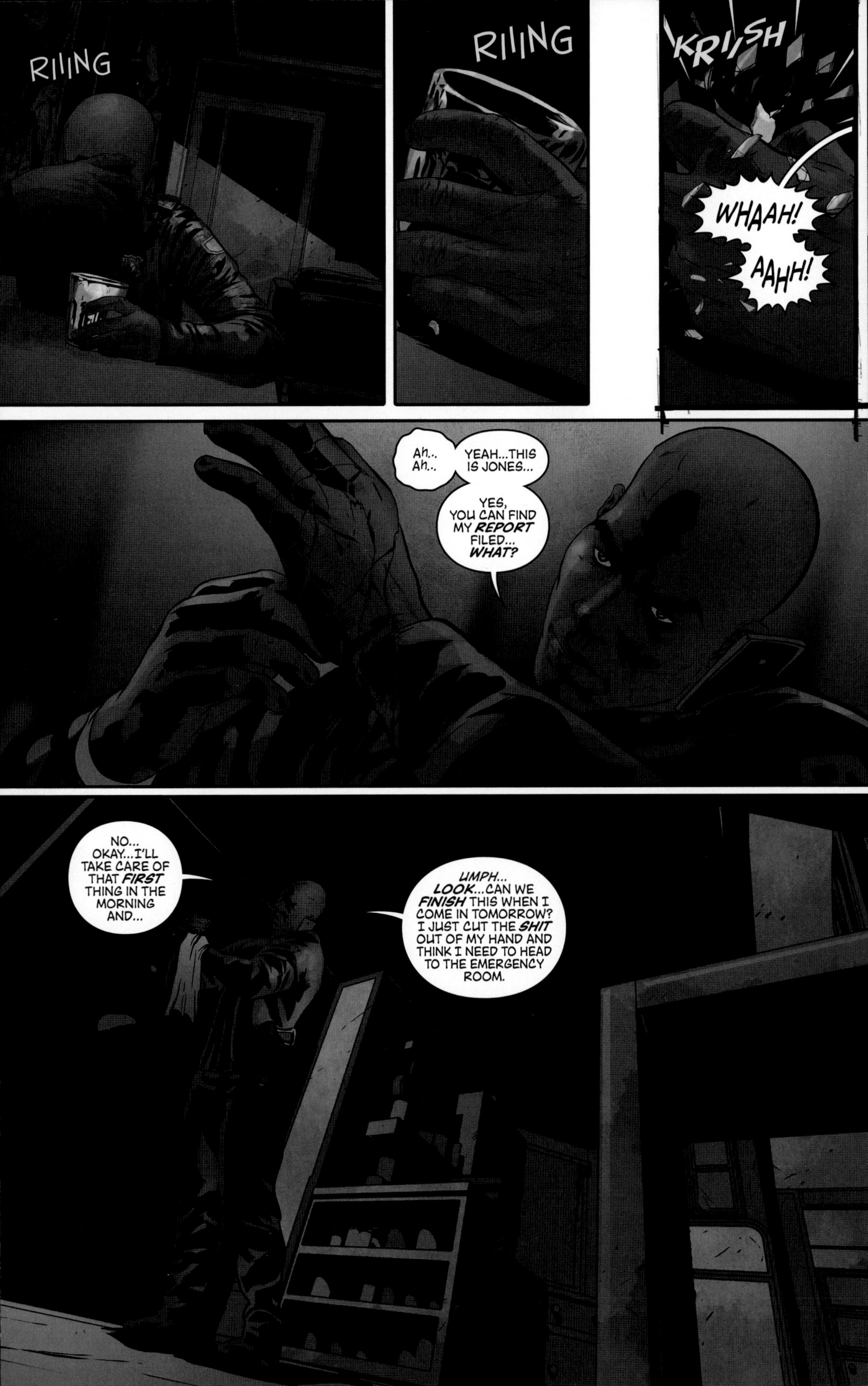
RIIING
RIIING
KRIISH
WHAAH!
AAHH!
Ah.. Ah..
YEAH...THIS IS JONES...
YES, YOU CAN FIND MY REPORT FILED... WHAT?
NO... OKAY...I'LL TAKE CARE OF THAT FIRST THING IN THE MORNING AND...
UMPH... LOOK...CAN WE FINISH THIS WHEN I COME IN TOMORROW? I JUST CUT THE SHIT OUT OF MY HAND AND THINK I NEED TO HEAD TO THE EMERGENCY ROOM.

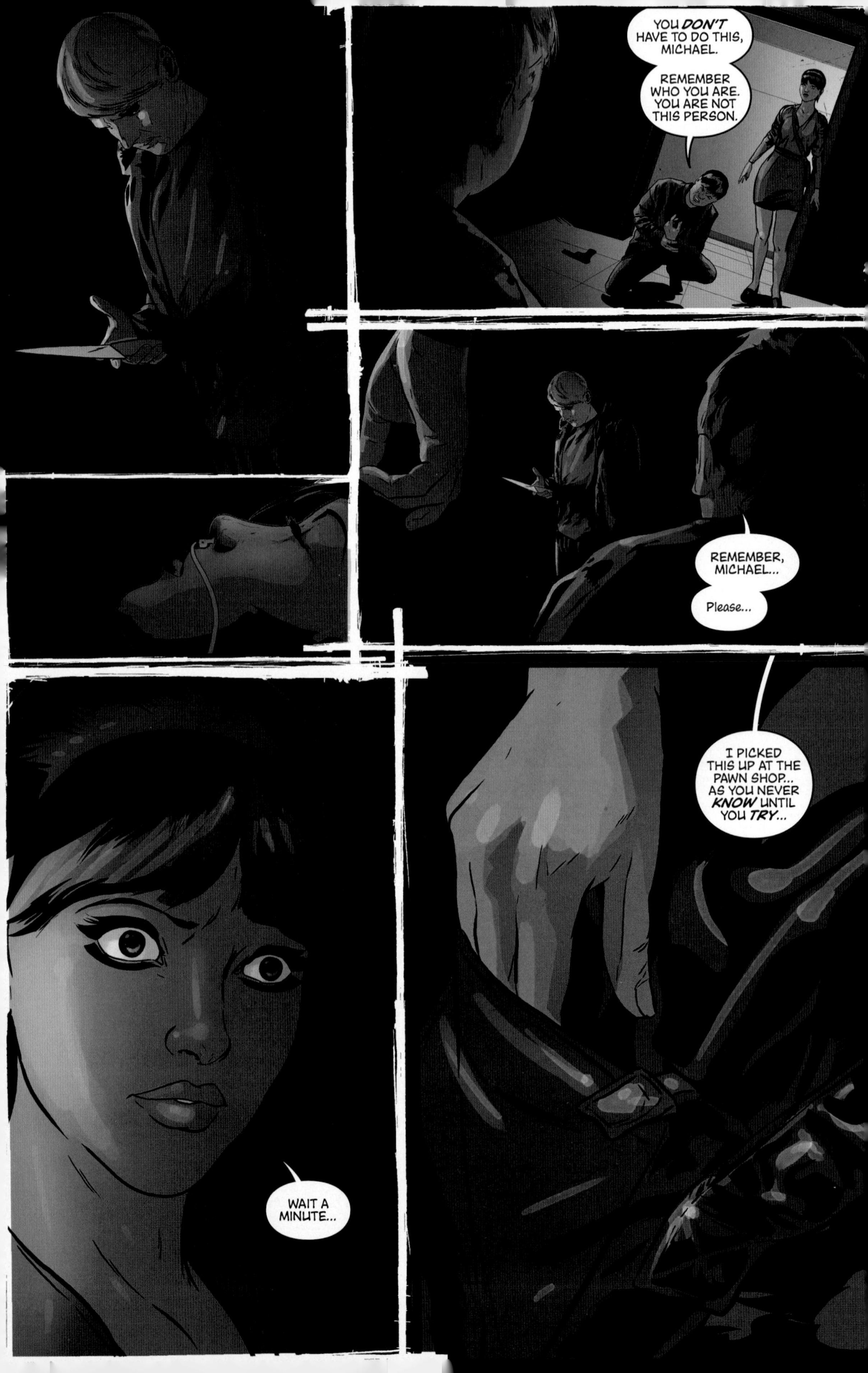
YOU DON'T HAVE TO DO THIS, MICHAEL.
REMEMBER WHO YOU ARE. YOU ARE NOT THIS PERSON.
REMEMBER, MICHAEL...
Please...
WAIT A MINUTE...
I PICKED THIS UP AT THE PAWN SHOP... AS YOU NEVER KNOW UNTIL YOU TRY...

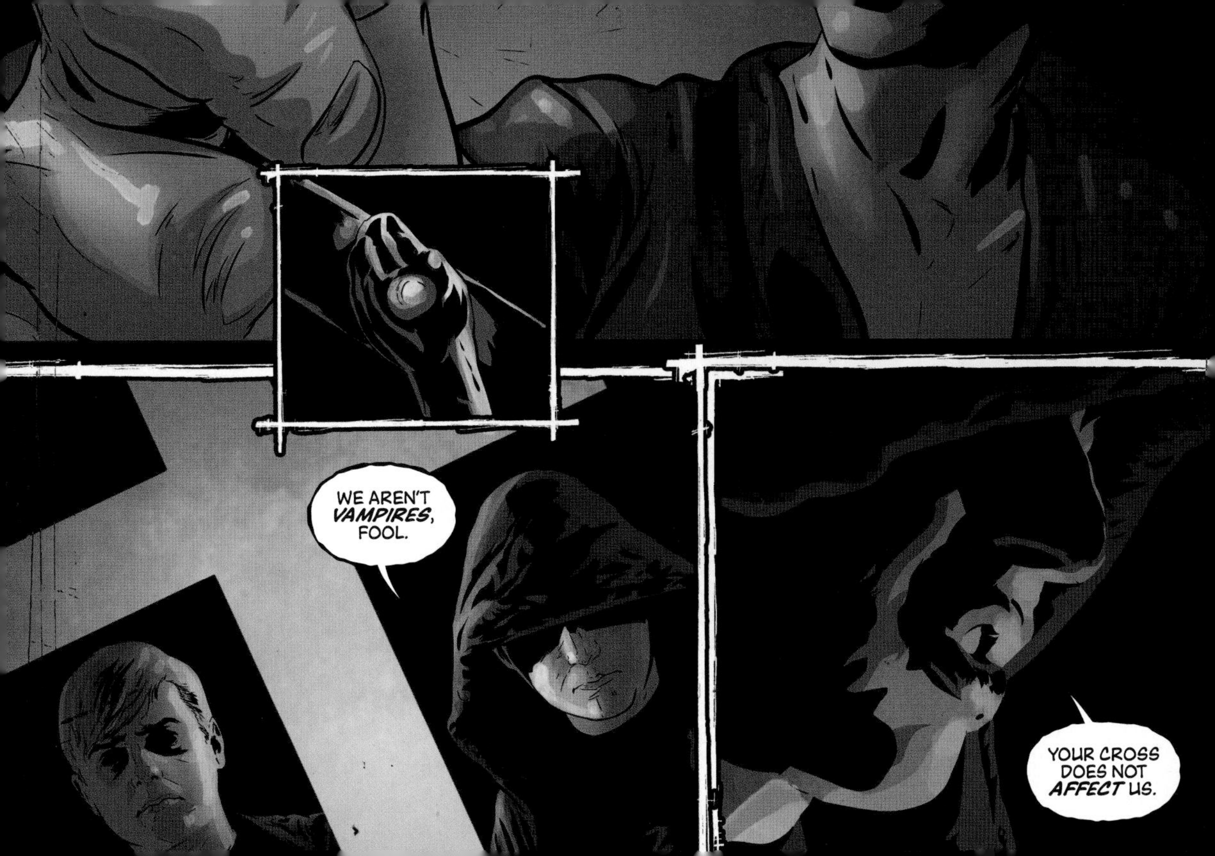
WE AREN'T *VAMPIRES*, FOOL.
YOUR CROSS DOES NOT *AFFECT* US.

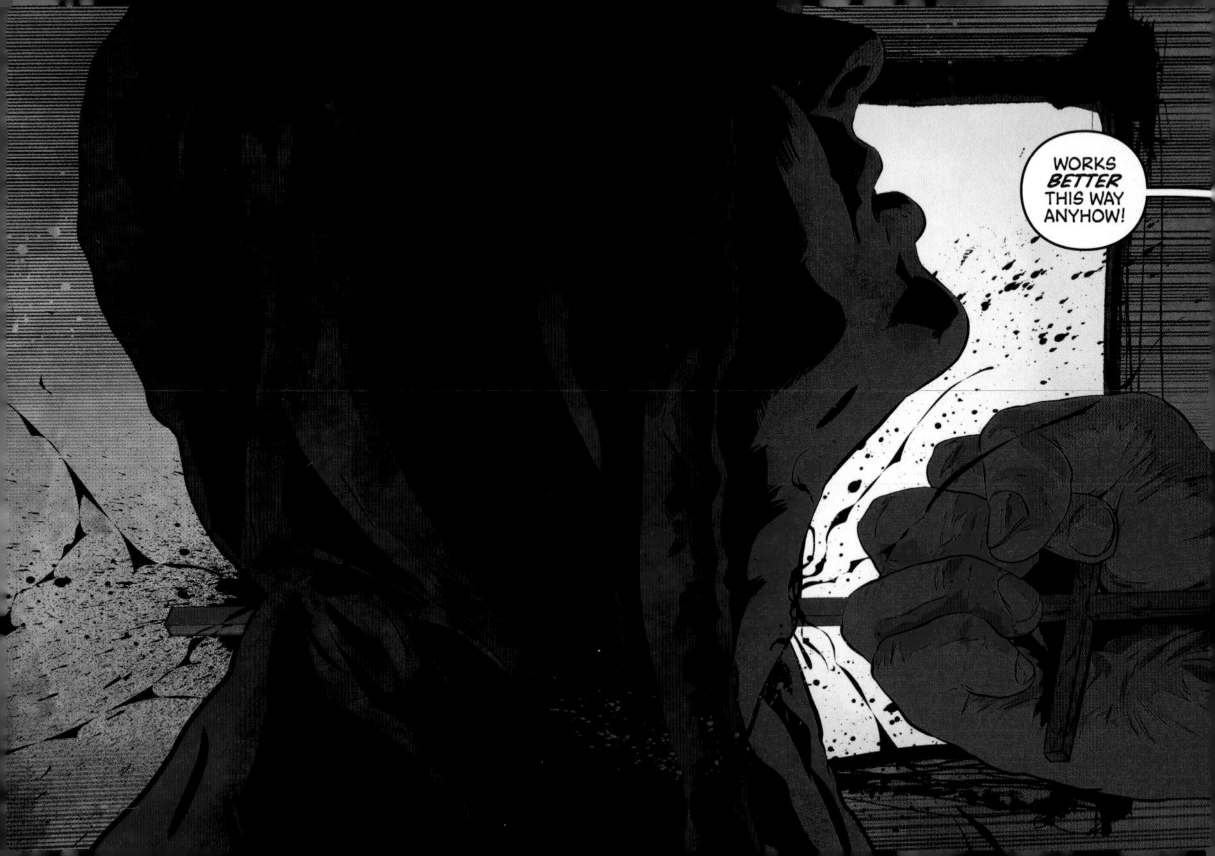
WORKS *BETTER* THIS WAY ANYHOW!

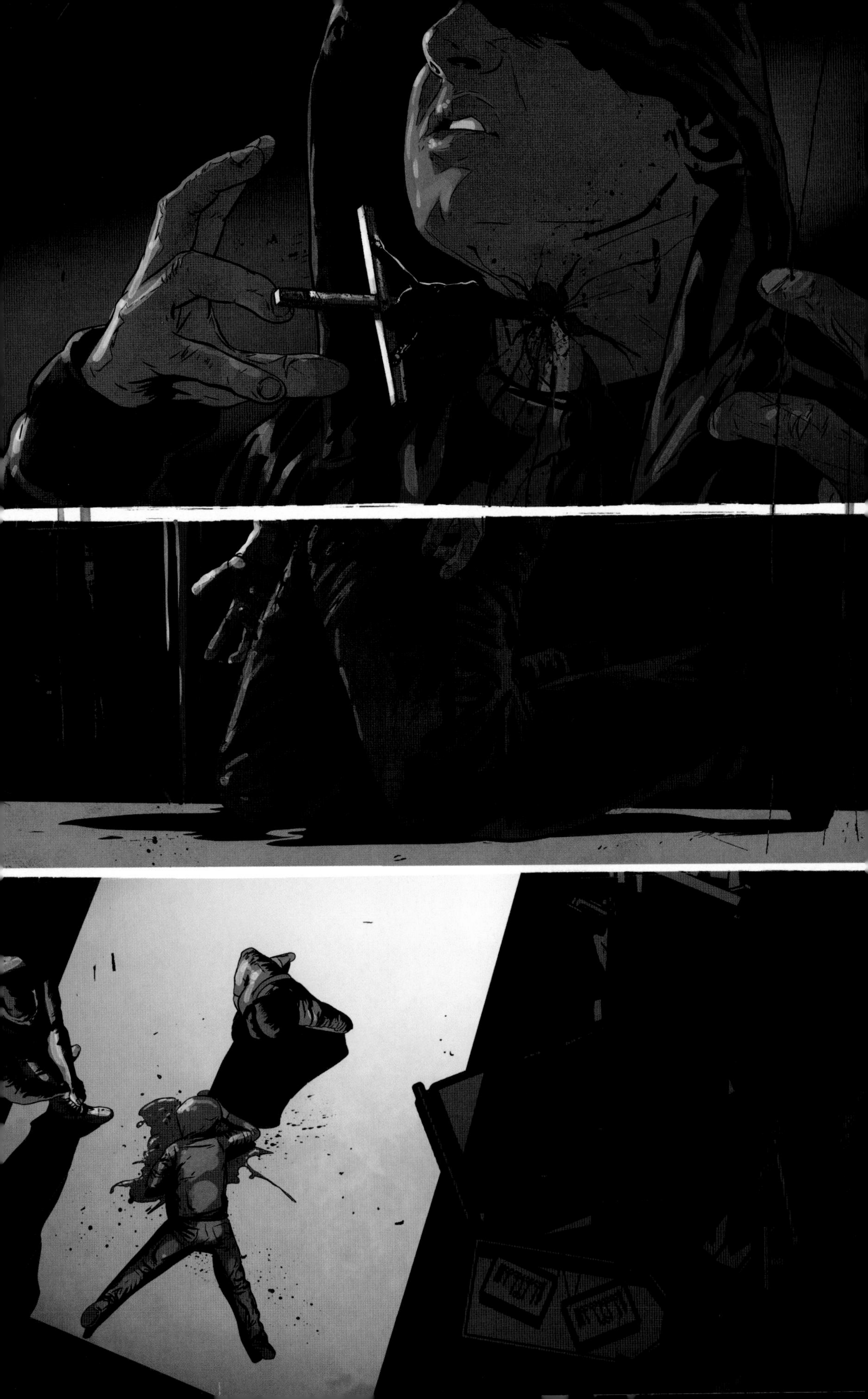

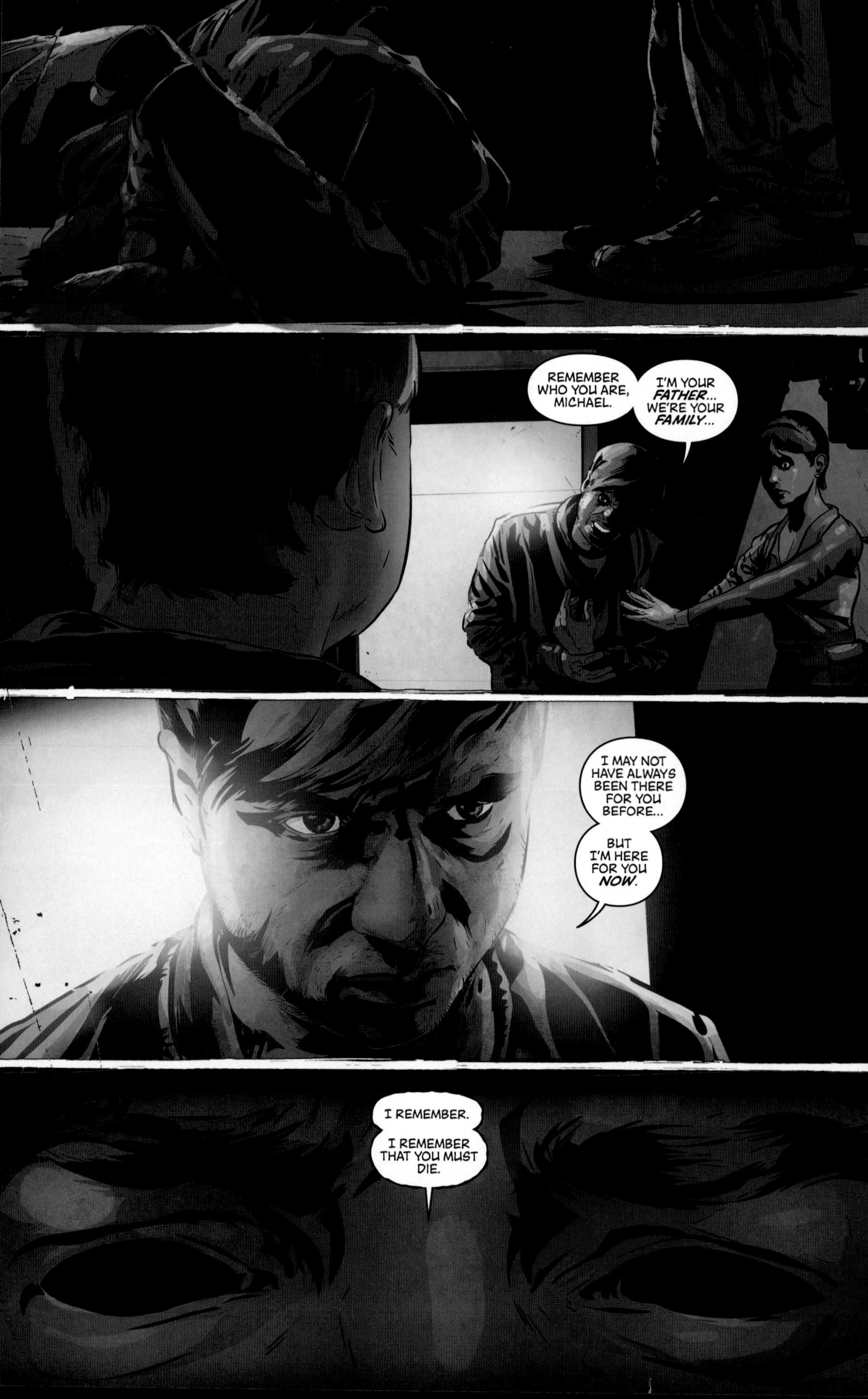

REMEMBER WHO YOU ARE, MICHAEL.
I'M YOUR *FATHER*... WE'RE YOUR *FAMILY*...
I MAY NOT HAVE ALWAYS BEEN THERE FOR YOU BEFORE...
BUT I'M HERE FOR YOU *NOW*.
I REMEMBER.
I REMEMBER THAT YOU MUST DIE.

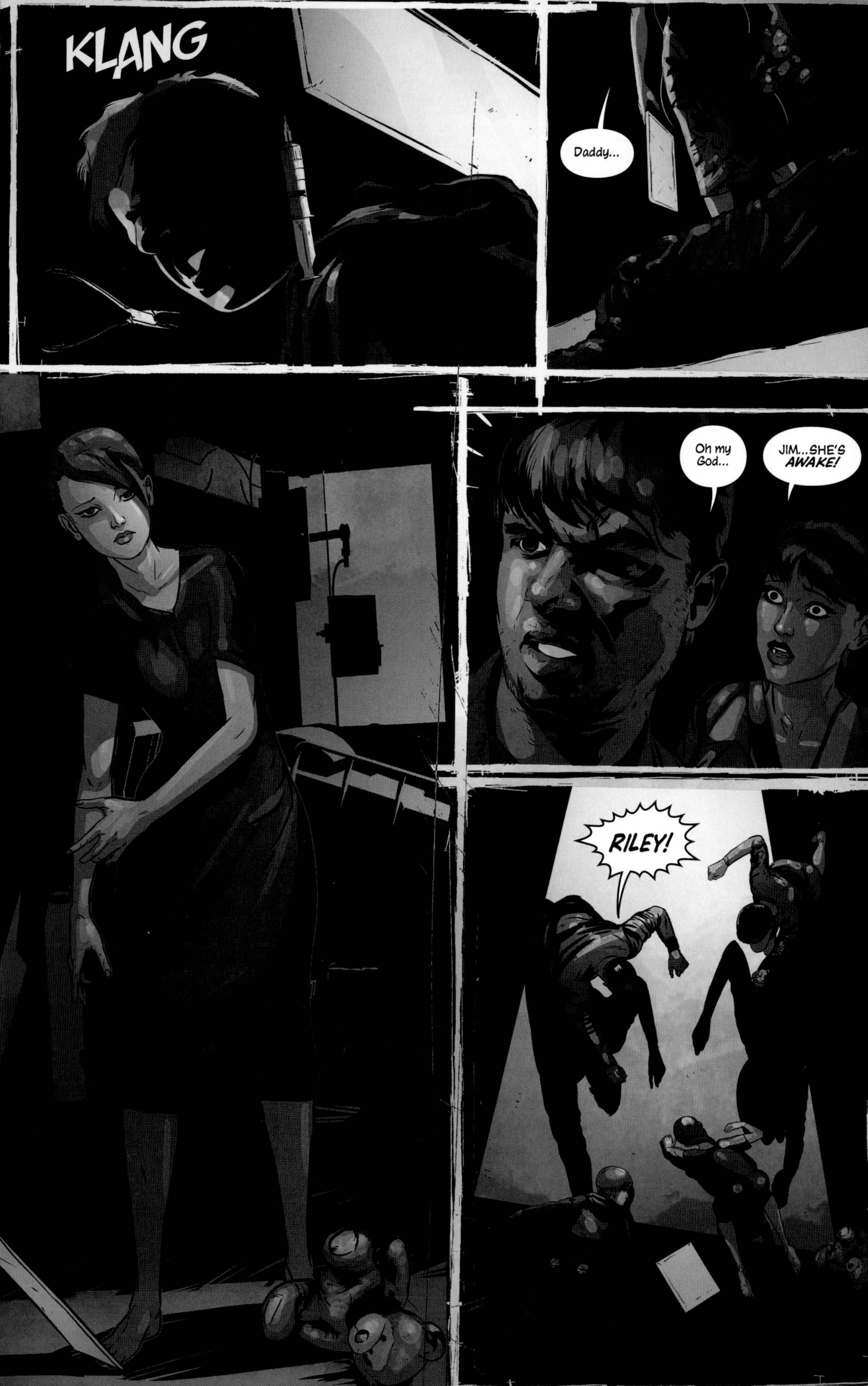
KLANG
Daddy...
Oh my God...
JIM...SHE'S *AWAKE!*
RILEY!

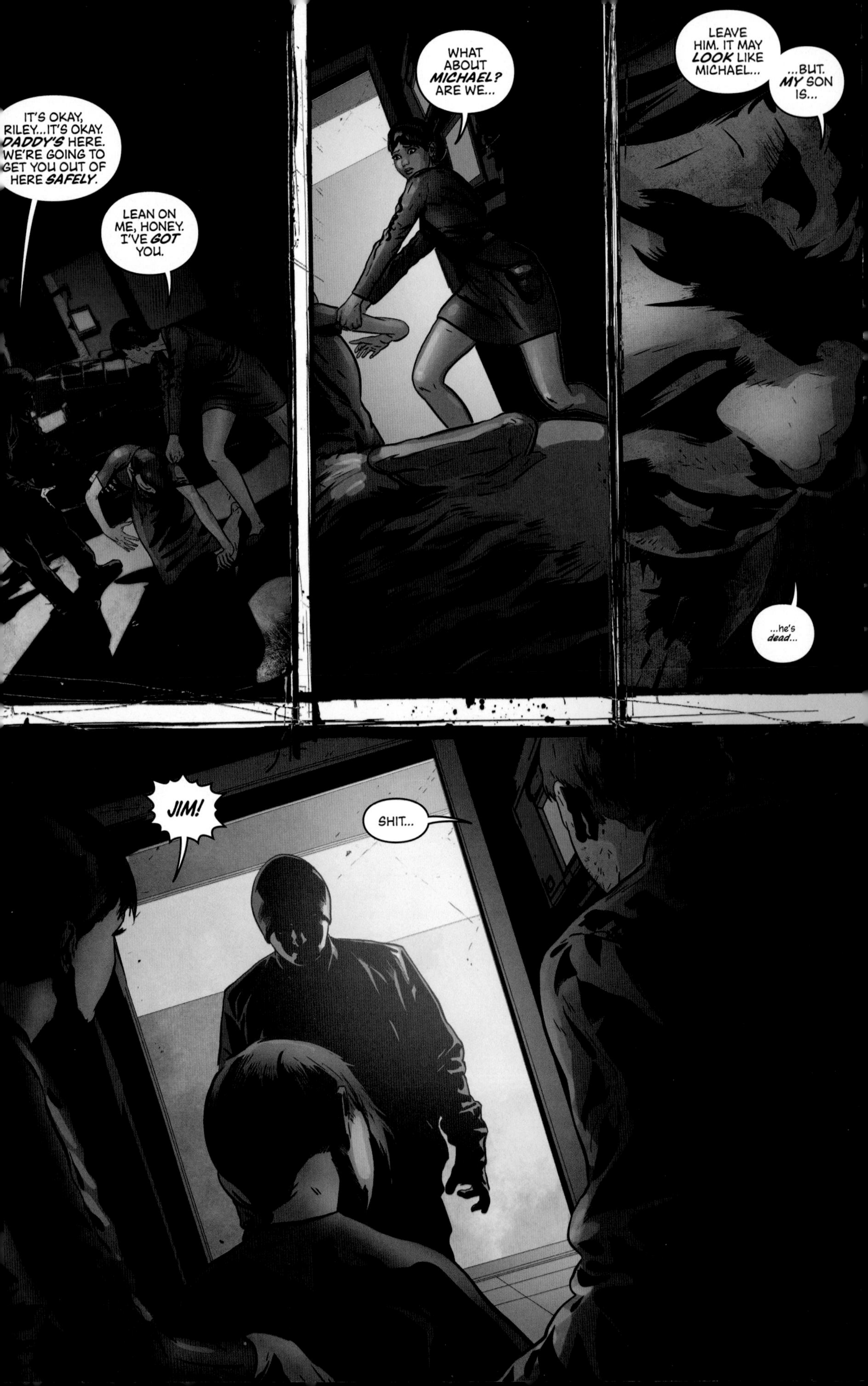
IT'S OKAY, RILEY...IT'S OKAY. *DADDY'S* HERE. WE'RE GOING TO GET YOU OUT OF HERE *SAFELY*.
LEAN ON ME, HONEY. I'VE *GOT* YOU.
WHAT ABOUT *MICHAEL?* ARE WE...
LEAVE HIM. IT MAY *LOOK* LIKE MICHAEL...
...BUT. *MY* SON IS...
...he's *dead*...
JIM!
SHIT...

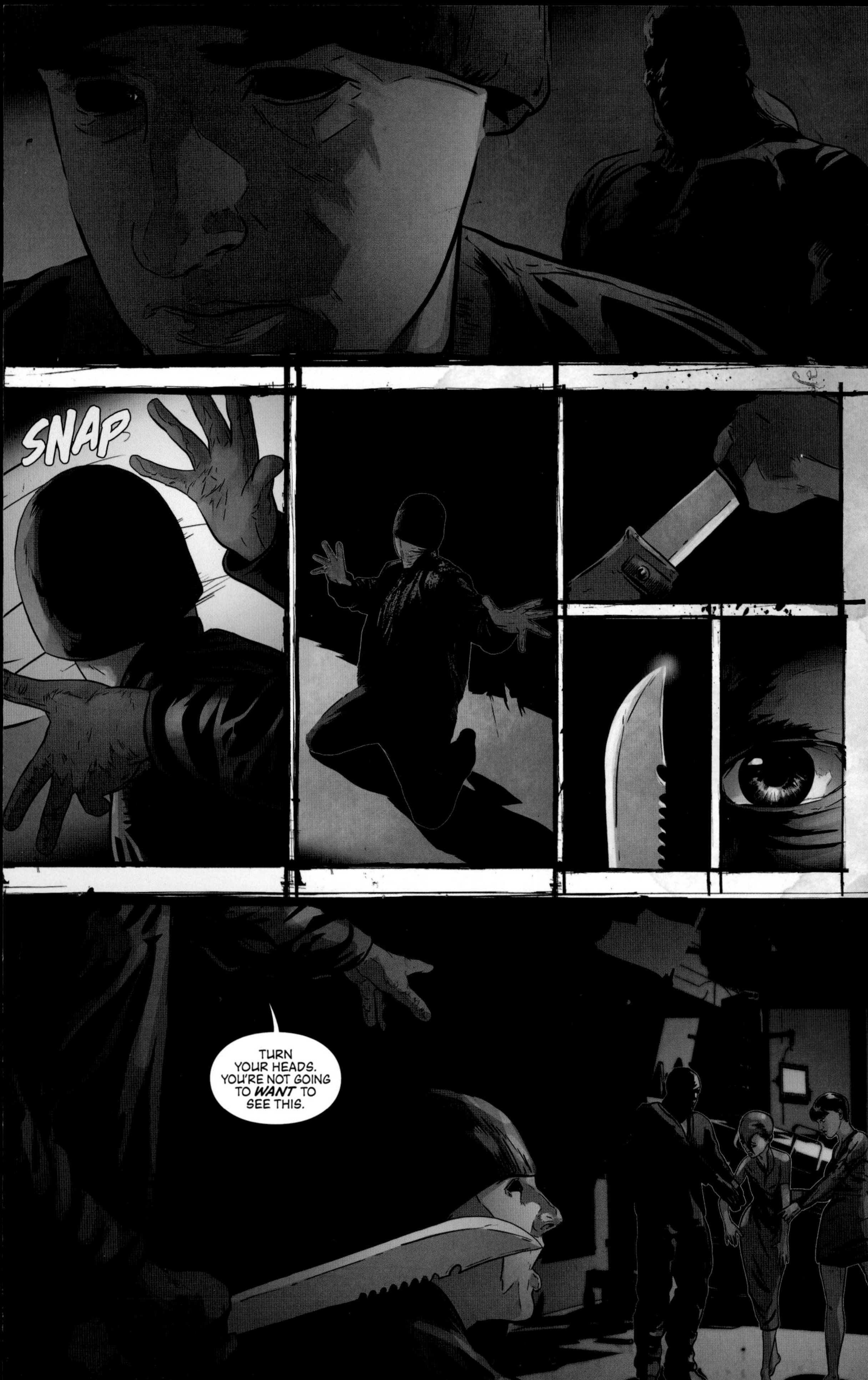
SNAP
TURN YOUR HEADS. YOU'RE NOT GOING TO *WANT* TO SEE THIS.

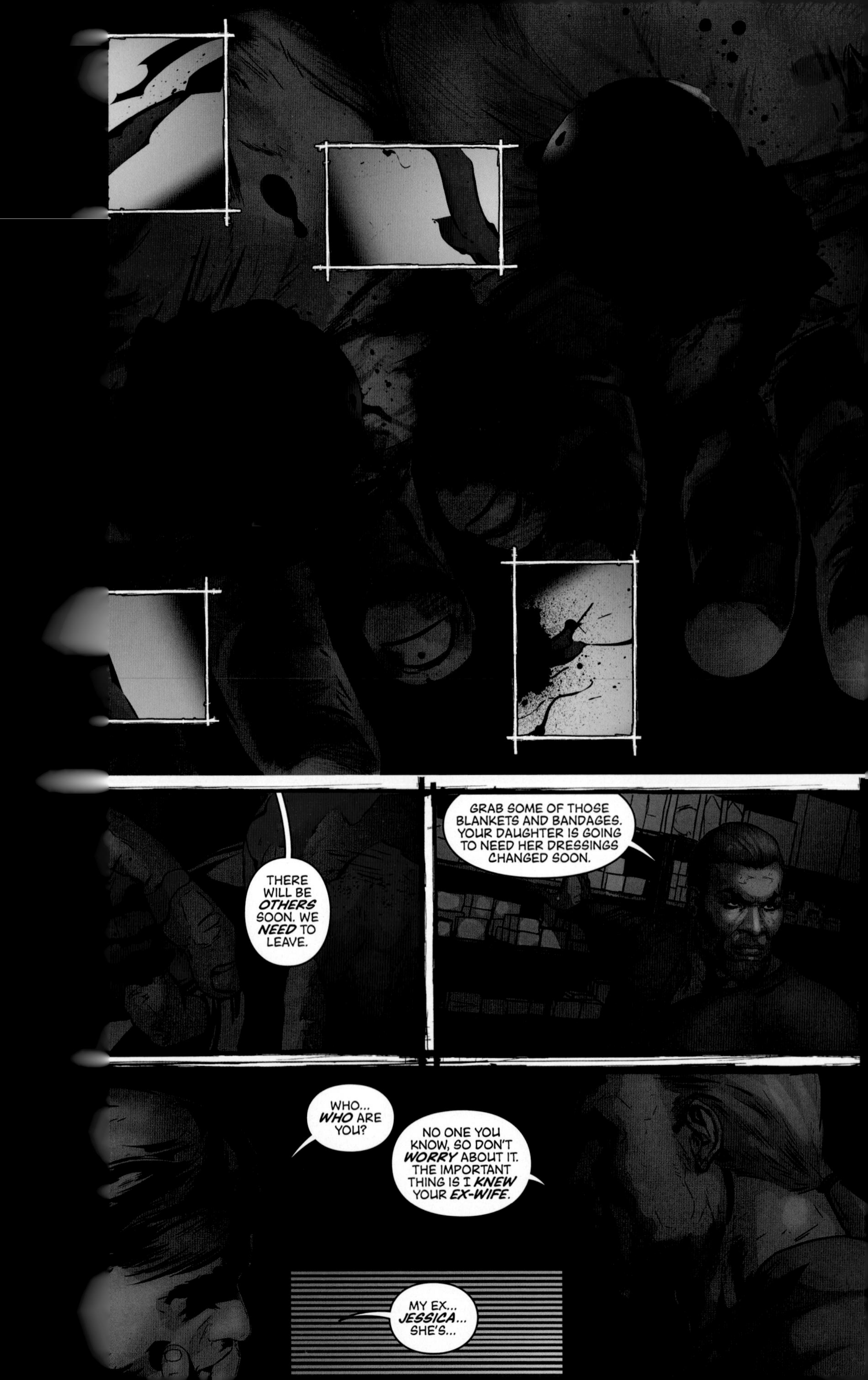
THERE WILL BE OTHERS SOON. WE NEED TO LEAVE.
GRAB SOME OF THOSE BLANKETS AND BANDAGES. YOUR DAUGHTER IS GOING TO NEED HER DRESSINGS CHANGED SOON.
WHO... WHO ARE YOU?
NO ONE YOU KNOW, SO DON'T WORRY ABOUT IT. THE IMPORTANT THING IS I KNEW YOUR EX-WIFE.
MY EX... JESSICA... SHE'S...

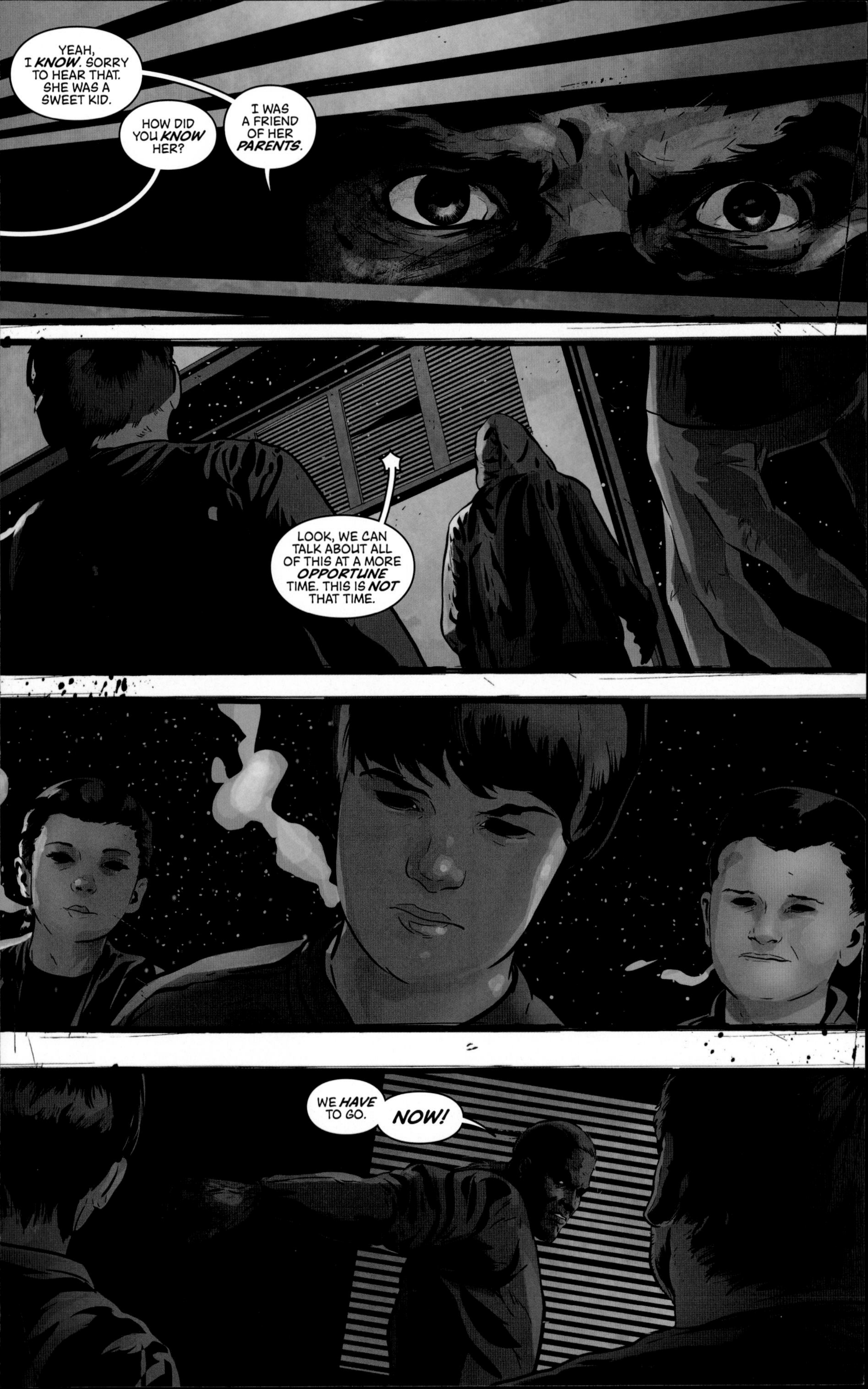
YEAH, I KNOW. SORRY TO HEAR THAT. SHE WAS A SWEET KID.
HOW DID YOU KNOW HER?
I WAS A FRIEND OF HER PARENTS.
LOOK, WE CAN TALK ABOUT ALL OF THIS AT A MORE OPPORTUNE TIME. THIS IS NOT THAT TIME.
WE HAVE TO GO.
NOW!

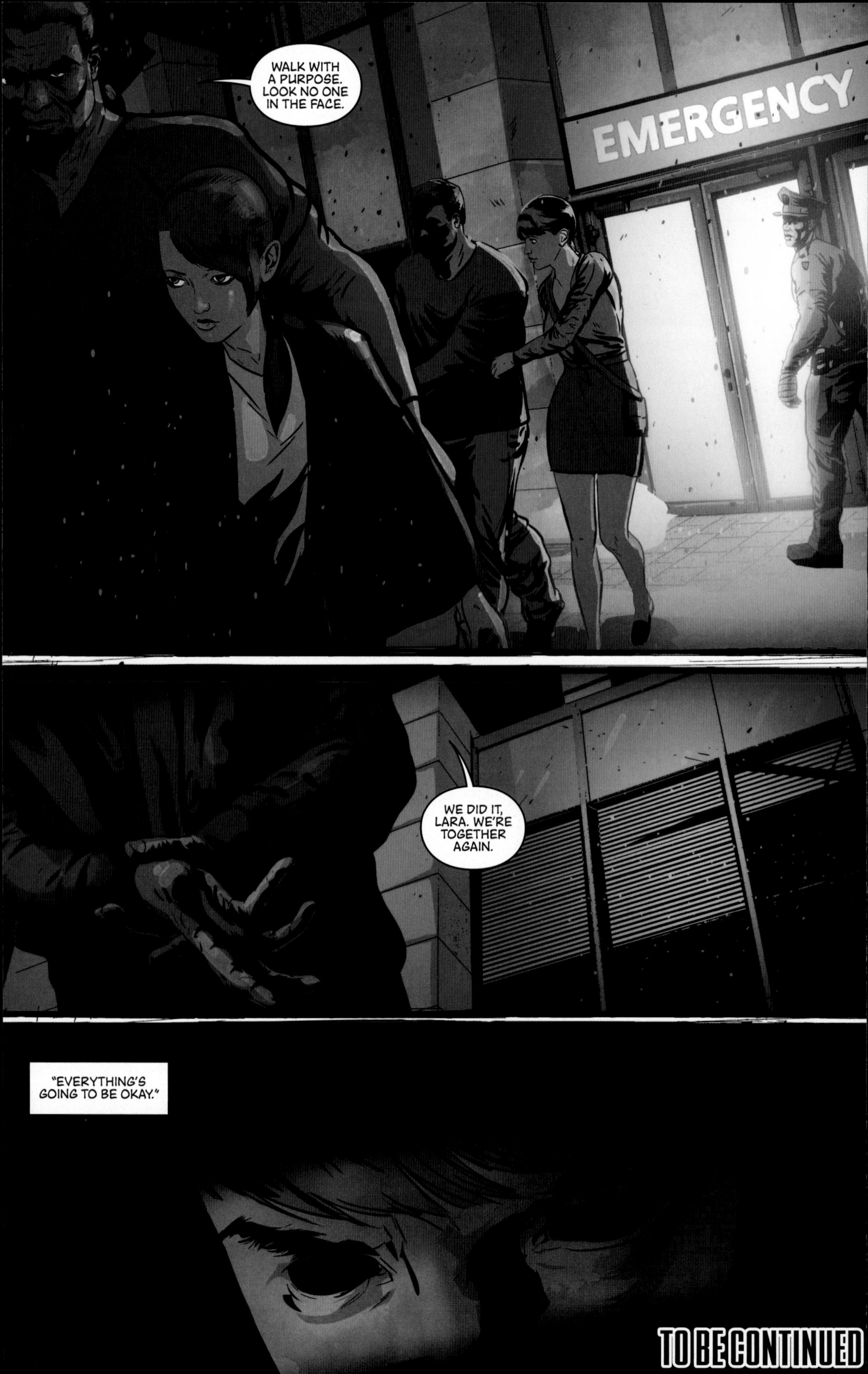
WALK WITH A PURPOSE. LOOK NO ONE IN THE FACE.
EMERGENCY
WE DID IT, LARA. WE'RE TOGETHER AGAIN.
"EVERYTHING'S GOING TO BE OKAY."
TO BE CONTINUED

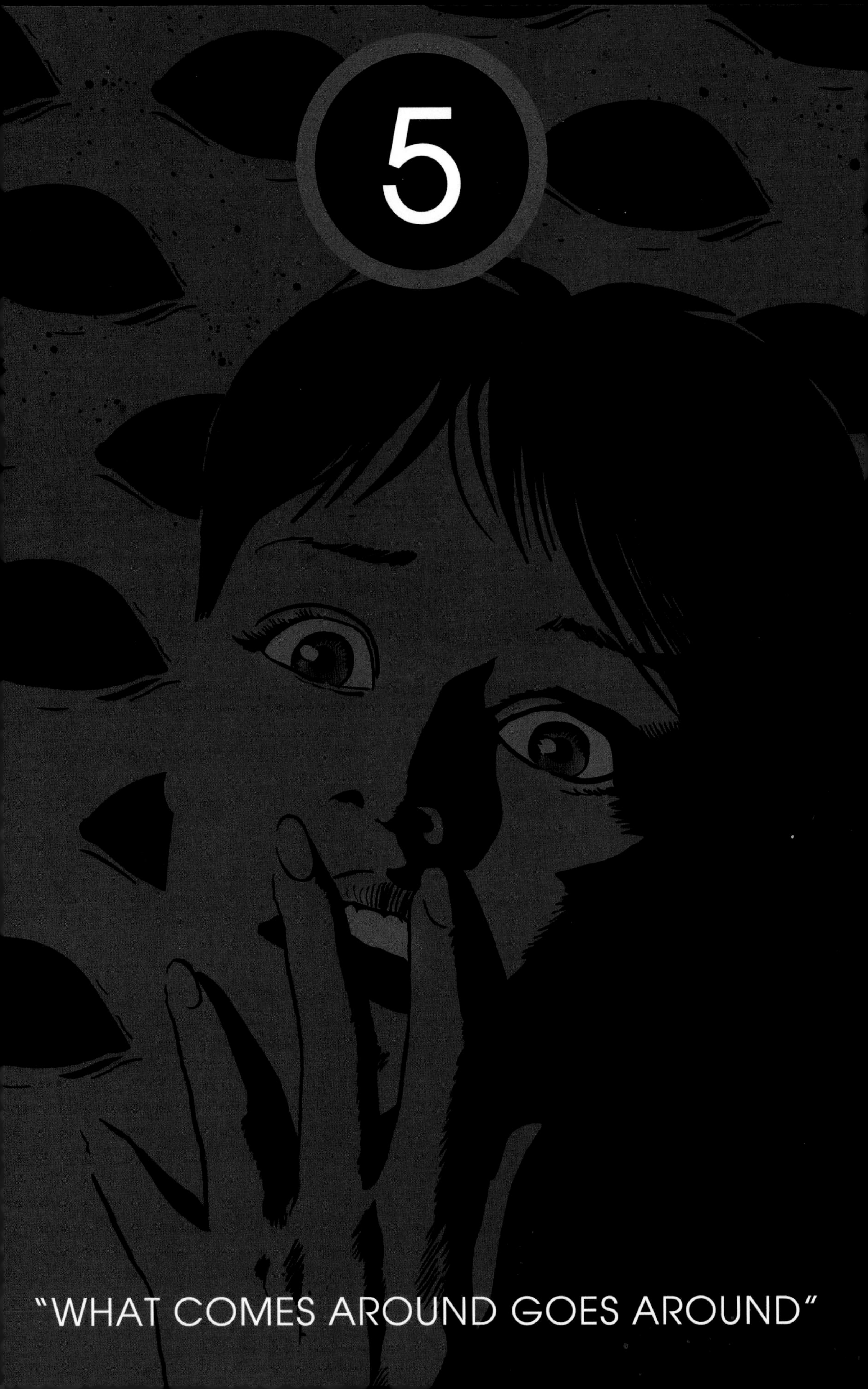

5

"WHAT COMES AROUND GOES AROUND"

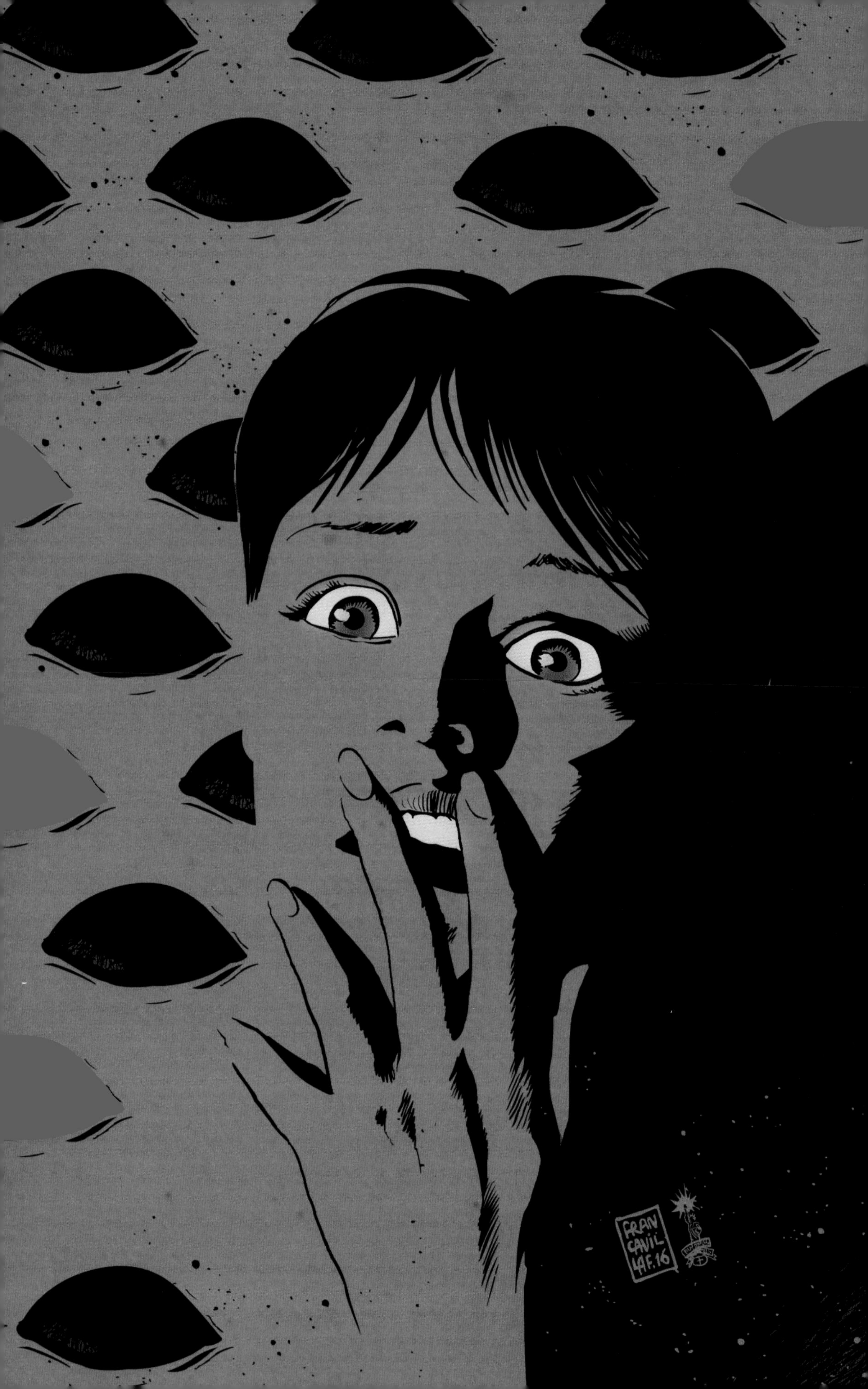

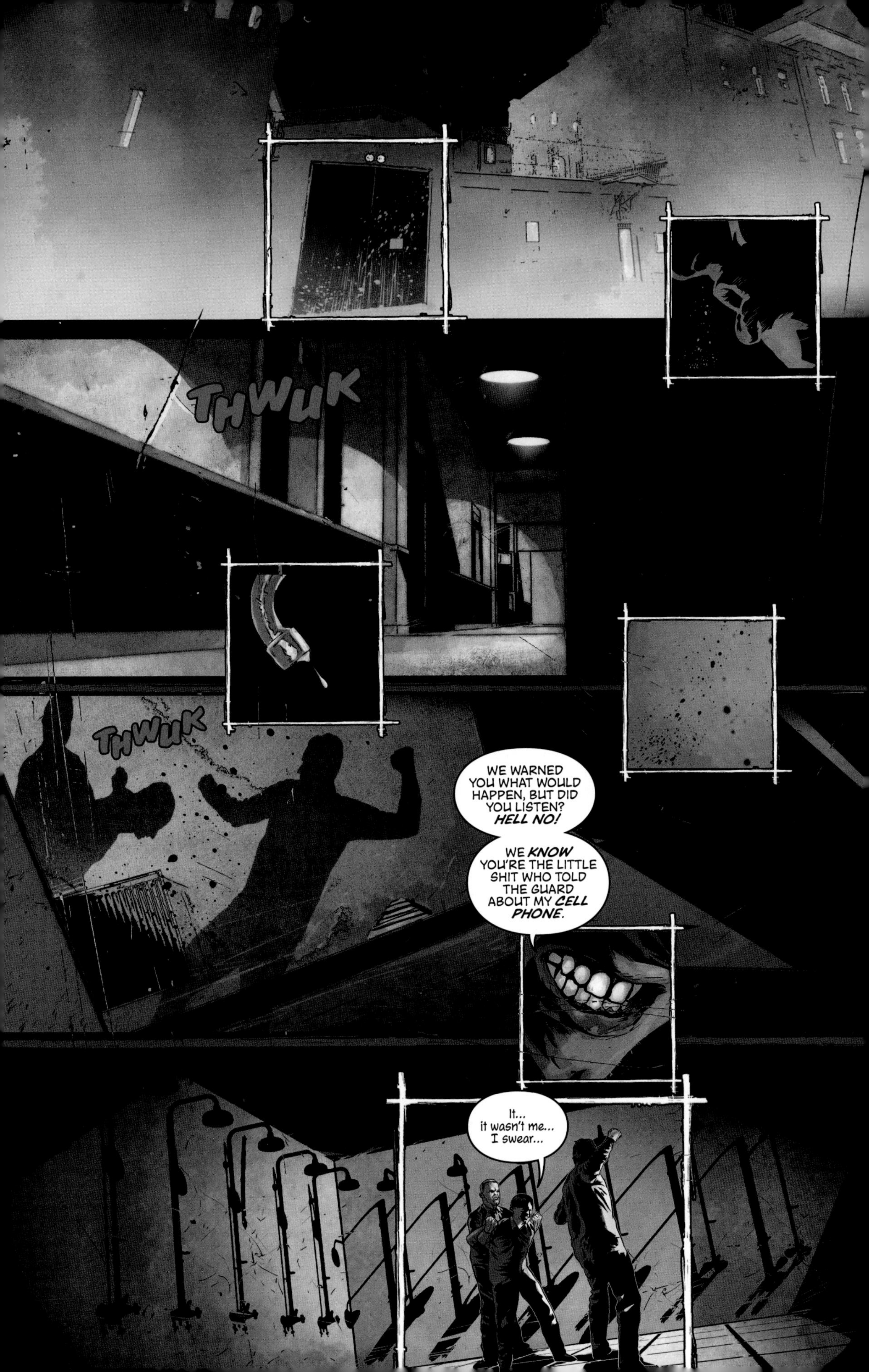
THWUK
THWUK
WE WARNED YOU WHAT WOULD HAPPEN, BUT DID YOU LISTEN? HELL NO!
WE KNOW YOU'RE THE LITTLE SHIT WHO TOLD THE GUARD ABOUT MY CELL PHONE.
It... it wasn't me... I swear...

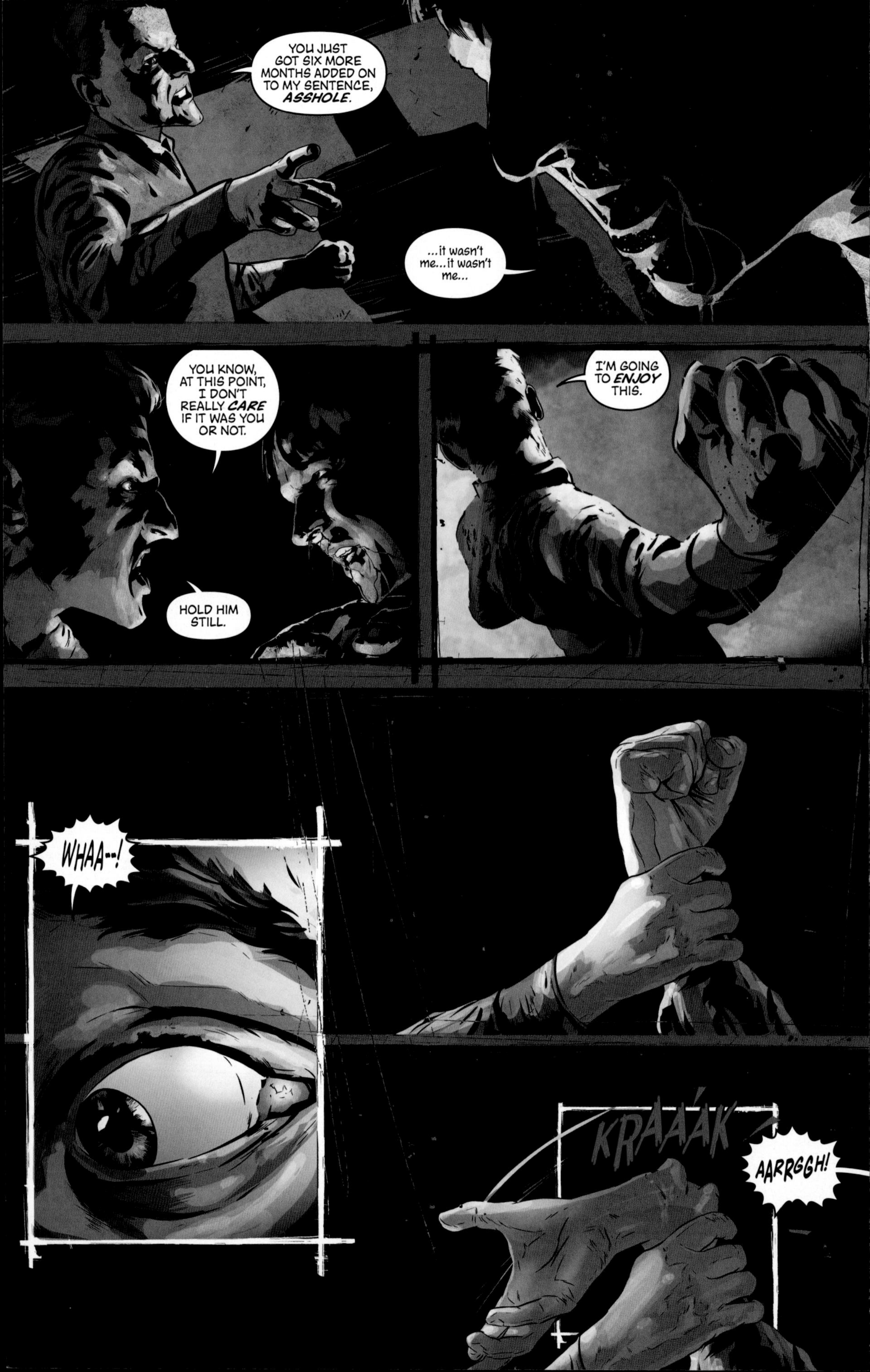
YOU JUST GOT SIX MORE MONTHS ADDED ON TO MY SENTENCE, *ASSHOLE*.
...it wasn't me...it wasn't me...
YOU KNOW, AT THIS POINT, I DON'T REALLY *CARE* IF IT WAS YOU OR NOT.
HOLD HIM STILL.
I'M GOING TO *ENJOY* THIS.
WHAA--!
KRAAAK
AARRGGH!

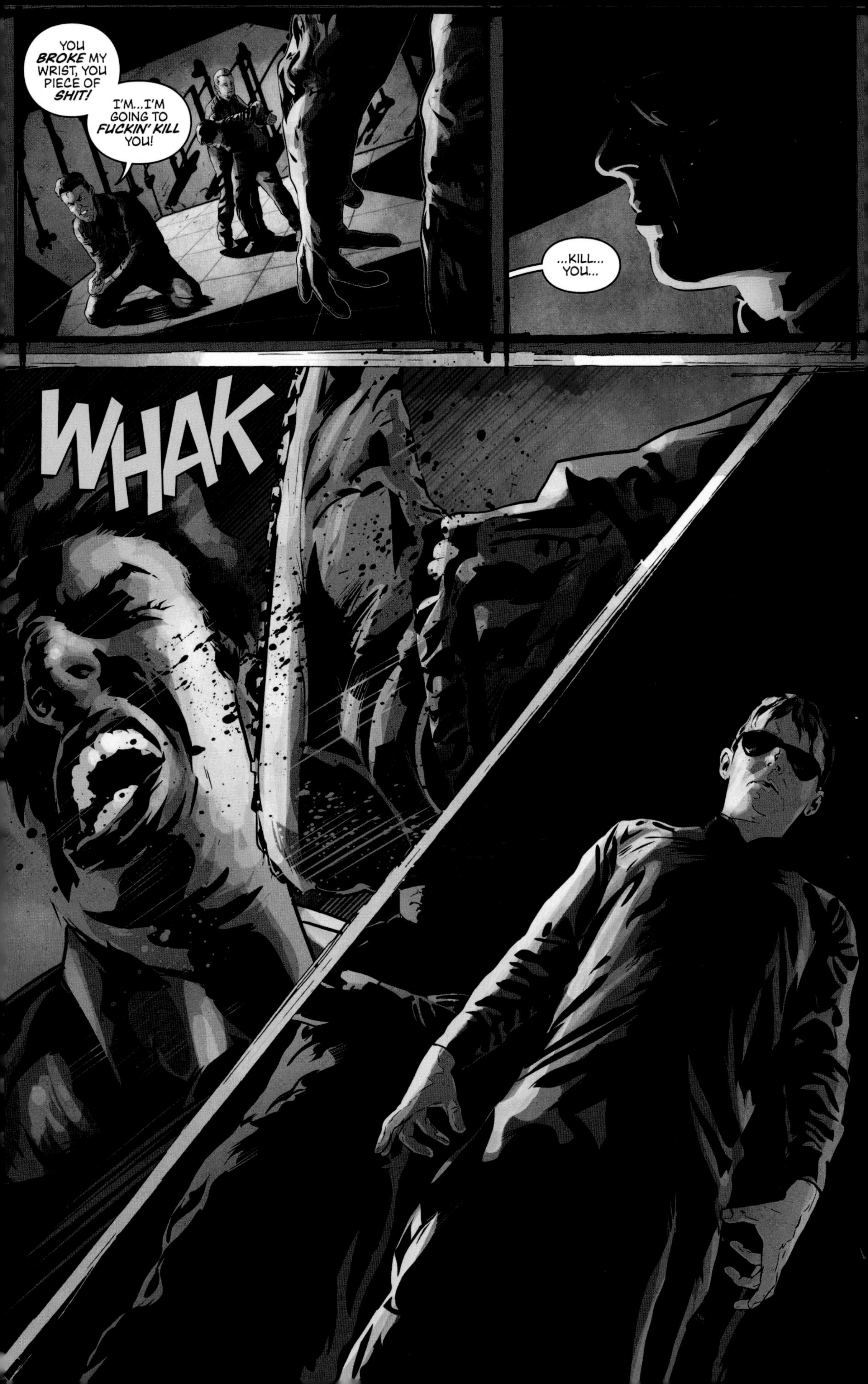
YOU BROKE MY WRIST, YOU PIECE OF SHIT!
I'M...I'M GOING TO FUCKIN' KILL YOU!
...KILL... YOU...
WHAK

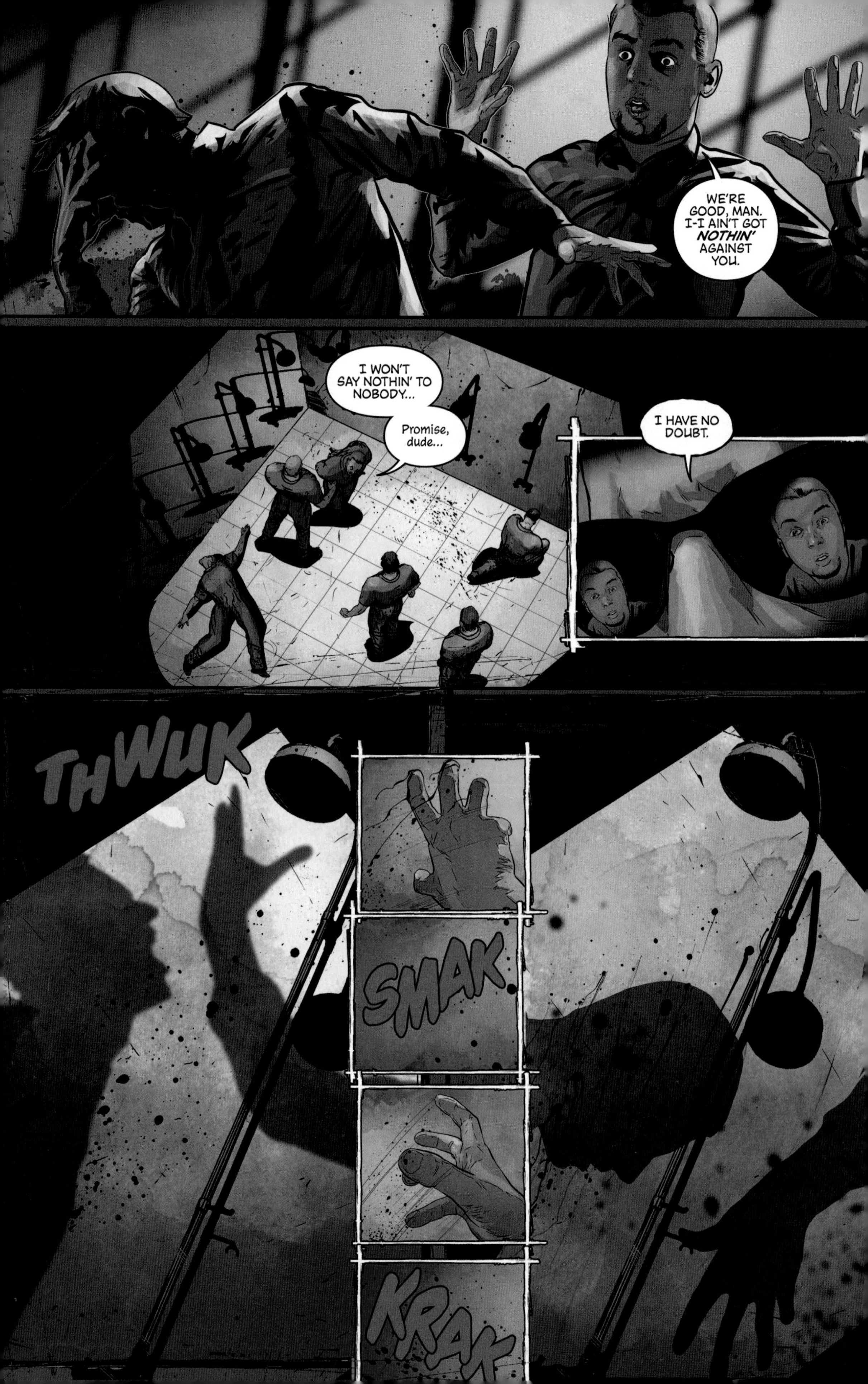
WE'RE GOOD, MAN. I-I AIN'T GOT *NOTHIN'* AGAINST YOU.
I WON'T SAY NOTHIN' TO NOBODY...
Promise, dude...
I HAVE NO DOUBT.
THWUK
SMAK
KRAK

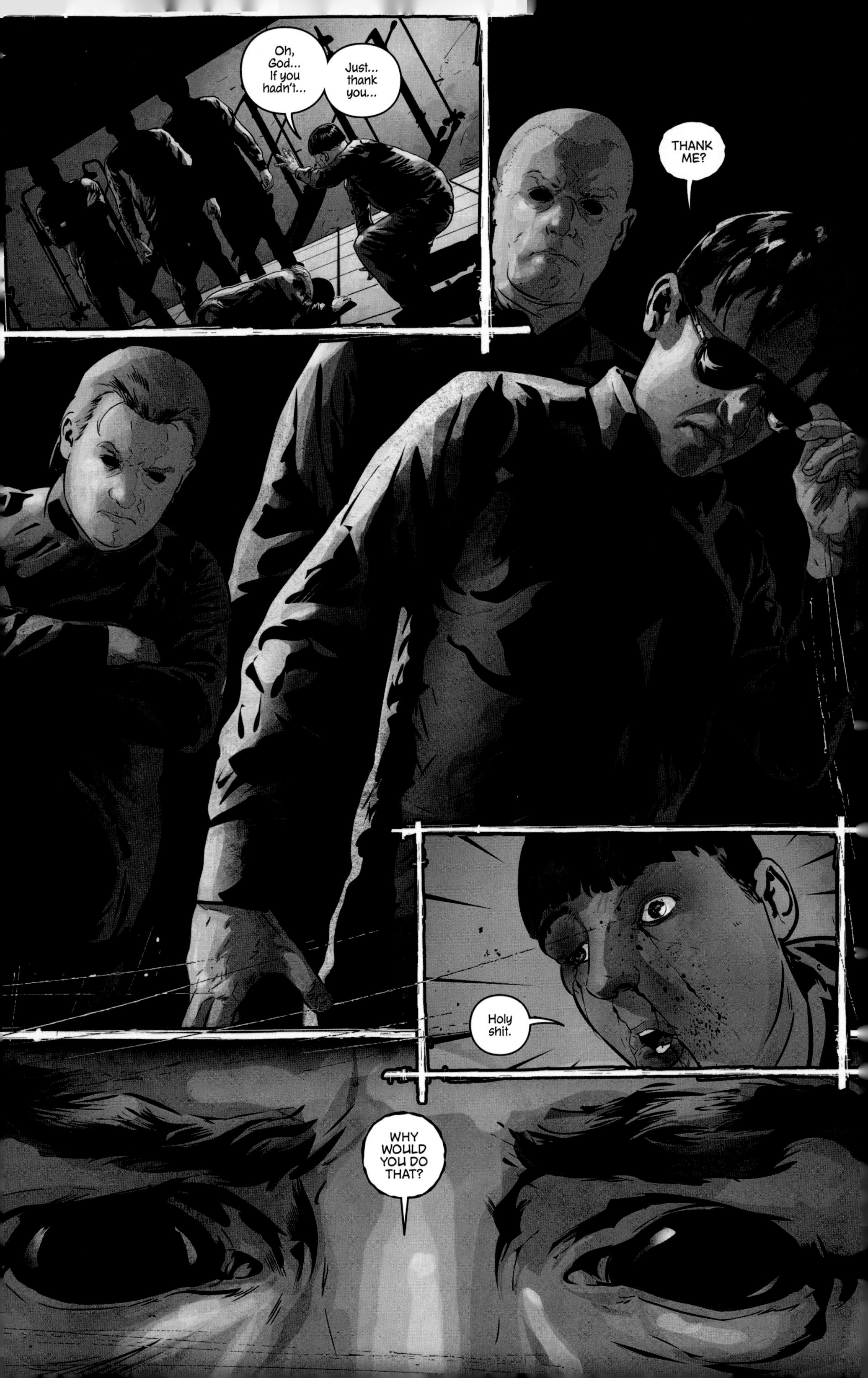
Oh, God... If you hadn't...
Just... thank you...
THANK ME?
Holy shit.
WHY WOULD YOU DO THAT?

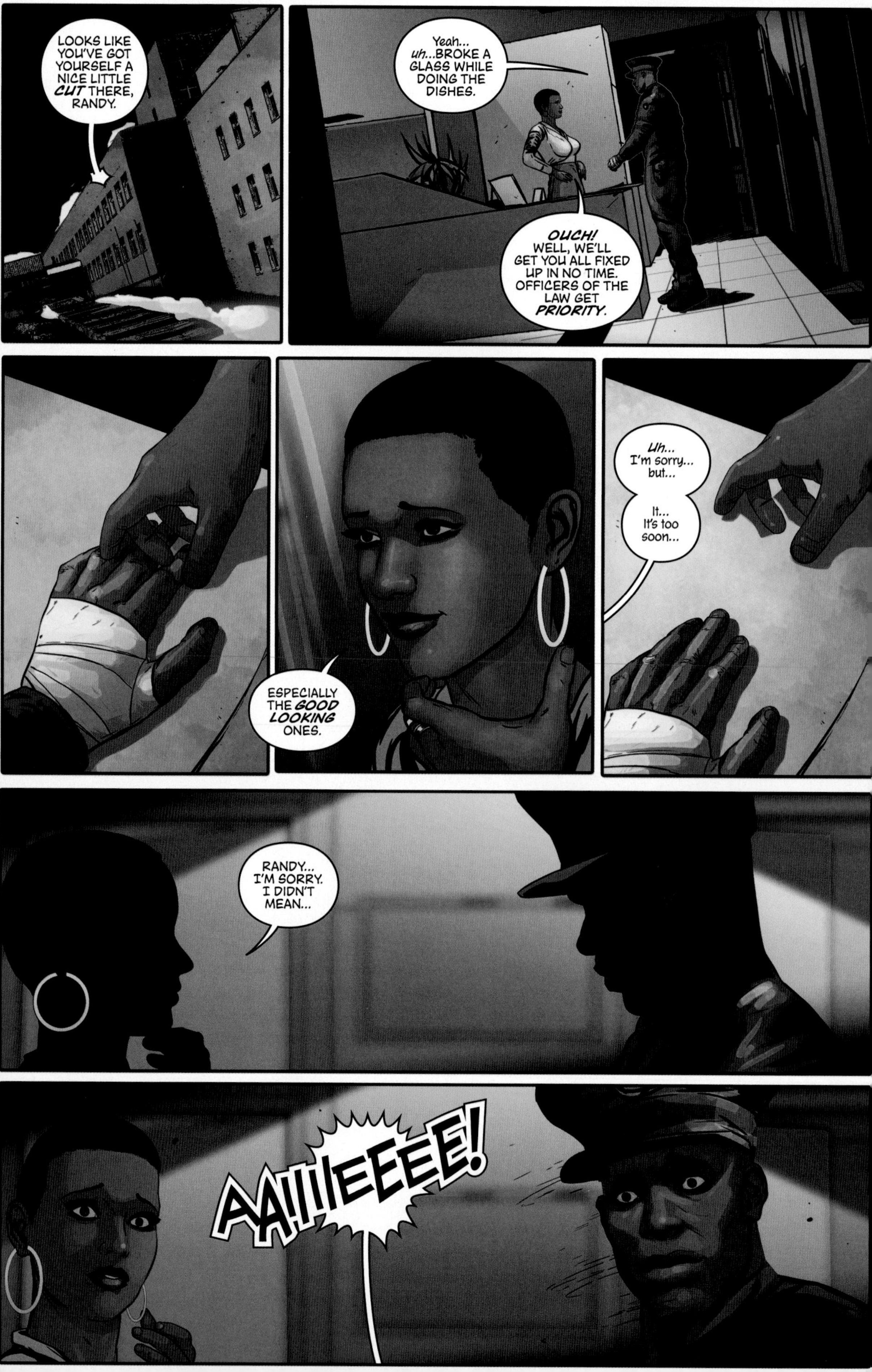
LOOKS LIKE YOU'VE GOT YOURSELF A NICE LITTLE CUT THERE, RANDY.
Yeah... uh...BROKE A GLASS WHILE DOING THE DISHES.
OUCH! WELL, WE'LL GET YOU ALL FIXED UP IN NO TIME. OFFICERS OF THE LAW GET PRIORITY.
ESPECIALLY THE GOOD LOOKING ONES.
Uh... I'm sorry... but...
It... It's too soon...
RANDY... I'M SORRY. I DIDN'T MEAN...
AAIIIEEEEE!

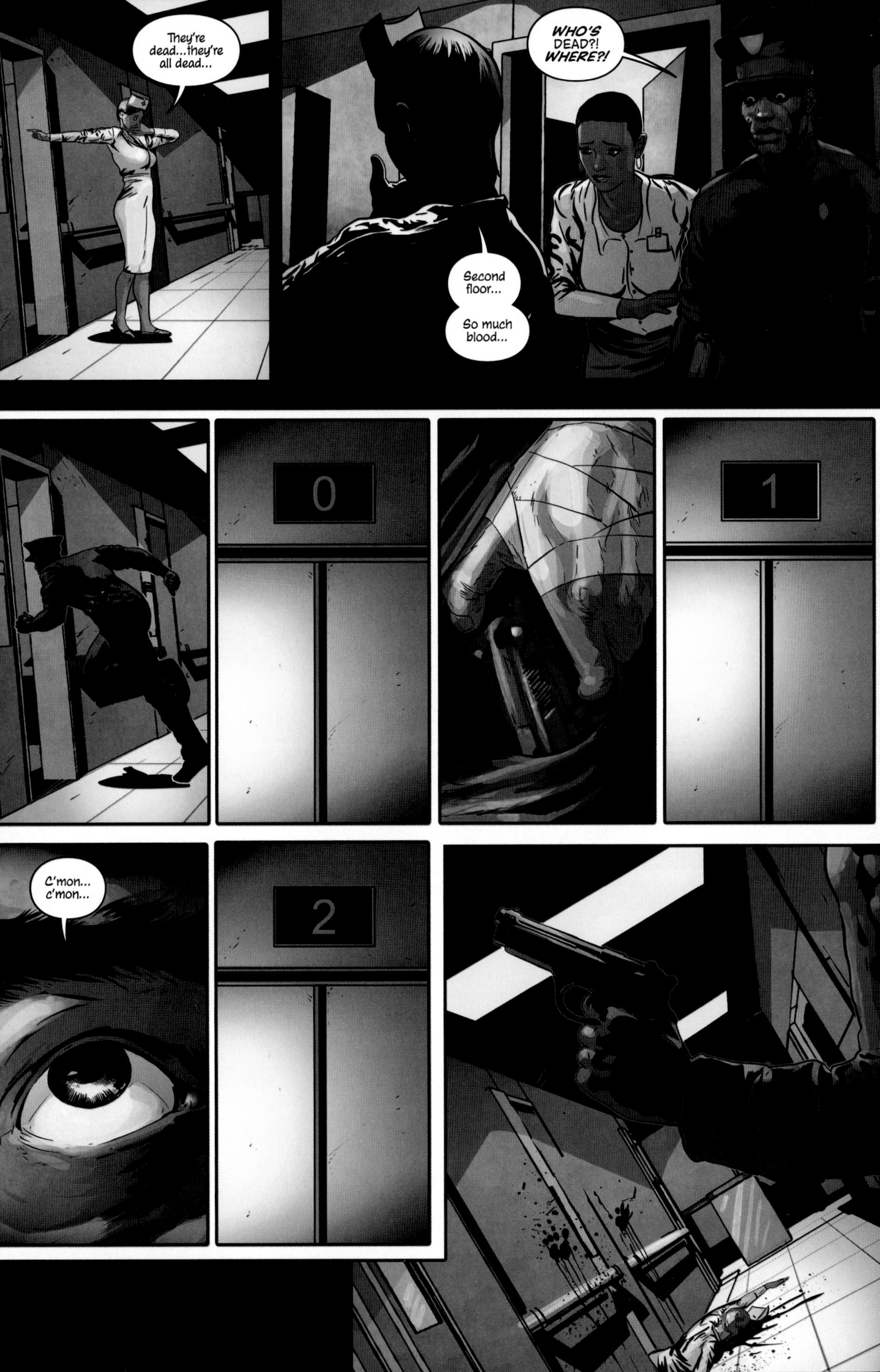
They're dead...they're all dead...
WHO'S DEAD?! WHERE?!
Second floor...
So much blood...
0
1
C'mon... c'mon...
2

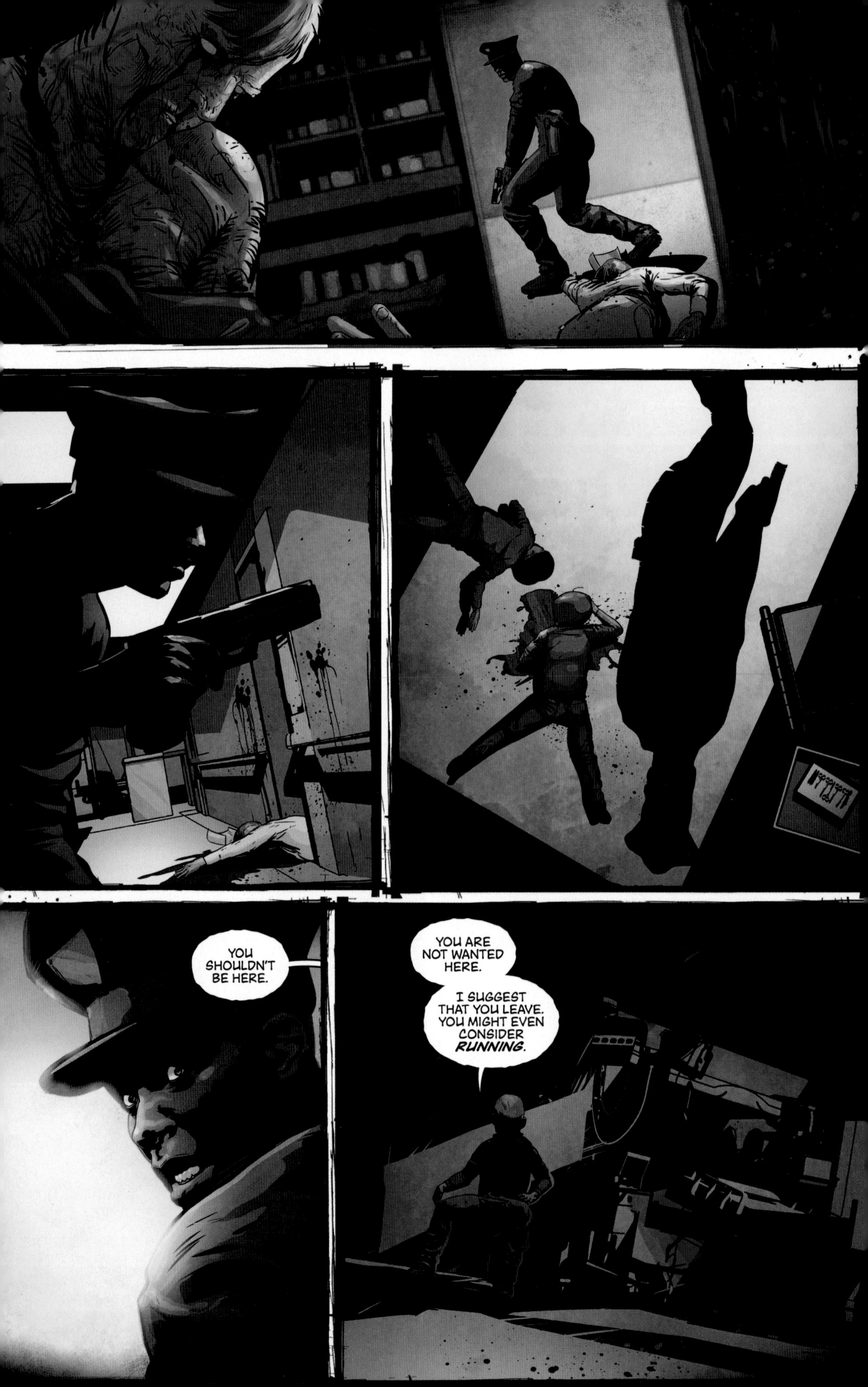
YOU SHOULDN'T BE HERE.
YOU ARE NOT WANTED HERE.
I SUGGEST THAT YOU LEAVE. YOU MIGHT EVEN CONSIDER RUNNING.

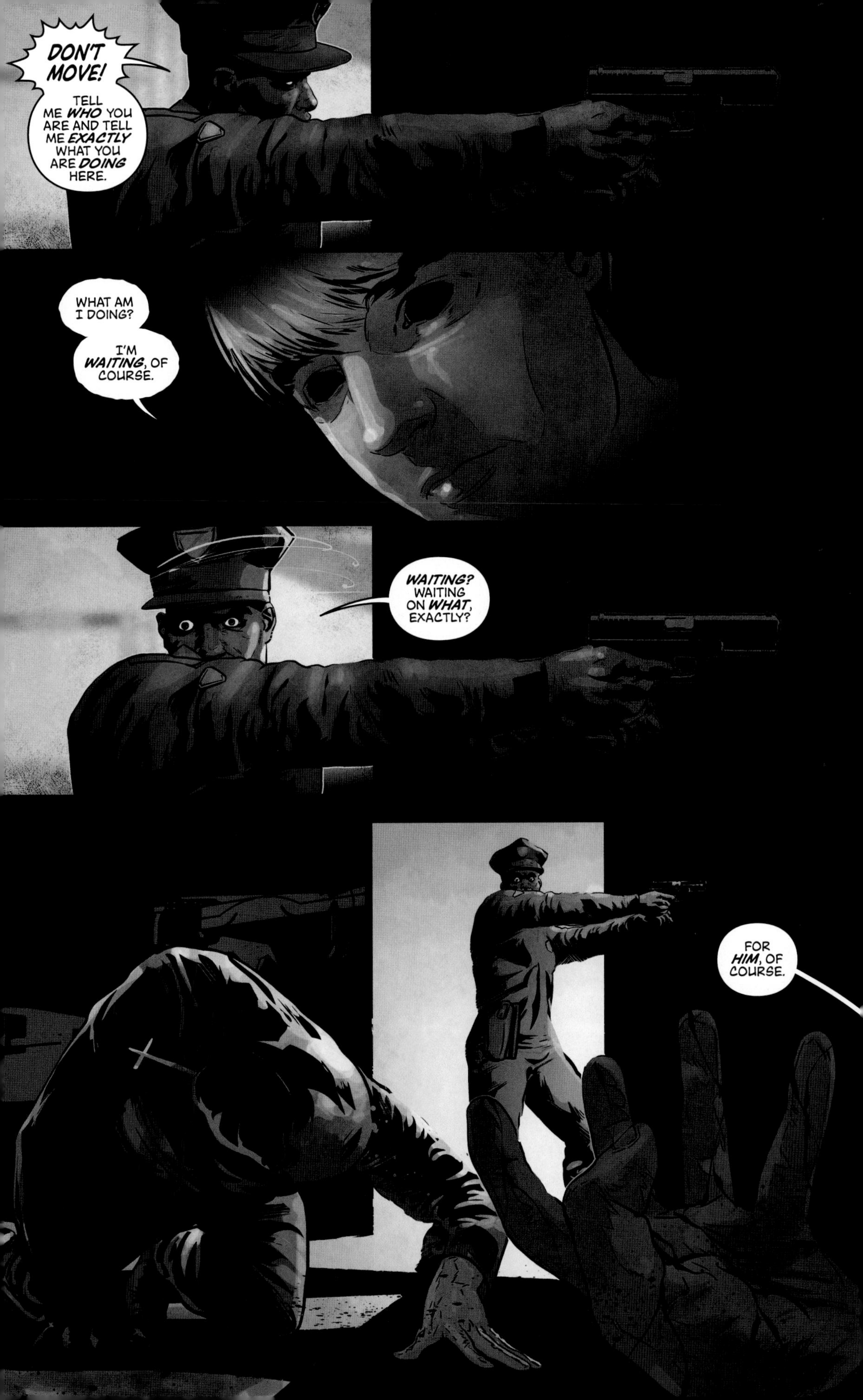
DON'T MOVE!
TELL ME WHO YOU ARE AND TELL ME EXACTLY WHAT YOU ARE DOING HERE.
WHAT AM I DOING?
I'M WAITING, OF COURSE.
WAITING? WAITING ON WHAT, EXACTLY?
FOR HIM, OF COURSE.

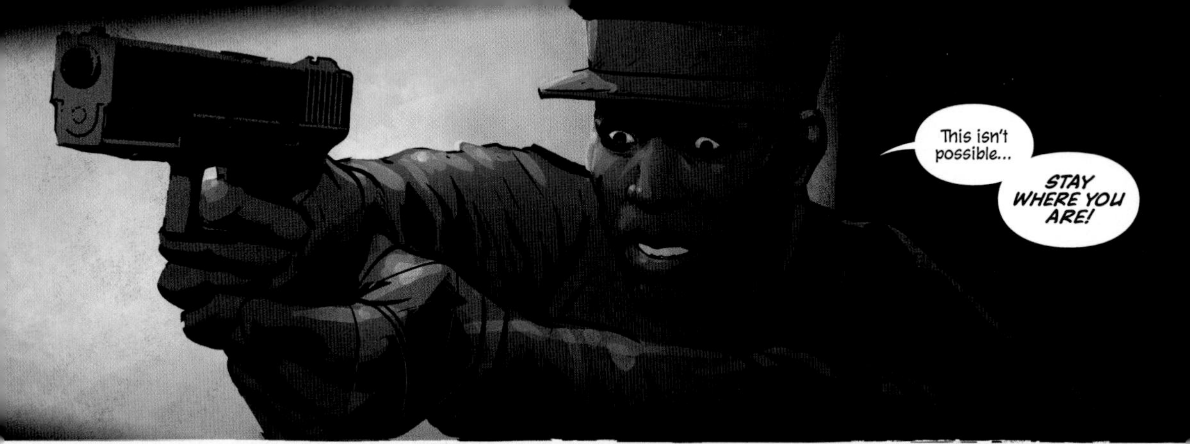
This isn't possible...
STAY WHERE YOU ARE!

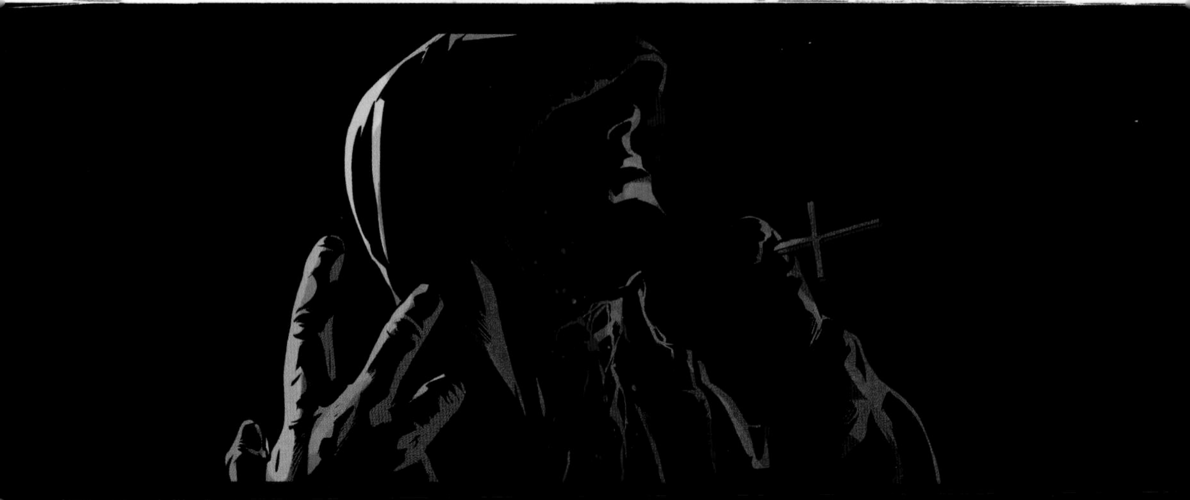

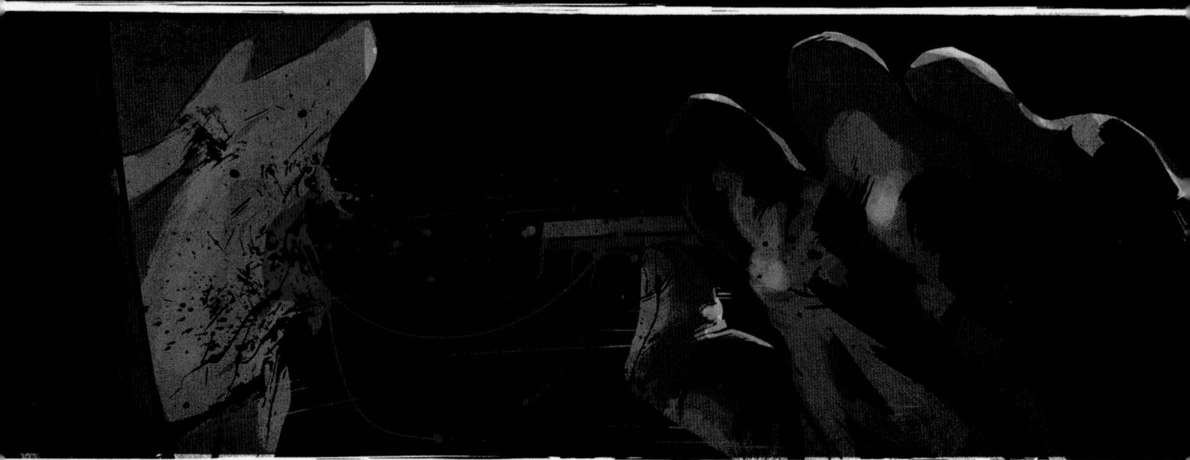

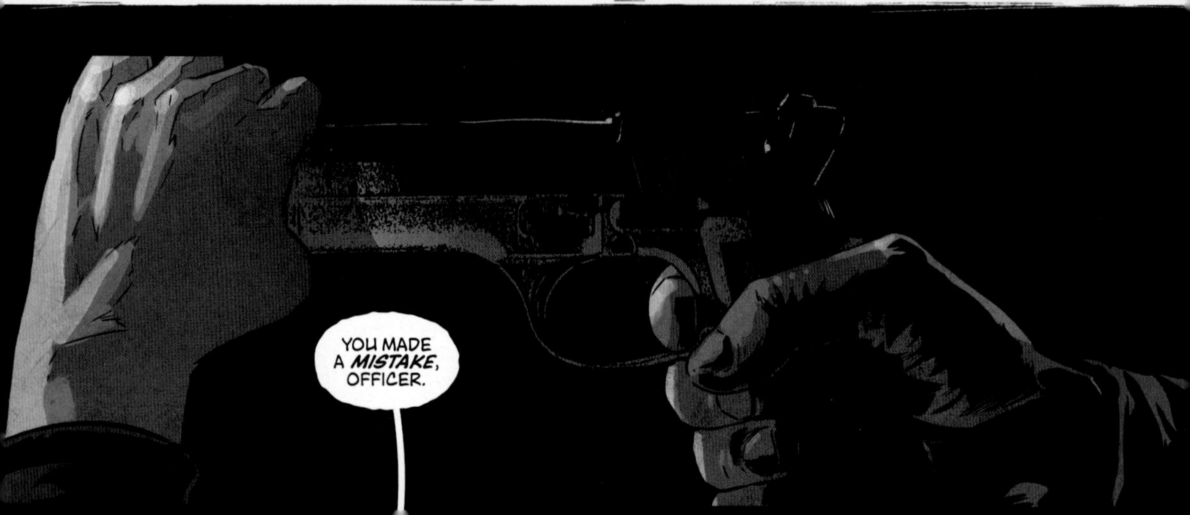
YOU MADE A MISTAKE, OFFICER.

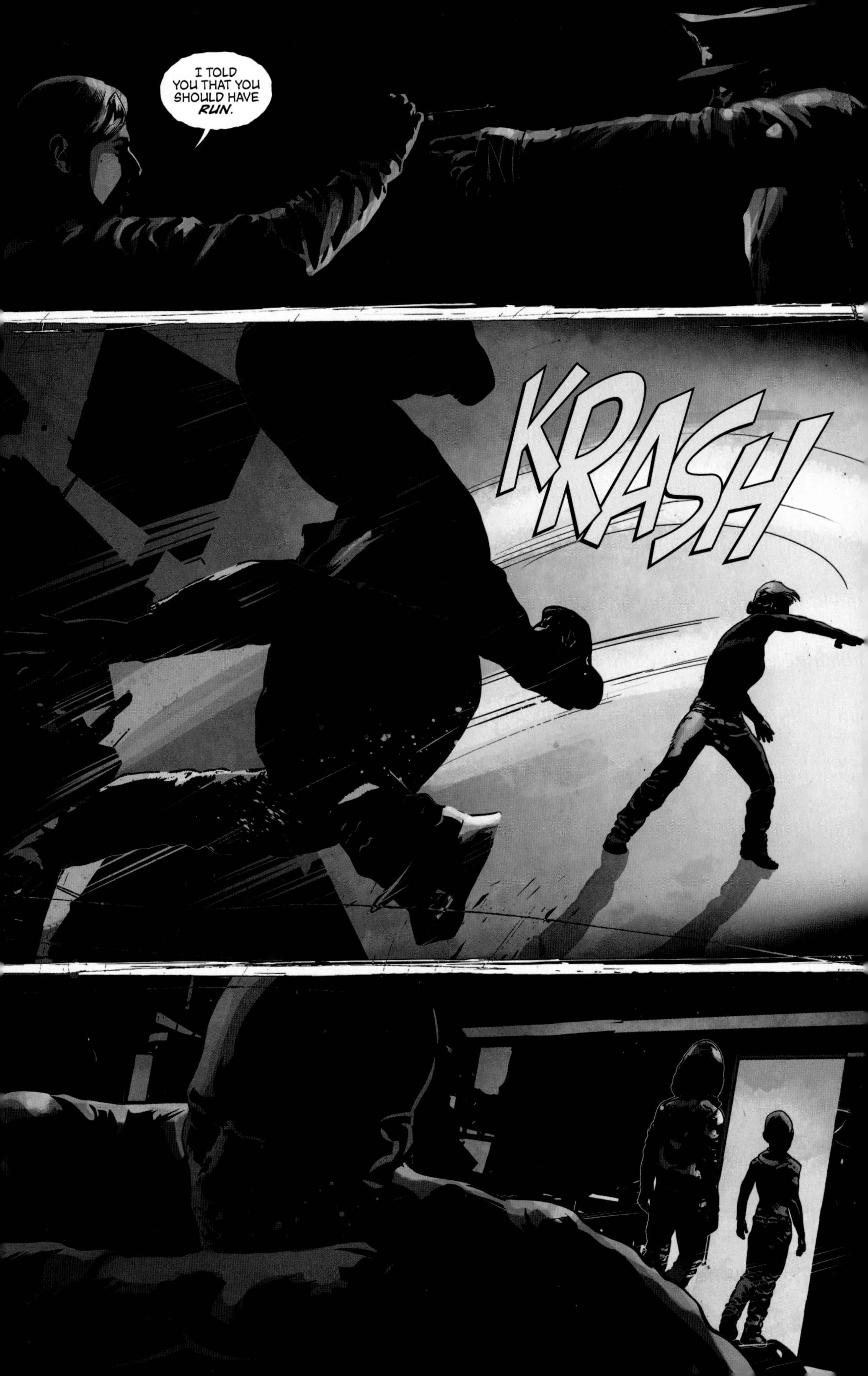
I TOLD YOU THAT YOU SHOULD HAVE *RUN*.
KRASH

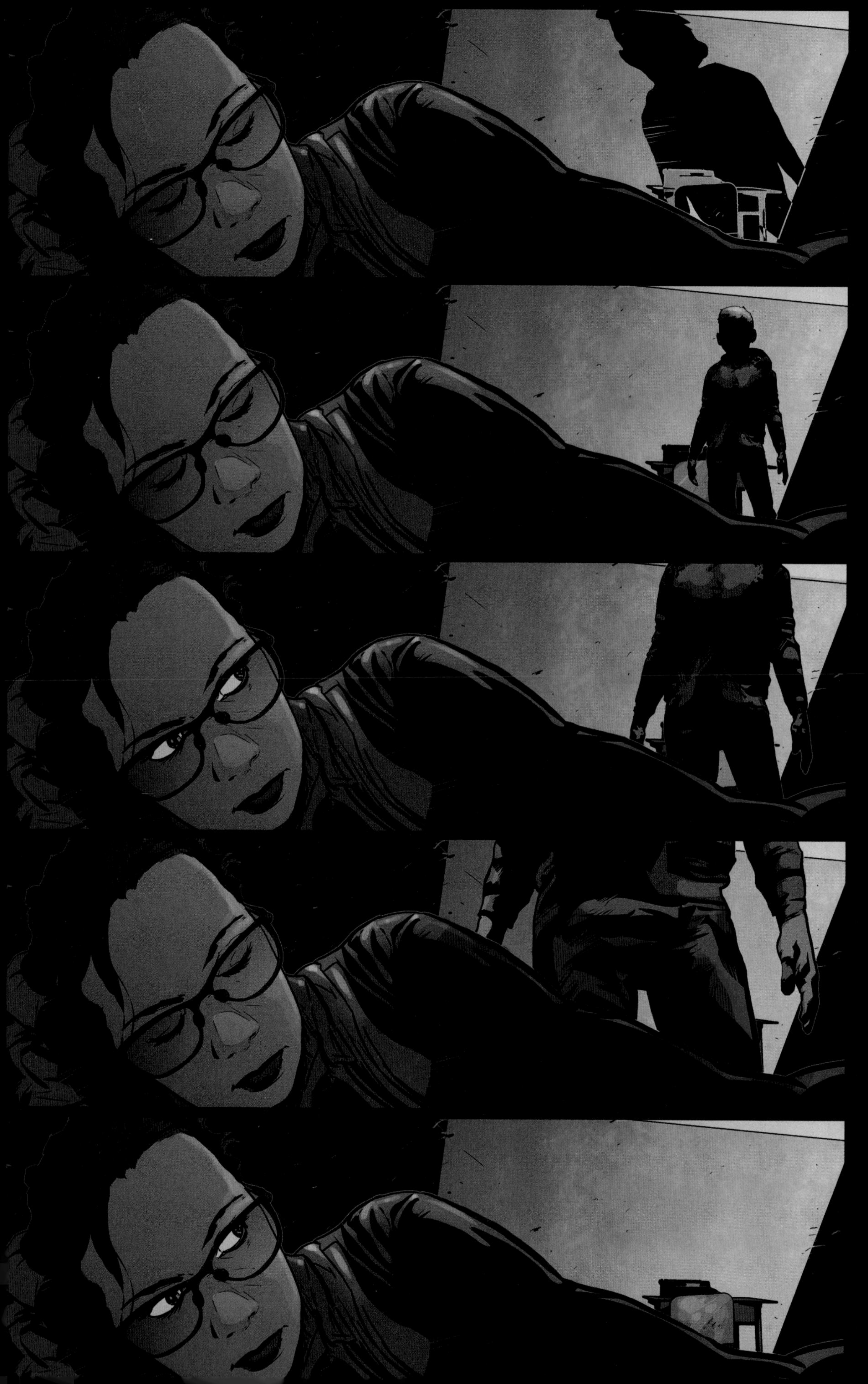

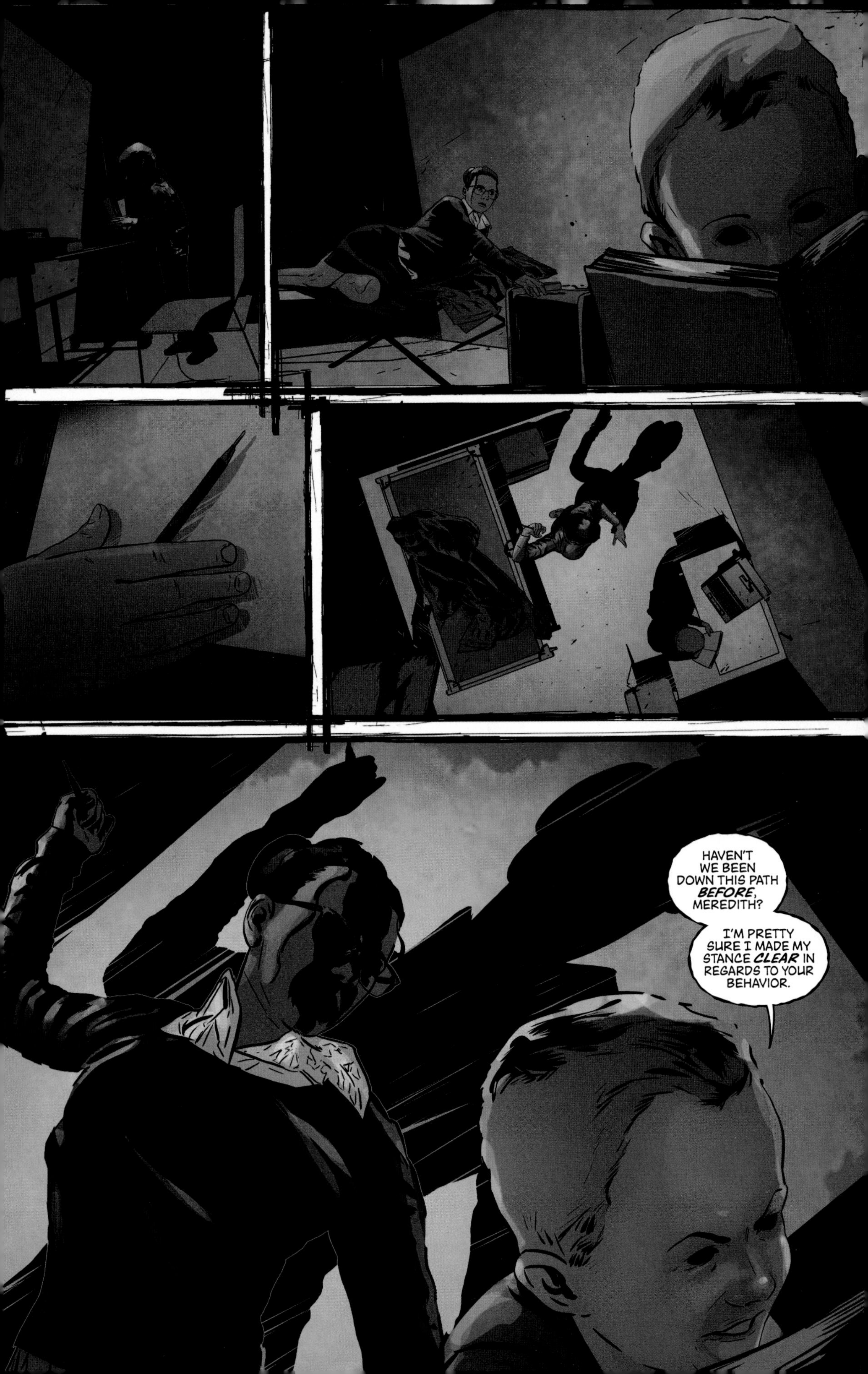
HAVEN'T WE BEEN DOWN THIS PATH BEFORE, MEREDITH?
I'M PRETTY SURE I MADE MY STANCE CLEAR IN REGARDS TO YOUR BEHAVIOR.

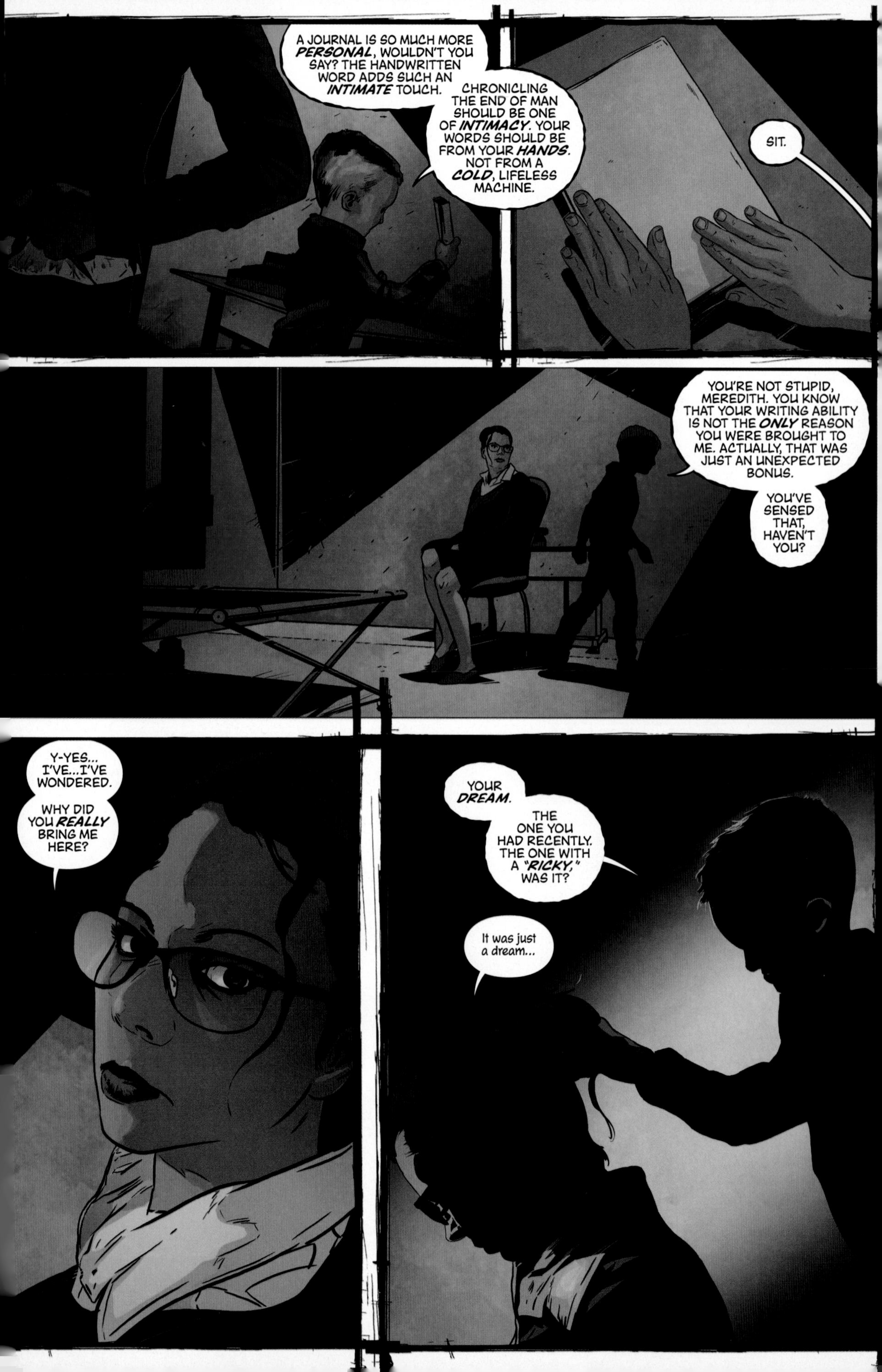
A JOURNAL IS SO MUCH MORE PERSONAL, WOULDN'T YOU SAY? THE HANDWRITTEN WORD ADDS SUCH AN INTIMATE TOUCH.
CHRONICLING THE END OF MAN SHOULD BE ONE OF INTIMACY. YOUR WORDS SHOULD BE FROM YOUR HANDS. NOT FROM A COLD, LIFELESS MACHINE.
SIT.
YOU'RE NOT STUPID, MEREDITH. YOU KNOW THAT YOUR WRITING ABILITY IS NOT THE ONLY REASON YOU WERE BROUGHT TO ME. ACTUALLY, THAT WAS JUST AN UNEXPECTED BONUS.
YOU'VE SENSED THAT, HAVEN'T YOU?
Y-YES... I'VE...I'VE WONDERED.
WHY DID YOU REALLY BRING ME HERE?
YOUR DREAM.
THE ONE YOU HAD RECENTLY. THE ONE WITH A "RICKY," WAS IT?
It was just a dream...

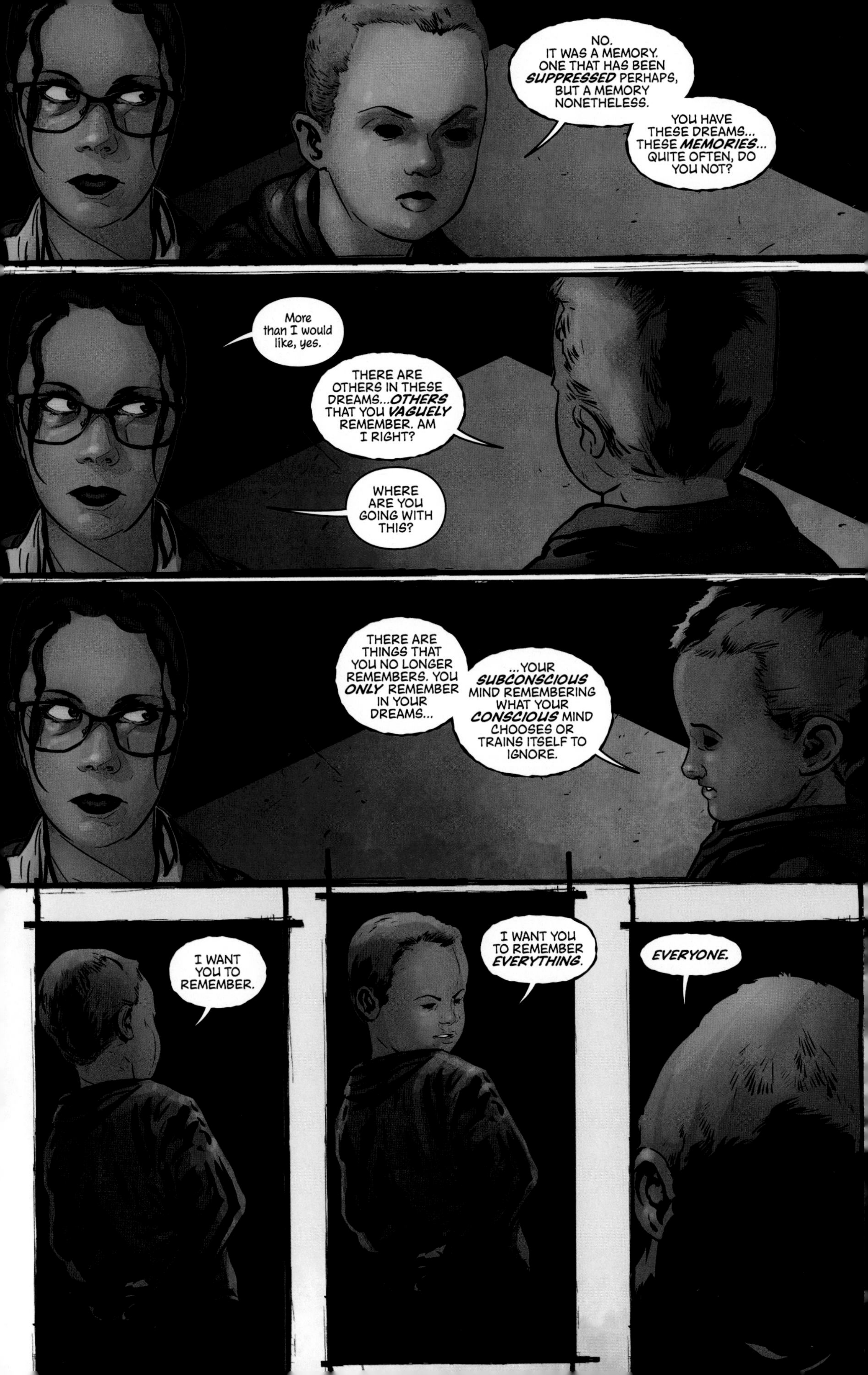
NO. IT WAS A MEMORY. ONE THAT HAS BEEN SUPPRESSED PERHAPS, BUT A MEMORY NONETHELESS.
YOU HAVE THESE DREAMS... THESE MEMORIES... QUITE OFTEN, DO YOU NOT?
More than I would like, yes.
THERE ARE OTHERS IN THESE DREAMS...OTHERS THAT YOU VAGUELY REMEMBER. AM I RIGHT?
WHERE ARE YOU GOING WITH THIS?
THERE ARE THINGS THAT YOU NO LONGER REMEMBERS. YOU ONLY REMEMBER IN YOUR DREAMS...
...YOUR SUBCONSCIOUS MIND REMEMBERING WHAT YOUR CONSCIOUS MIND CHOOSES OR TRAINS ITSELF TO IGNORE.
I WANT YOU TO REMEMBER.
I WANT YOU TO REMEMBER EVERYTHING.
EVERYONE.

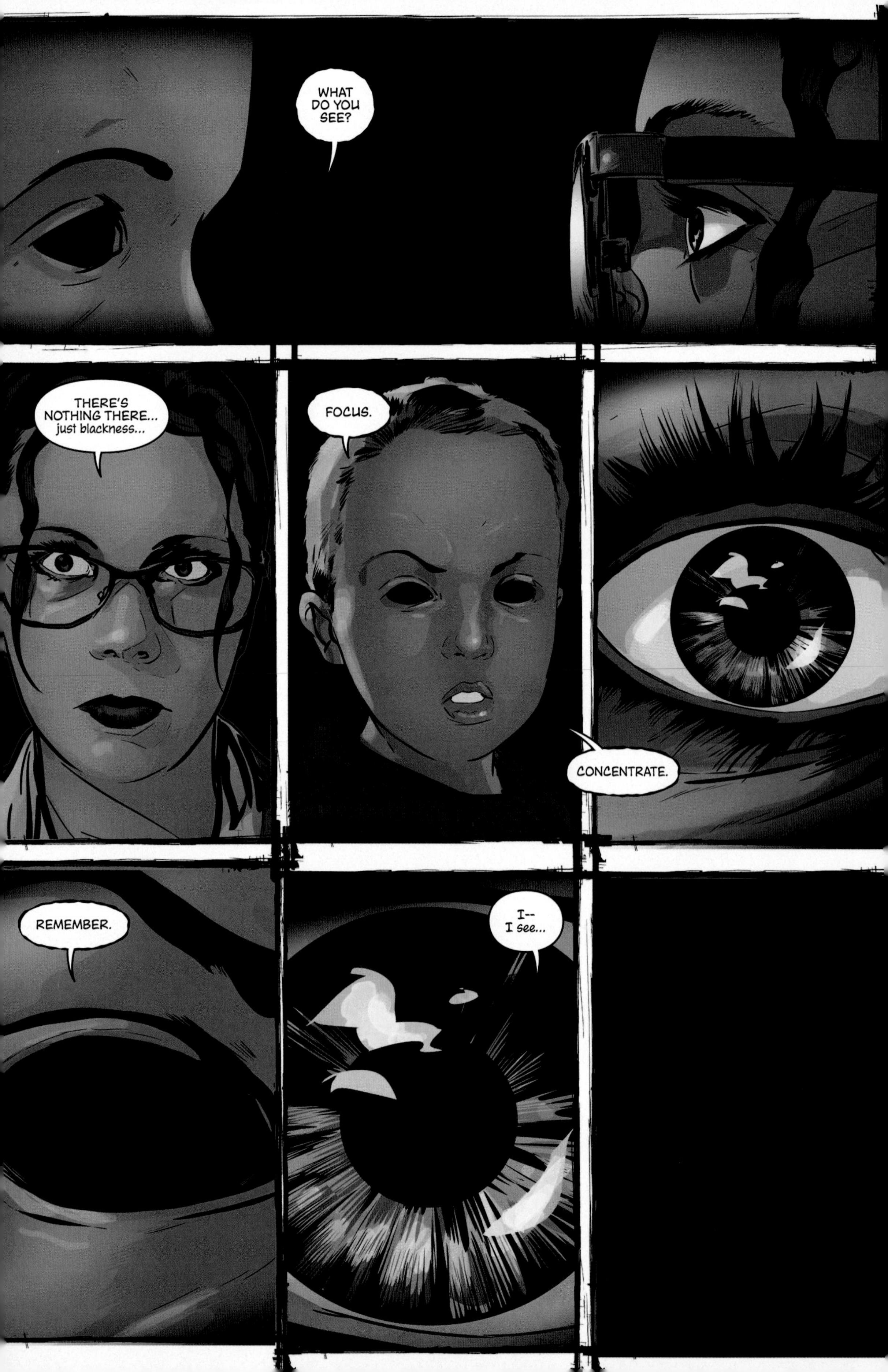
WHAT DO YOU SEE?
THERE'S NOTHING THERE... just blackness...
FOCUS.
CONCENTRATE.
REMEMBER.
I-- I see...

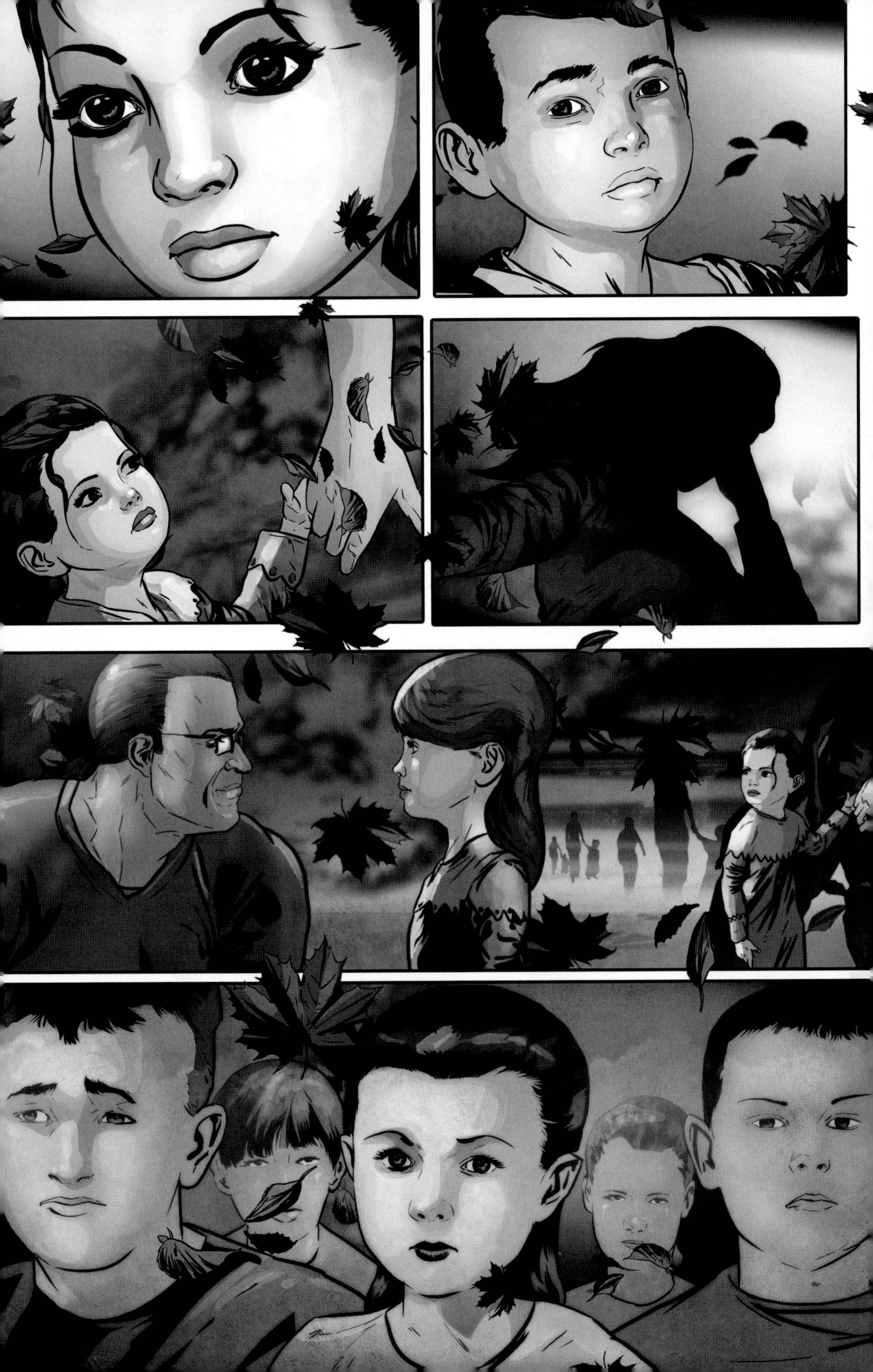

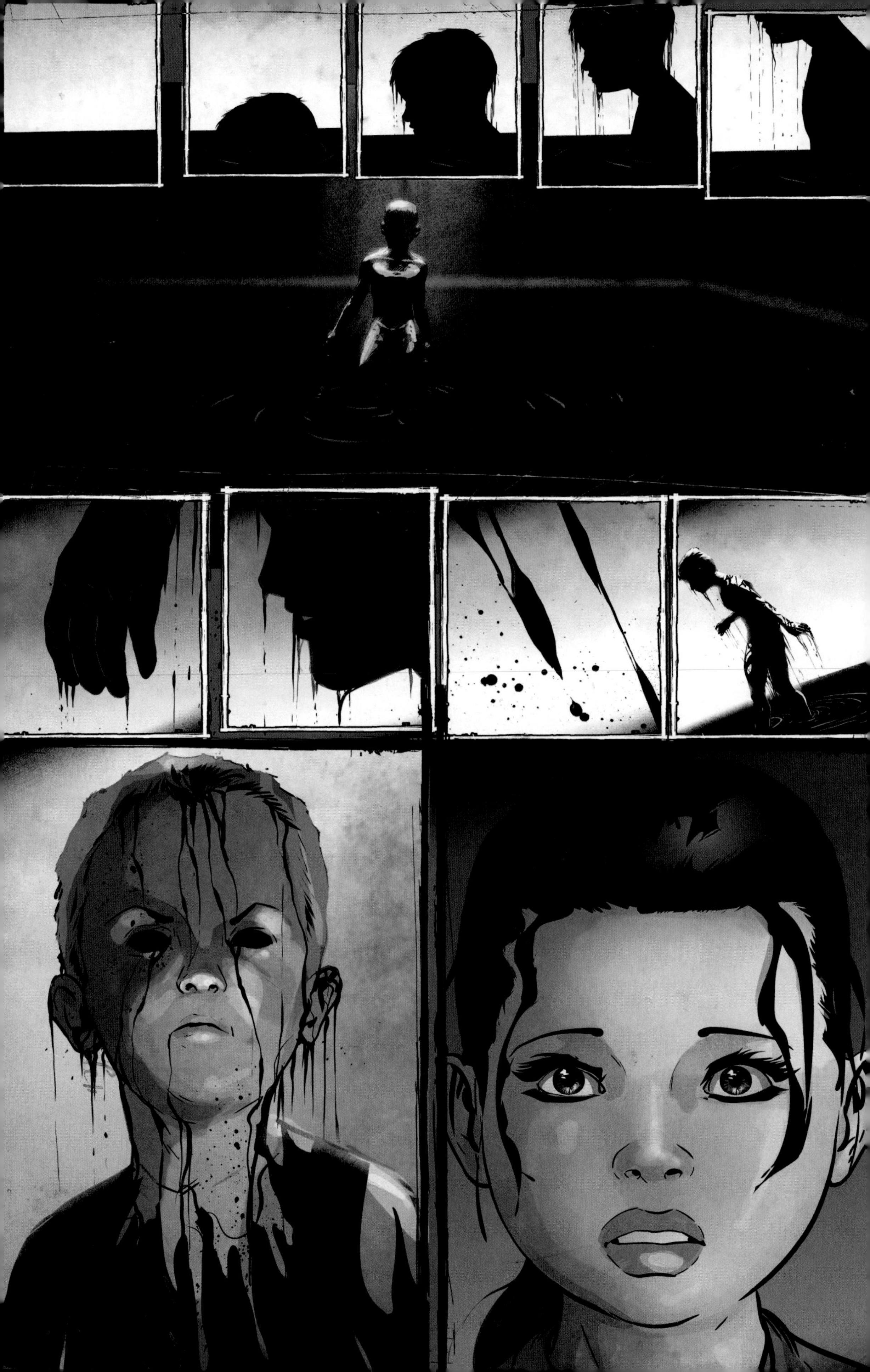

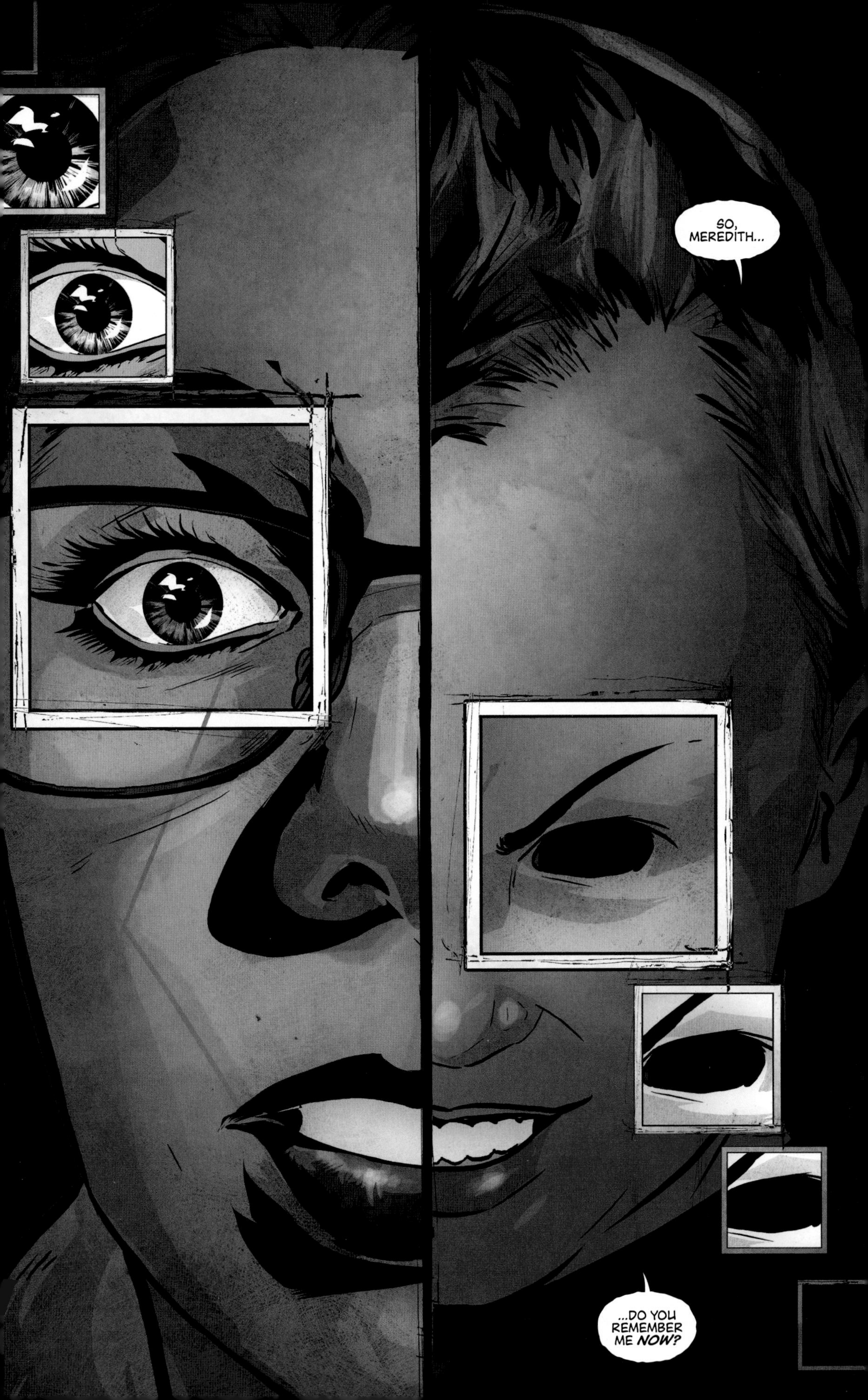
SO, MEREDITH...
...DO YOU REMEMBER ME **NOW?**

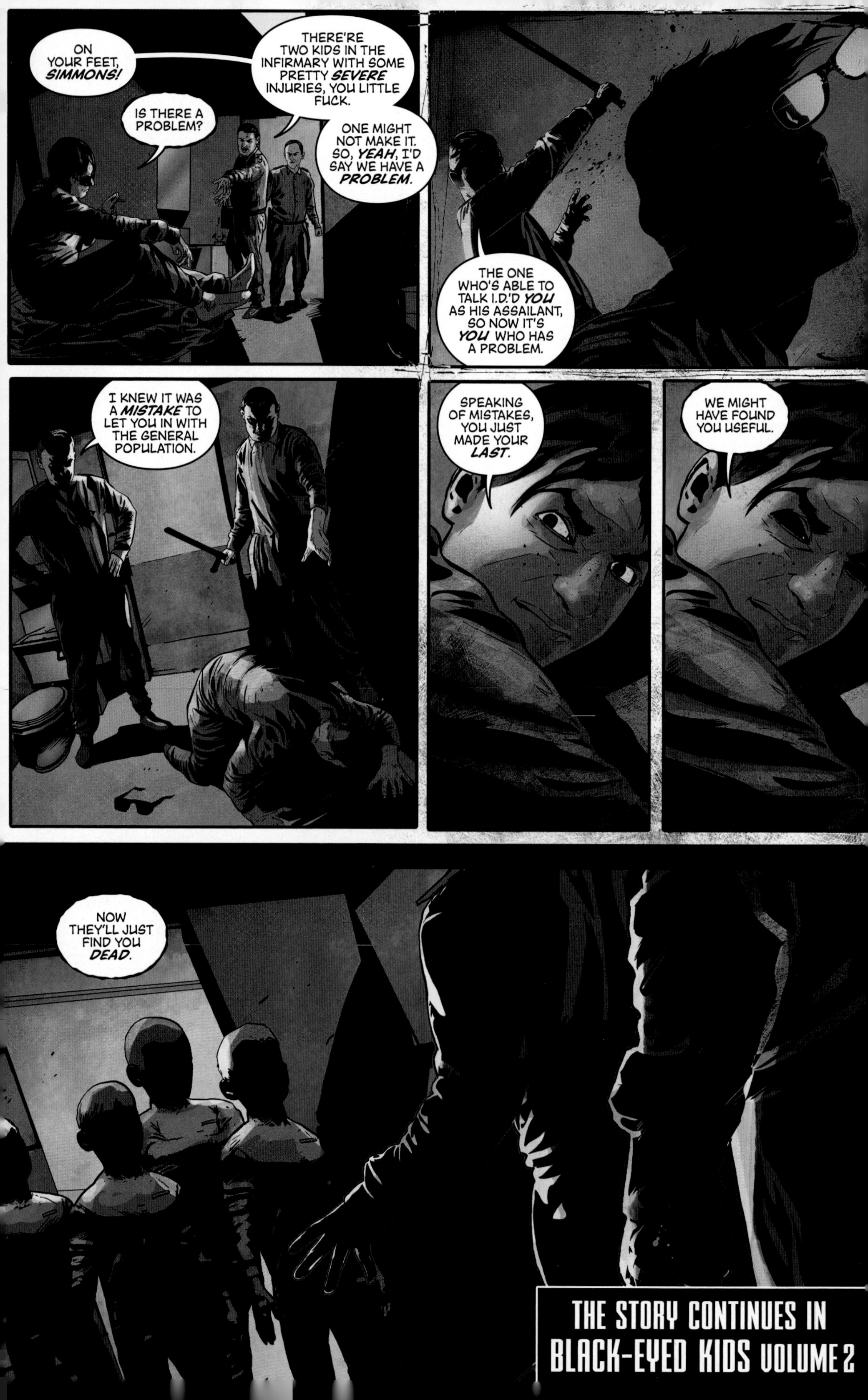
ON YOUR FEET, SIMMONS!
THERE'RE TWO KIDS IN THE INFIRMARY WITH SOME PRETTY SEVERE INJURIES, YOU LITTLE FUCK.
IS THERE A PROBLEM?
ONE MIGHT NOT MAKE IT. SO, YEAH, I'D SAY WE HAVE A PROBLEM.
THE ONE WHO'S ABLE TO TALK I.D.'D YOU AS HIS ASSAILANT, SO NOW IT'S YOU WHO HAS A PROBLEM.
I KNEW IT WAS A MISTAKE TO LET YOU IN WITH THE GENERAL POPULATION.
SPEAKING OF MISTAKES, YOU JUST MADE YOUR LAST.
WE MIGHT HAVE FOUND YOU USEFUL.
NOW THEY'LL JUST FIND YOU DEAD.
THE STORY CONTINUES IN BLACK-EYED KIDS VOLUME 2

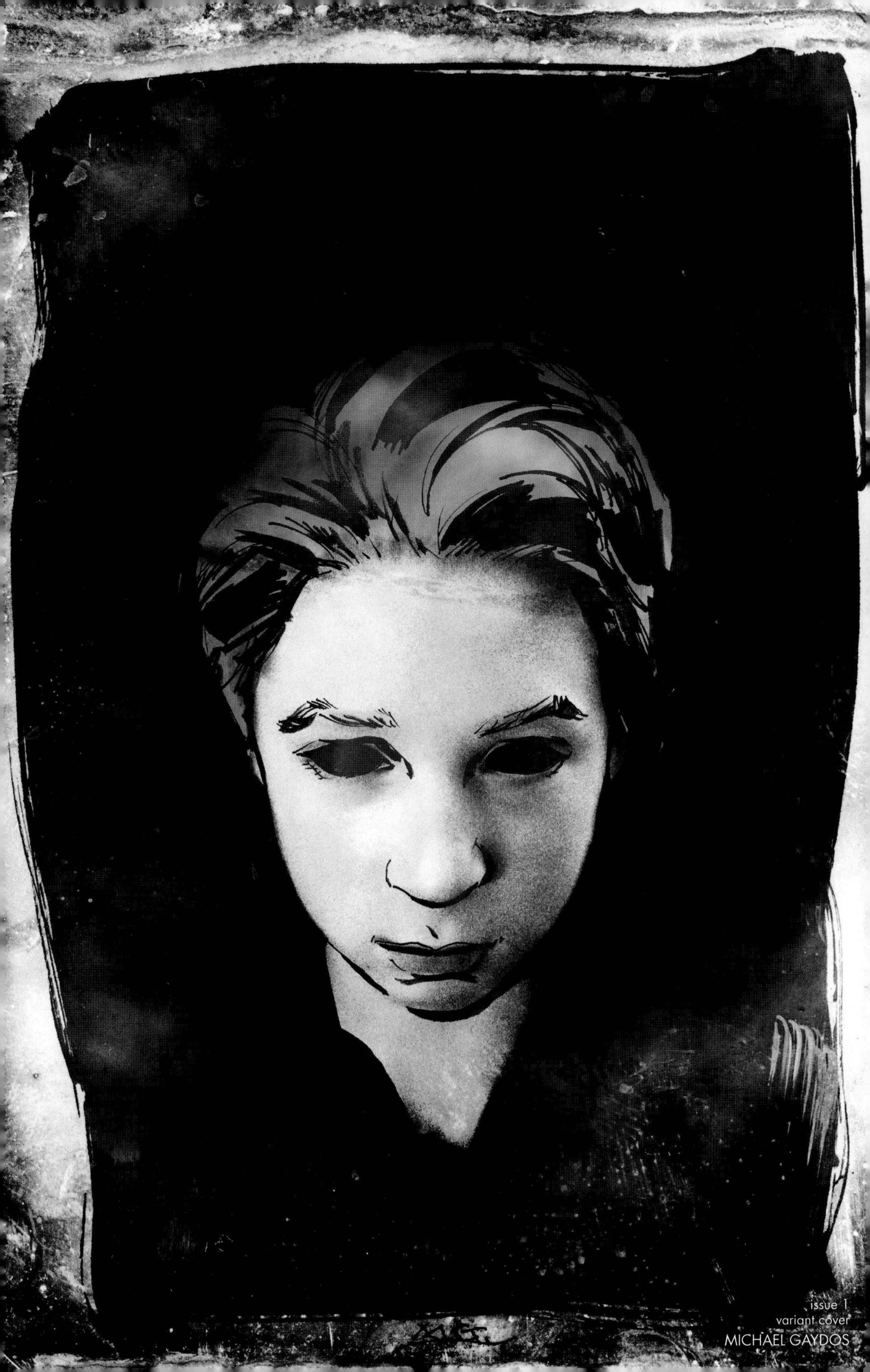

issue 1
variant cover
MICHAEL GAYDOS

issue 1
variant cover
SZYMON KUDRANSKI

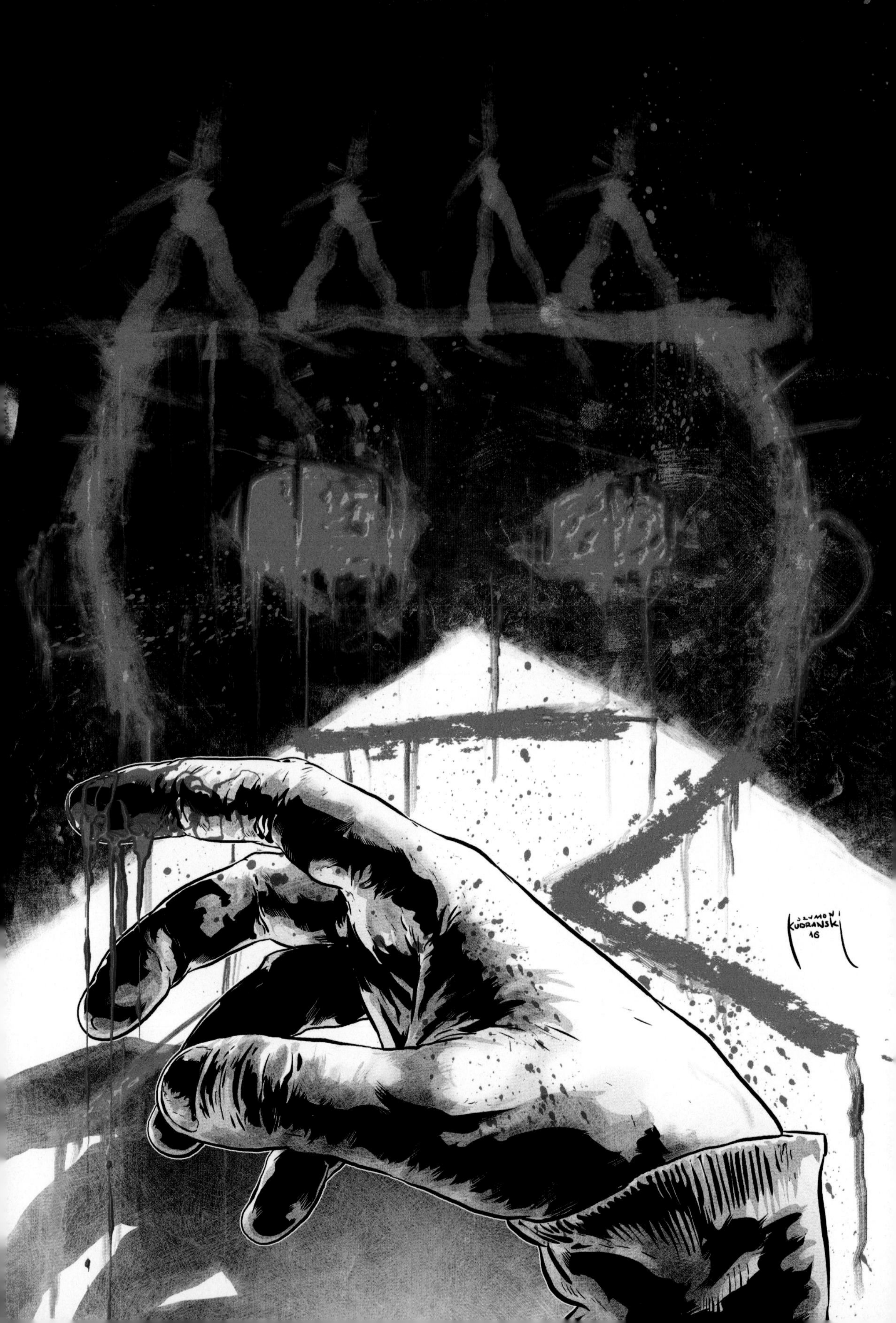
SZYMON KUDRANSKI 16

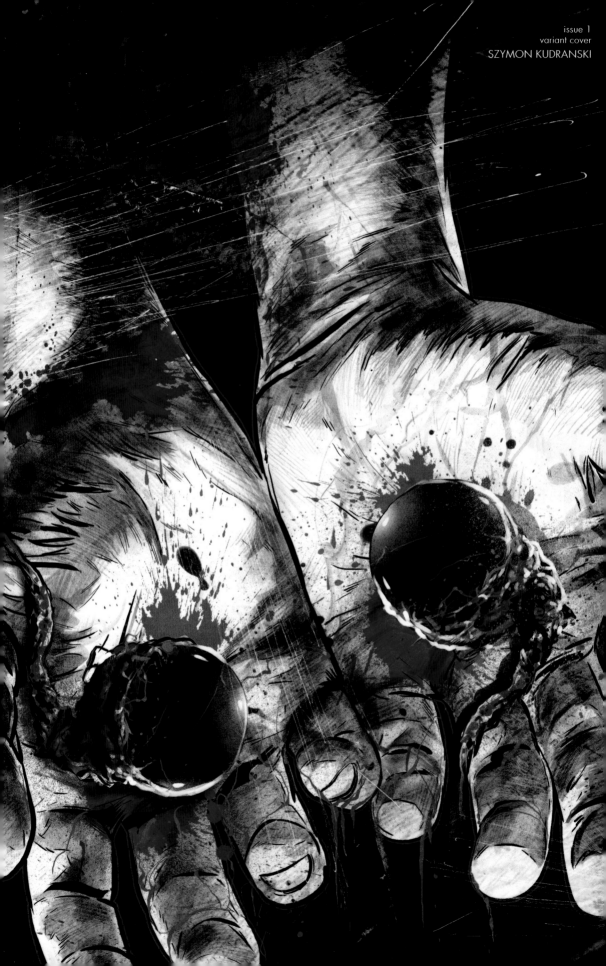

issue 1
variant cover
SZYMON KUDRANSKI

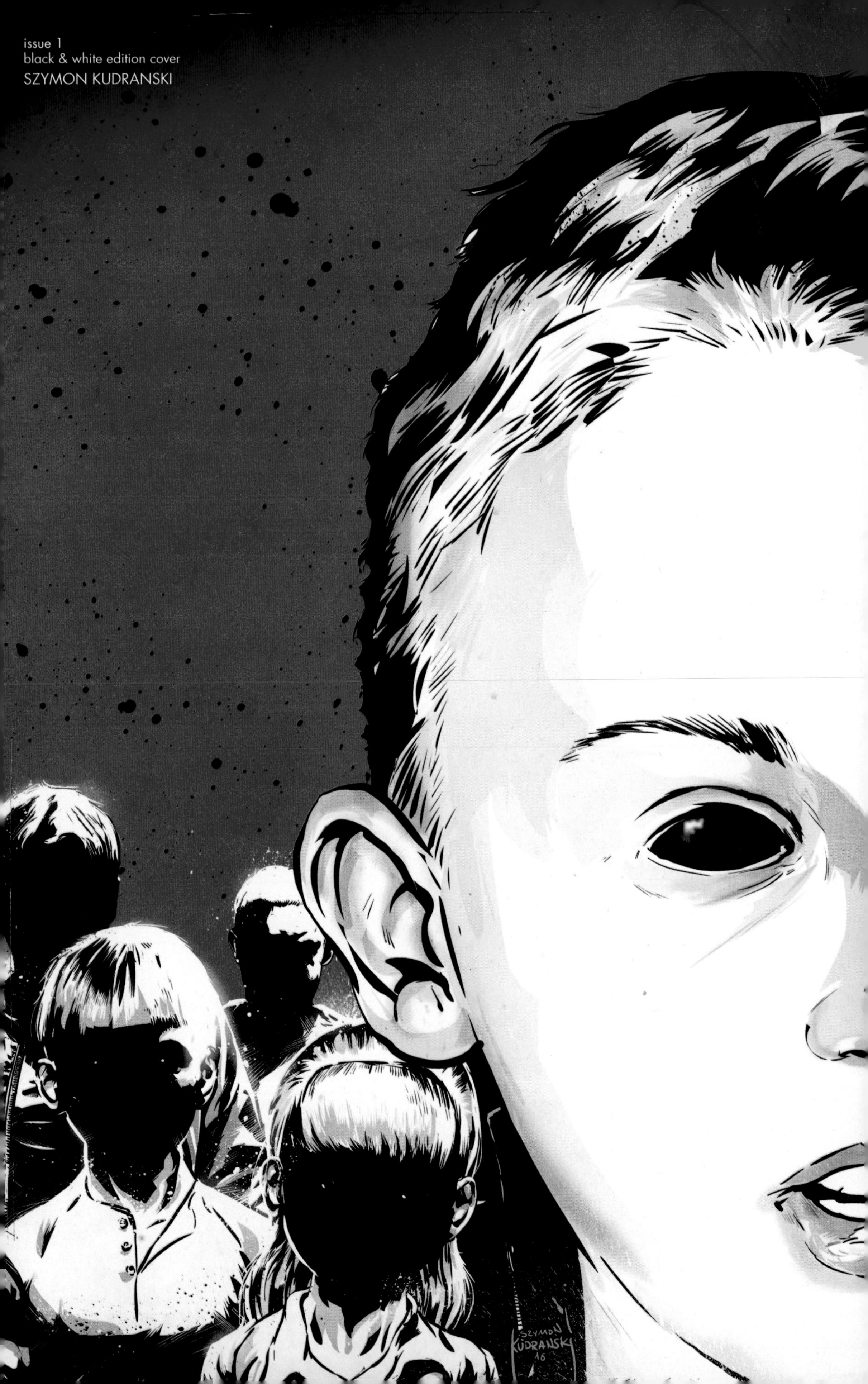
SZYMON KUDRANSKI 16

issue 1
black & white edition cover
SZYMON KUDRANSKI

issue 3
variant cover
PHIL HESTER

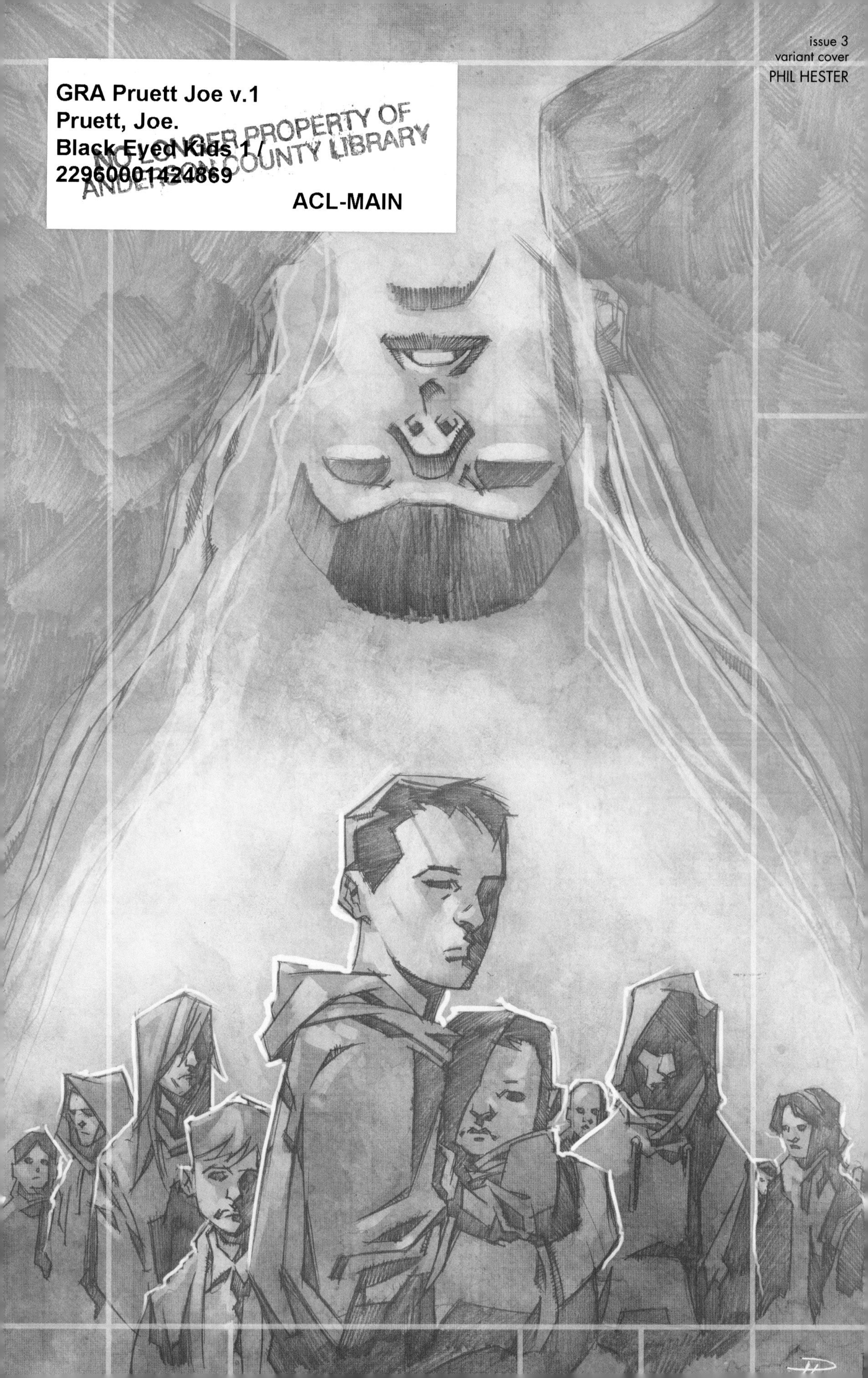

JOE PRUETT writer

🐦 @pruett_joe

Joe Pruett is an Eisner Award-winning comic book editor, publisher, and writer, having been nominated for numerous Eisner, Harvey and Eagle awards for his work on *Negative Burn* at Caliber Comics. He is also known for his writing work at Marvel, where he wrote for *X-Men Unlimited*, *Cable* and *Magneto Rex*. In addition to his X-Men writing work, Joe has written for virtually every other major comic publisher, including Image, Vertigo and IDW.

SZYMON KUDRANSKI artist

🐦 @SzymonKudranski

Born in Poland in 1986, Szymon got his big break into comics eighteen years later when writer Steve Niles asked him to draw a story featured in 2004's *30 Days of Night Annual*. Since then, Szymon has worked with many other comic publishers, including DC Comics *(Green Lantern, The Dark Knight)*, Marvel Comics *(Daredevil/Punisher)* and Image Comics, where he was personally asked by Todd McFarlane to take over art duties on the long-running *Spawn* series.

GUY MAJOR colorist

🐦 @guymajor

Guy Major is an artist and photographer who has been working in comics since 1995, when he responded to an add looking for colorists for Wildstorm's *WildC.A.T.S.* series. He worked for Homage Studios until 1998 when he became a freelance color artist. He has worked on just about every character from Batman to Barry Ween. When not working on comics or out with his camera, he is studying about, tasting or drinking wine. He currently lives in Oakland, CA with two amazing women— his wife Jackie and their daughter Riley.

MARSHALL DILLON letterer

🐦 @MarshallDillon

A comic book industry veteran, Marshall got his start in 1994, in the midst of the indy comic boom. Over the years, he's been everything from an independent self-published writer to an associate publisher working on properties like *G.I.Joe, Voltron* and *Street Fighter*. He's done just about everything except draw a comic book, and has worked for just about every publisher except the "big two." Primarily a father and letterer these days, he also dabbles in old-school paper & dice RPG game design. You can catch up with Marshall at firstdraftpress.net.